To Ryan

Best wishes

(Alastair ...)

Jim Rodger

GREAT SAINTS

St Mirren heroes of the past six decades

By Alastair MacLachlan

macdonald media publishing

First published in November 2006 by **macdonald** media publishing
22 Roxburgh Road, Paisley, PA2 0UG

ISBN 978-0-9553126-1-8
ISBN 0-9553126-1-2

Design: Cameron Heggie
Sub-editing: David Macdonald

Printed and bound by Bell and Bain Ltd., Glasgow

Acknowledgements

Paisley Daily Express

Scottish News and Sport Agency

Jim Jeffrey

Paisley Library

Norrie Jamieson

Kenny Pointon

Bobby Kerrigan

Willie Hunter

Allan Marshall

Malcolm Brodie

Willie Todd

Douglas Lamming

George Pratt

Kathleen Sinclair

Donnie Kerrigan Junior

Jim Crawford

Hugh Gibson

Belfast Telegraph

Jim Rodger

David Roberts

SFA

and finally... to all the players who have been subjected to numerous idiotic questions and opinions.

Foreword

IT is both a privilege and an honour to provide a foreword for a book that profiles the careers of one hundred St Mirren players over the last 60 years. Many were legends in their playing careers and still are today. To appear in a list which contains a number of all-time St Mirren greats leaves me feeling immensely proud and not a little humble.

First and foremost, I wish to congratulate my friend and the author of this book, Alastair MacLachlan. When I first learned of his desire to profile one hundred St Mirren players over the post war period, I realised that he was about to undertake a task of Herculean proportions that would involve innumerable interviews and thousands of journey miles and, at the same time, require a relentless drive to achieve his objective. I was always confident, however, that he would produce an informative and accomplished product which is a must read for Buddies of all generations.

Every footballer can identify a particular highlight in his career, that never to be forgotten moment in time, unrivalled by any other. I have discussed this occasionally with my band of brothers in that very special Saints team of 1959-61. Some of them pinpoint the winning of the cup as the apex of their career, others favour the 3-1 victory at Ibrox in October of the same year, the first time this was achieved in over half a century, and the record breaking 8-0 victory at Cathkin in 1961 claims a lot of support.

For me, personally, my magic moment is located in the 4-0 victory over Celtic at Hampden Park in that memorable 1959 semi-final. Ten minutes from the final whistle, with the game done and dusted, the thousands of Saints fans there that day, like a massive and resonant male voice choir, gave a rousing and triumphant rendition of 'When the Saints go marching in'. Nothing in my experience comes close to the thrill and euphoria of that moment. It merely underlined what we already knew – that the St Mirren fans are the inspirational life blood of the team – always have been, always will be!

I had the pleasure of meeting Alex Linwood a few years ago and was hugely impressed by the modest demeanour and friendly nature of this St Mirren star whose name is still revered in Paisley folklore. We spoke about St Mirren, about the deep affection engendered by the Club, and we agreed, after some reflection, that this intangible, unique and ubiquitous family atmosphere at Love Street is derived from the total and wholehearted involvement of everyone associated with the Club – Board members, admin and domestic staff, coaches, players, ball boys, etc. and, most important of all, the fans. It was there fifty years ago and is still very much to the fore at the present time. Its legacy is to instil in players like myself, who sought pastures new after their time with St Mirren, a life-long love affair with the Club which can be best summed up in the words – Once a Buddie, always a Buddie.

My final word is to the fans. Alastair MacLachlan's book will take you back through time on a 60-year journey and will stir in your hearts and minds some magic moments and allow you to relive great deeds by the men in the black and white stripes. It is a journey you will cherish and I recommend this splendid book to you without reservation.

Jim Rodger

Introduction

IT was a somewhat bizarre ambition that opened the door to match programme editing and publication. To watch a match on every senior Scottish ground in the course of one season was the target.

Fortunately, the season in question was before Ross County, Elgin City, Inverness Caledonian Thistle, Gretna and Peterhead entered the Scottish soccer landscape.

The exercise provided the opportunity to assess the various club programmes, and a survey of the Premier League clubs' publications revealed the Motherwell FC production to be in need of major editorial surgery.

That August, Holyrood MSP and champion of the Scottish Senior Citizens Unity Party, John Swinburne – who was both the Fir Park commercial manager and programme editor at the time – endorsed my views. He doubled the size of his programme and asked for help to fill the pages. It was a pleasurable task and one I undertook for some five years.

It was during season 1992-93 that St Mirren came calling. And once Bill Campbell had been elevated from programme editor to commercial manager, a 12-year editorial association with St Mirren began.

It has been a privilege and a pleasure to have had the opportunity to interview many of the top officials, players and administrators in the great game. I would express my very real thanks to them for fending numerous interview questions, many innocuous, some fanciful and a few that yielded nuggets of pertinent information.

I have tried to veer away from a statistically heavy publication, but there is a common spine to each interview. One is players are born, they play at school, Juveniles and boys' clubs follow, perhaps a spell with a Junior club before entering the Senior stage.

Some players had short stays at Love Street, but their contribution to the Scottish game as a whole merited the expansion of their overall careers.

Many readers will take on board the opportunity to verify the dates, the stats and general data provided. Much has been gleaned from the players themselves. Consequently, I would endorse the contents with a substantial E & OE!

I trust you will find it interesting. Enjoy.

Alastair MacLachlan

GERRY BAKER

IT'S doubtful if Gerry Baker was ever timed over 100 metres, or yards as they were in his playing days. Metres or yards, the clockwatch would surely have clicked at around the 10 second mark. That was the Baker specialty - speed!

Tutors at his Alma Maters - firstly at Motherwell's Park Street School and, latterly, at St Joseph's Secondary - having failed to keep up with him, would probably have been relieved when the speed merchant moved on to play with Craigneuk Boys' Guild before entering the Junior ranks with Larkhall Thistle.

Ted Drake was the man in charge at Chelsea at the time and his West of Scotland scouting team sent back glowing reports to Stamford Bridge of one jet propelled centre forward. Gerry was only 15 and his tender teenage years at the Bridge were perhaps not fully attuned to appreciate the cosmopolitan lifestyle of the "Big Smoke". In truth, he was homesick.

Bobby Ancell's Motherwell Babes, a collection of prodigious soccer talent, were anxious to augment their ball playing trickery and the Fir Park side offloaded a cheque for £750 to bring Gerry back up to the then Lanarkshire steel town.

One particular truism in football is the need to be in the right place at the right time. Gerry's move to Motherwell earned him almost instant fame, the 19-year-old winning a Second Eleven Cup medal and making his claret and amber debut against Dundee in April 1958.

However, the Baker skill factors were overshadowed by the established residents of the Ancell Babes regime. Ian St John, Pat Quinn, Andy Weir and Willie Hunter were ahead of him in the Motherwell pecking order. Clearly he had arrived at the wrong time and after a mere 10 Fir Park appearances he moved to St Mirren in 1958.

He cost Saints and manager Willie Reid in particular the princely sum of £2,000. But in the light of what was to follow, that was money well spent.

The Baker move to Love Street was made all the more sweeter when he found himself on his debut in opposition to Hibernian in Edinburgh, with his more illustrious brother Joe in the Easter Road line up. The atmosphere in the Baker household that evening was possibly somewhat tense - Gerry scored the winning goal!

His scoring exploits won applause from even the most hardened of the Paisley fans as Gerry's goal contributions eased the Love Street relegation worries.

But in the words of a certain Irish comic - there's more...!

It came the following season. Saints were drawn to play Peebles Rovers in the second round of the Scottish Cup at Love Street. The final score of 10-0 terminated the hopes of the wee Borders side and Baker notched four of the best.

Motherwell were overcome in the round three, followed by Dunfermline, with Gerry on target in each tie.

Celtic beckoned in the semis at Hampden and the Parkhead men were thumped 4-0, Baker again a marksman in what many believe to be St Mirren's finest hour.

And so to the final. Aberdeen had travelled down to Hampden with one question on everybody's lips - could Gerry Baker score in every round of the Cup? He did, and with additional scoring help from Tommy Bryceland and Alistair Miller, the Northern Lights were truly dimmed.

Could such a scoring feat ever be surpassed? It could and it was.

Cue the following season's Scottish Cup and the students of Glasgow University forsaking their campus for a first round tie at Love Street.

Blizzard conditions made both playing and spectating extremely difficult but those who managed to peer through the driving snow were witness to a cameo of record-breaking proportions - St Mirren's 15-0 thrashing logging in their highest ever score in a first class game.

One newspaper was perhaps over euphoric in suggesting "Bryceland and Gemmell were the male nurses in an operating theatre, where Gerry Baker was the surgeon who amputated the 'Yoonie' students' dream of cup glory!"

Baker netted 10, his input being the highest individual scoring performance in the 20th century. No other player in the UK has managed to net double figures.

Conceivably, the Saints hitman might have scored more, but had to leave the field in some pain just after the 10th goal went in. Gerry ruefully recalls the moment.

He said: "A St Mirren corner had been swung over and their keeper, instead of clutching the ball, took an almighty swipe at it. It hit me in that part of the male anatomy that offers almost instantaneous transition from basso profundo status to the shrill tones of some screaming soprano!"

Younger sibling Joe almost emulated his elder brother's feat. Hibernian were drawn to met the luckless Peebles Rovers a couple of years later in the 1961 Scottish Cup. Joe scored a remarkable NINE to compound an astonishing family scoring feat, the Easter Road side winning 15-1.

On the international front, Joe, who first saw light of day in Liverpool, qualified for England selection and went on to collect eight full caps, scoring on his debut against Northern Ireland in 1959.

Bother Gerry's international affinity was somewhat different. Born in New York in 1938 and thus qualifying for USA selection, the Americans were highly delighted in having a player with Gerry's credentials in their national squad. Sixteen full caps followed and global acceptance was generated with participation in the World Cups of 1966 and 1970.

In 1960, Gerry moved to Manchester City to team up with Dennis Law, the transfer cheque of £17,000 significantly boosting the coffers at Love Street.

But the Baker balloon was never fully inflated at Maine Road and Hibernian came calling. One of his early Hibee appearances was against Saints at Love Street. However, the warm greetings proffered on his return quickly changed to a cacophony of derision as Gerry netted the Easter Road winner in a 3-2 result.

The wanderlust continued with subsequent pegs being offered at Ipswich Town, Coventry City and Brentford. Keen to stay in the game, Gerry tried management with Racing Club Warwick and Nuneaton in the English non-Leagues. It wasn't particularly to his liking and he chose to renegade on any further managerial involvement.

The Coventry playing association at Highfield Road saw Gerry, his wife Ann and daughters Lorraine and Karen set down their family roots in Lady Godiva's historical township. Lorraine clearly inherited her father's genes and her athletic prowess earned her a national vest for the UK team.

Arguably her athletics zenith came at Glasgow's Kelvin Hall, where she ran a close second to the Russians in the 800 metres.

Early retirement at the Coventry Jaguar plant saw Gerry go on to mastermind the fortunes of a thriving horticultural business. Only occasionally did he return to Paisley but the reunion of the 1959 Cup winning side at St Mirren's 125th anniversary celebrations in October 2002 clearly demonstrated him as one of St Mirren's finest and one of the club's hospitality suites was named after him.

THEROLF BECK

ONE would have to admit season 1960-61 wasn't exactly top drawer. Fifth bottom in a First Division of 18 teams plus an early exit from the League Cup courtesy of bottom spot in a section containing Clyde, Hearts and Motherwell was hardly a successful operation.

Some solace was gleaned from the Scottish Cup, where Dunfermline ended the St Mirren hopes in the semi-final after a replay. However, Saints' star turn in that competition came in the third round with the remarkable 8-0 replay win over Third Lanark at Cathkin Park, Jim Rodger adding to the Paisley folklore with four of the best.

These performances hardly merited a "thank you and well done" end of season trip, so the subsequent tour of Iceland in June had to be classified more as a pre-season activity than a holiday pick-me-up!

Conceivably, any pick-me-up went on hold on June 7, 1961. Facing a South West Iceland Select, St Mirren floundered to a humiliating 7-1 defeat. What was of interest was the fair haired striker leading the Icelandic attack.

He scored a hat-trick. He had talent. He was Therolf Beck.

The reaction to the hammering was to blame it on lack of sleep. Clearly the midnight sun had affected the players' body clocks, although it hadn't bothered Dundee the previous week - they won 3-1!

The Beck achievement indicated there was a talent and the frontman was anxious to expand his playing level, with signing overtures from St Mirren now evident.

Ironically, manager Willie Reid wasn't with the Saints touring party but he soon flew out at the beginning of July to run the rule over this available talent.

Club captain Jimmy Brown, the former Hearts and Kilmarnock keeper, also joined the boss on the Icelandic safari to provide informed comment on the Beck capabilities.

Brown's assessment classified Icelandic football as that of Scottish Second Division standard. But what Reid had to determine was did Beck have the speed, strength and skill to shape up to the treatment meted out to attack leaders in this country?

A firm transfer approach was made by Saints but difficulties arose in obtaining the necessary work permit to bring him over to Paisley.

Tottenham Hotspur had beaten Leicester City in the 1961 English FA Cup and the Filbert Street side were then invited to contest the Paisley Charity Cup on August 5. Even with such icons as Gordon Banks and Frank McLintock on board, St Mirren were too good, winning 3-1.

While that result brought a warm glow to the Paisley community, of more importance on the day was the receipt of the relevant documentation to bring Beck to Love Street, the blonde one signing on September 25.

With the North Bank supreme in the composition and rendering of cat calls, melodic insults and nicknames, it wasn't too long before Therolf had been realigned to "Tottie" - perhaps a remote reference to his compact physique...

Tottie made his Saints debut in a league match against Airdrie at Love Street but the Diamonds won 2-0. The St Mirren forward line read McDonald, Beck, Kerrigan, Henderson and McFadzean.

Jim McDonald was only in the team due to an injury to winger Jim Rodger and the school teacher well remembers Tottie's introduction to the Scottish game.

He said: "Tottie was a strong lad who played hard but clean. Popular with his team-mates, he was adept at taking remote chances and was nippy in the goalmouth.

"He wasn't a rowdy lad but was a good speaker and soon picked up the communicative essence of parliamo Paisley.

"One slightly negative memory of Tottie was a November visit to Celtic Park. We were thrashed 7-1 but it was Tottie that scored our only goal."

The Beck goal machine continued in a productive vein with a memorable quartet recorded against Raith Rovers in a 5-1 win at Love Street.

His four-season term at Love Street saw him net 35 goals from 110 appearances, a remarkable and more than acceptable scoring rate for any striker.

In Beck's initial season with the Buddies, St Mirren reached the final of the Scottish Cup, with goals from Tottie, Willie Fernie and Don Kerrigan seeing off Celtic at the semi-final stage.

However, on the day Rangers were too strong in the final, winning 2-0.

There is no doubt, though, the Ibrox management team went on to mark their card in favour of the Beck expertise.

Such was the charisma of the Icelander and his committed approach to the game that he picked up the St Mirren Player of the Year trophy for the 62-63 season. And it was no surprise when Rangers persuaded him to don a light blue shirt on Armistice Day 1964, in exchange for a reported £20,000 transfer fee.

The Ibrox relationship wasn't quite so fruitful, Tottie playing only 11 games for a two-goal return. He left Ibrox in 1966 to return home.

In later years, with Tottie being a former KR Reykjavik player, he was introduced to former Saint David Winnie, and the pair of them enjoyed sharing some nostalgic memories over their joint KR and St Mirren connections.

David was impressed with the former Saints striker. He said: "Therolf was a lovely man but he was quite ill at the time and I believe he eventually died from Alzheimer's disease around 1999."

At the KR club they have established a little memorial to Tottie, with press cuttings on show covering his time at both St Mirren and Rangers. He is well remembered in Paisley as the Icelandic Buddie.

ALEX BECKETT

YOU'D have to admit that St Mirren's away days to Parkhead have never been over fruitful in the points gathering business. Indeed, the fundamental ability to plank the ball in the Celtic Park net has been generally conspicuous by its absence.

Saints were due at the ground fondly known as Paradise by the green and white faithful on Saturday November 22 1980. Manager Jim Clunie would have pointed out to his troops that it was nearly 23 years since St Mirren had last harvested the full points on offer at Parkhead.

Would the 1980 encounter at last break the mold? It could and it did, thanks to the monumental goal manufacturing skills of full-back Alex Beckett.

The game was teetering towards a bland 0-0 draw when, six minutes from time, Celtic failed to clear a cross ball and the effervescent Lex Richardson drove in a low shot that completely deceived Packy Bonner in the Hoops goal.

The travelling Buddies were ecstatic at the prospect of Saints at last breaking their 23-year hoodoo. However, their euphoria had hardly died down when Jack Copland was adjudged to have tripped Tommy Burns in the box.

Jack would tell you it was a blatant dive.

"Tommy wasn't going anywhere and I eased him out of the goal scoring zone," Jack has said of the incident. He added: "He went down rather easily, too easily in fact, and you had to say it was a pretty soft penalty."

As some would utter under their breaths – a penalty against Saints at Parkhead – what's new?

The sure footed George McCluskey did the business with the spot-kick, giving a glimmer of hope to those with investments in the day's treble chance lists.

But no, the game took an amazing twist two minutes from time. Celtic centre-back Tom McAdam headed a cross away from the apparent danger zone. The ball fell kindly for Beckett to take a crack at it and from all of 25 yards the ball screamed into the net reminiscent of an exocet missile on heat.

It was Alex's first goal since November 6, 1976. He'd never scored a better and never did again.

Two points for Saints at Parkhead – dreams are made of this.

The irony of such a meritorious win was that manager Clunie was sensationally sacked the Tuesday after the game!

One of a family of five, Beckett drew his first breath in 1954 in Glasgow. With the family home on the eastern Glasgow precincts, it was St Jude's and St Gregory's in Barlanark that supplied the early Beckett educational needs.

After primary schooling, the Beckett family moved to Dennistoun, where the emerging full-back talents were enlisted by Rob Roy Thistle.

Alex recalled: "My dad was always helpful in the planned routing of my career and he helped me get a trial for the famed Eastercraigs club.

"My pal went on to get a trial for Kilsyth Rangers. I was only 17 and I ended up not only getting a trial but they signed me provisionally. I was farmed out to the Juvenile side Milton Battlefield for six months before returning to Kilsyth. In between, I had been invited down on trial at Coventry City for three weeks."

It was then that a touch of the blarney took over. Willie Cunningham, the Northern Ireland and former Saints full-back, was the manager of Falkirk and the then Brockville side took Alex on board.

Alex went on: "I played for the Bairns for a full season but was given limited opportunities of first-team football. I had just completed my apprenticeship as a joiner and was planning to go down to London when Willie Cunningham phoned me. He had moved to St Mirren in May 1973 and I think it was the following year that I signed on at Love Street.

"I spent almost eight years at St Mirren and had in addition to Cunningham, Alex Ferguson, Clunie and Rikki McFarlane as my managers.

"Eventually, St Mirren gave me a free transfer and I went south to play for Queen of the South. When the senior career began to dip, I moved back down to the Juniors and played with St Roch's and Vale of Clyde."

Beckett will always be remembered for his full-back role, and in particular that Parkhead goal. But it was McFarlane who felt the Beckett expertise would be more beneficial to Saints in midfield.

Alex said: "What brought that move to a speedy conclusion was a game against Arbroath. The Gayfield club had a wee flier who could run a bit and I couldn't cope with his pace. Clearly midfield was a bit outside my comfort zone, so it was soon back to full-back beat."

The Beckett view of the Alex Ferguson is in marked contrast to the current goldfish bowl climate of controversy manufactured on a daily basis by the media.

He explained: "He gave us a bit of freedom with the opportunity to change tactics and express ourselves. Any game plan has to be fluent and Alex gave us licence to adapt it according to how the game was going. He obviously liked to attack and score goals."

Beckett's one major unfulfilled ambition was to have won the Scottish Cup with Saints. Leaving Love Street in the early 80s left him a few years short of appearing in that 1987 epic.

Rarely did he return to watch St Mirren in Paisley. With such a conurbation of Junior clubs in the east end of Glasgow, the Beckett watching brief would see him regularly take in the efforts of Vale of Clyde, Cambuslang Rangers, Baillieston or Shettleston – all being geographically close to the Beckett homestead in Carmyle.

Working latterly as a driver for the Arnold Clark organisation, Alex was reluctant to hang up his boots. Even into his 40s, he never lost the urge and played every second Sunday for Avonbridge Over-35s.

As to the frequency of these games, Alex had the last word: "It took me a couple of weeks to recover!"

TOM BLACK

IF David Lapsley was the penalty kick king of the 1950s, his ermine mantle of creating successful spot-kick conversions was an easy fit on the broad shoulders of Tom Black in the 80s and 90s.

A late developer physically, Tom's modest teenage proportions saw him readily earmarked for the centre-forward slot or wide on the left wing.

A Bellshill Academy boy with school soccer in the morning and a football affinity with the local YMCA in the afternoon, it was Bobby Watson, then the Airdrie manager, who elevated the 16-year-old to the pro ranks with the Broomfield club by passing the norm of the "S" Form route.

Prior to joining the Diamonds, Tom had stirred up considerable interest in a number of senior clubs, not the least of whom were Rangers.

Tom revealed: "I was invited to play a trial for the Ibrox side against an Icelandic team. John Greig was the Rangers manager at the time and I played alongside the likes of Dave McPherson and wee Billy Davies.

"I had a good game but this was the era when Ally Dawson had sustained a fractured skull and was in process of regaining his match fitness. By now the puppy fat had been replaced with modest brawn, with my playing role now redefined as a left sided defender, so my chances of further Ibrox trials hinged on Ally's recovery."

The anticipated telephone call from Govan failed to materialise. Keen to advance his career, Tom was offered a trial with Airdrie in a bounce game against Celtic and he was in a quandary.

He explained: "Airdrie were domiciled in Division One and the Premier League was a more exciting proposition. So at the back of my mind was the thought, would Rangers ever make contact?

"However, I decided to go with Airdrie and signed on as a 16-year-old on the Tuesday night. But believe it or not, Rangers phoned on the Thursday evening asking me to play another trial for them against, of all clubs, Airdrie.

"I played in that trial game, my first as a signed pro for the Broomfield side, and with Rangers at full strength, we were thumped 10-0!"

In almost 10 seasons in an Airdrie jersey, Tom posted over 170 league outings, spiced with a handful of goals – mostly penalties.

However, it was time for pastures new. Airdrie had proposed a joint Testimonial for Tom, Brian McKeown and John Martin. The Testimonial saw Rangers visiting Broomfield and the first ever outing in light blue by Maurice Johnston, who had just signed for the club. His appearance would have most certainly have boosted the gate takings.

It was a tempting proposition but Tom had his heart set on Premier League fayre. Tony Fitzpatrick was in the process of rebuilding St Mirren. Peter Weir, Davies, Roddy Manley and then Guni Torfason had dropped anchor in Paisley, with Ian Cameron and Brian Hamilton exiting.

Tom's transfer from Airdrie to Love Street in July 1989 was somewhat contentious. The clubs couldn't agree a fee and the move was finally settled by a Tribunal, resulting in £75,000 going to the Broomfield exchequer.

Tom recalled: "Lord McCluskey was the Tribunal judge and there were parties there from the SFA, Airdrie and St Mirren. Airdrie had an extensive dossier on me, extolling my virtues, while the Love Street file played down my strong points. In essence, it was a straight tug-of-war between Airdrie boss Jimmy Bone and Tony Fitzpatrick. I believe Tony won!"

What was remarkable in Black's time at Love Street was his regular selection for the first team. Only once was he on the bench in a league encounter, with his 73 outings as a Saint yielding a four-goal return. One of these strikes was particularly memorable. His first for St Mirren came when he pinged a 25-yarder into Andy Goram's postage stamp against Hibs at Easter Road. However, it wasn't enough – Saints lost!

By now, David Hay had taken over Fitzpatrick's managerial throne and, as is the norm, began bringing in his own style of player. One of those was Mark Reid, secured from Charlton Athletic, who had served under Hay at Celtic.

Tom admitted: "With Mark's arrival, I knew I was on my way. I had a good meeting with David and asked him not to over price me to the extent of freezing me out of the game. He played fair and I joined Kilmarnock in November 1991."

Again the steady approach of Black's game saw him become an almost total absentee from the subs' bench, appearing from there only once in nearly 150 Rugby Park league outings.

In fact, the 1993-94 season saw him record a 100 per cent league match record. The penalty and free-kick content also flourished, with 17 being notched in Killie colours.

A playing colleague at Rugby Park was Mark Reilly, later to join St Mirren. Mark spoke highly of the Black skill factors.

He said: "Tom was a great lad. He was a bit of a laid back character – nothing ever phased him. He was a very underrated player and possessed a great left foot that contributed a considerable number of free-kicks and penalties. He did a great job at left-back for Kilmarnock but was never given the credit he deserved for the job he did."

Kilmarnock went on to win the Scottish Cup in 1997 but Tom missed out on a winners medal, having just moved to Stranraer on a part-time basis.

He was in good company with former Saints Campbell Money, Paul McIntyre, Paul Archdeacon and Johnny McMillan all in residence at Stair Park.

Tom recalled: "I only went to Stranraer because of my former association at Love Street with Campbell. Of course, the move necessitated a switch to normal working life for me."

It wasn't quite so normal in consideration of the Stranraer league programme. Tom joined the team from the ferry boat town in July 1996 and his first season necessitated the winning of their last game against Stenhousemuir or be relegated to the Third Division.

Tom said: "We were losing 1-0 with 15 minutes to go and managed to score twice to stay up.

"The next season was even more bizarre. It came to February and we were sitting second bottom and come May we'd won the league. It took a run of 19 games, winning 16 of them, to clinch the title."

Also on display amongst Black's soccer souvenirs is a winners medal from the 1996 Challenge Cup, Stranraer defeating St Johnstone 1-0 in the final.

With over 40 career league goals to his credit, one might muse that a particular penalty against Hibs at Easter Road could have energised the Black emotions.

It was a vintage David and Goliath confrontation. Hibs had just been relegated in 1998 from the SPL, Stranraer had just earned their First Division stripes. Clearly here was a home banker in the second league game of the 1998-99 season. It wasn't. Tom's penalty made it 2-0 for The Blues and the Edinburgh side could only manage a late consolation goal.

Another that retains a high affection in Black's goal collection was a strike against Rangers for Kilmarnock on May 7, 1994.

He recalled: "It was the second last game of the season and Killie were in a relegation fight with St Johnstone. We won 1-0 and I scored from a free-kick. From the point of view of the tension of the occasion, that goal was a bit special. It gave Kilmarnock a solid footing for further SPL activity."

Tom downed his playing tools after four seasons at Stair Park but couldn't be persuaded to take up arms on the Junior front, despite a plea from the Stonehouse Violet officials.

Once the necessities of part-time football had kicked in, Tom's day job was secured as a financial advisor with the CIS Insurance Group.

Now Tom, the complete family man, is happily ensconced in Larkhall with wife Michelle, son Thomas and daughter Morgan, from where he commutes to his latest posting as a logistics and distribution official with the Ross Electrical Group.

EDDIE BLYTH

FOR those born in the early 1920s and having a genetic hereditary that swung the compass point in the direction of professional football, the likelihood of a playing career interruption was an inevitability.

The Second World War created a career abyss for Eddie Blyth, whose birth certificate was date stamped on May 4, 1924, with Adolf Hitler's delusions of world domination creating a considerable dent in Eddie's soccer progression.

The early days were idyllic enough. A successful secondary curriculum at Govan High School generated adequate grey matter to tackle a future pharmaceutical course while the pacy teenager with an eye for goal had already implanted his skills in the minds of the national schoolboy selectors.

Eddie recalled: "I was happy playing as either a wing half or an inside forward. I was fortunate to be selected to play for the Rest of Scotland Schools in a game where I faced up to big John McPhail of later Celtic fame.

"My school teachers had me earmarked for a number of trials and I played briefly as an amateur on the Junior stage with Yoker Athletic at Holm Park."

Usage of the Blyth ball skills was eventually directed towards the amateur kingdom at Hampden Park, before the aforementioned Herr Hitler provided a major coffee break in the development of a latent football career.

Eddie found himself bedecked in khaki with the Royal Artillery operating under the banner of the very English sounding Berkshire Yeomanry. Army training in the south of England preceded a posting to India and any football activity was confined to Battalion bounce games.

Demobbed in 1945, Eddie returned to soccer civilisation and to the successful post-war Queen's Park side who boasted considerable ability with such stalwarts as Ronnie Simpson, Bobby Brown and David Letham.

As a returning serviceman, Eddie found himself playing with the Queen's Park third team - affectionately known as the Hampden Xl - a more than useful side who had just won the Scottish Amateur Cup.

22

A further step up the Queen's Park ladder found Eddie operating with the Strollers prior to gracing the first team and their time honoured lack of sartorial elegance in the wearing of their jerseys outside their shorts.

Around half a dozen games for the Spiders' top squad and the black and white career (Hampden style) looked rosy - at least for a while.

Eddie explained: "Latterly, I was being quoted as the reserve to travel with the first team. This selection process happened so often that I was fast becoming frustrated and disillusioned.

"I made my feelings clear but the Queen's Park committee told me they couldn't guarantee me a game, so I left and joined the Babcock & Wilcox team. They used to play in the Renfrewshire Cup competition, as well as regularly competing in the Scottish Cup."

Life with the engineering company side provided a moderate slap on the wrist for the Queen's Park committee. The Scottish Amateur side were regularly populated by the entire Queen's Park side, with only occasionally an outsider being included in the team. Eddie Blyth was one that broke the mould.

He said: "I was selected firstly to play against Northern Ireland before playing England at Hampden in 1949. I missed a penalty in the first half but scored three in the second period and we won 3-2."

Shades of embarrassment in the committee rooms of down town Mount Florida.

It was after that game that St Mirren director Willie Waters and manager Bobby Rankin persuaded Eddie to throw his lot in with the Paisley Saints.

Clearly future confrontations between St Mirren and either Babcock & Wilcox or Queen's Park would be games of relish for Mr Blyth.

Eddie's first competitive outing for Saints saw Paisley's finest travel to Cathkin Park for a match against Third Lanark. Thirds were a feared team immediately post war. Harry Mooney was a veritable pocket dynamo, Matt Balunas a resolute full-back while the pint-sized Jocky Robertson belied his inches to become a top-rated keeper.

Adam Forsyth was a commanding centre-half in the Third Lanark defence but one subsequent head to head with Blyth was far from a harmonious encounter.

Eddie explained: "A through ball was played to me. I went after it and tried to flick it past the keeper but only succeeded in catching the Forsyth ankles and bringing the Cathkin colossus crashing down in ton of bricks fashion.

"Adam was none too pleased with my effort and offered me some pertinent advice - 'See that Stand over there son, try that business once more and I'll kick you over that f***** thing!'"

More a provider than a goal scorer, Eddie was on target on 17 occasions for St Mirren, with one particular goal in a match against Airdrie still fresh in his mind.

He said: "We were playing the Diamonds at Love Street and both teams were relegation candidates. We won 3-2 and I managed to poke the winner past their keeper Willie Fraser, who later played for Third Lanark, Sunderland and Scotland. Fortunately, both Airdrie and Saints beat the drop."

Life as a winger in a St Mirren strip conjured up numerous tetchy battles with full-backs of the day. George Young and Eric Caldow were both established in the national side, with the clean kicking Willie McNaught, always a difficult opponent, going on to establish a Raith Rovers record of 430 League appearances. But for sure bedrock opposition, Jimmy Mitchell down at Morton, formerly of Queen's Park and later to join Aberdeen, was, in Eddie's eyes, an enthusiastic player !

Eddie's time at Love Street coincided with the Irish shenanigans of the leprechaun that was Gerry Burrell.

On one league safari to play Queen of the South at Dumfries, the St Mirren party made the journey by train. These were the days before team buses and the motorway network had arrived at an amicable fusion.

Blyth remembers: "Gerry, as per normal, had been his usual over zealous self. The referee called him over and said 'Name please?' The Burrell response was of pantomime proportions. 'My name is McCoubrey'. 'How do you spell it,' queried the ref. 'Ah, that's my problem,' blurted out Gerry!"

The follow up found both the St Mirren party and the match referee on the Dumfries station platform awaiting the Glasgow train.

The red came over to the diminutive Irishman and said, "Don't for one minute think you can get away with that performance. I know your real name and it isn't McCoubrey."

Eddie concluded: "Gerry was fined £5 by the SFA, but we all chipped in to clear his fine. It wasn't just the phoney name, it was the fact he couldn't spell it!"

These were the days of £10 a week and bonuses of £2 for a win and £1 for a draw, and Eddie supplemented his part-time status with pharmaceutical studies at Glasgow's Royal Technical College, later to become Strathclyde University.

Six years at Love Street and a stand-off with the St Mirren management ensued.

Eddie said: "I didn't sign and trained on my own, which generated some pertinent headlines such as 'It wouldn't take too many aspirins to solve this headache'."

The contractual headache wasn't resolved and Eddie refused to sign as a matter of principle. He simply stopped playing, hung up his boots and embarked on the running of his Renfrew-based pharmacy.

A man with a Renfrew homestead, he occasionally takes in a St Mirren game. Perhaps there is more personal pleasure being generated at the Erskine Golf Club, though, battling to reduce a handicap of 17.

JIMMY BONE

IT was a time for a little self confession. Jimmy Bone, the lad born in Bridge-of-Allan and who went to the rugby playing establishment that is Stirling High School, was a nippy stand-off in the oval ball game.

He admitted: "I never really started to play competitive football until I left school. I could run a bit and was school captain at rugby. I must have had something as I was given a trial for the Scottish Schoolboys side but got no further.

"In truth, in my later years in professional football, those that could stand up to a colourful earfull would be happy to tell you I played all my football like a rugby player!"

The competitive element in the soccer scene surfaced with the 14th Stirling Boys' Brigade Company, Jimmy's first season input giving the devotees of Sir William Smith's boyhood ideals a league and cup double.

The Bone BB skill factors also earned him a representative call up for the Stirling Battalion. That match against their Irish counterparts was the first time Jimmy had ever been on a plane.

Although he went on to taste the Juvenile menus with Airth and Bannockburn, offers of trials at senior level were sparse in the extreme - his socks to Brylcreem measurement of 5'-7" being considered as somewhat minute for the senior game.

The needs of a wage earning future were partially eliminated with a time served apprenticeship as an electrician down the pits in the local Stirling coal mining operation.

But the realisation of senior football finally surfaced in 1968 when Jimmy secured a peg at Firhill. Just over 100 league outings for the Maryhill Magyars saw him rack up a goal tally of 62.

One particular strike that regularly massages the Bone memory banks was the 1971 League Cup final. Celtic at Hampden - a walkover for the Parkhead side - no need for Thistle to turn up. But the Jags did just that and swept four into the Celtic net before half-time. Bone was in on target, aided and abetted by Alex Rae, Bobby Lawrie and Dennis McQuade.

With such a goal sniffing pedigree, it wasn't surprising some of the bigger fish began to take notice. One such soccer marine mammal was Norwich

City - a dubious analogy the Carrow Road club relish in the nickname of The Canaries!

Jimmy recalled: "I left Partick in February 1972 to join Norwich, who went on to win promotion to the First Division for the first time in their history. It was nice to land a league, despite only being a short time at the club."

A further historical memento befell Jimmy when he scored the Carrow Road club's first ever goal in the First Division.

Such scoring inputs generated a triple call up for the Scotland Under-23 team. But it was only a short time in Norwich colours before a letter inviting him to join the full national side landed on the Bone doormat.

Jimmy came off the bench to replace the legendary Denis Law in the 2-2 draw with Yugoslavia in 1972 and followed up with a full cap the next year. He also scored in the 4-1 turnover of Denmark in Copenhagen.

However, life in East Anglia had reached a crossroads for Jimmy.

He said: "Norwich had managed to reach the final of the League Cup but I wasn't guaranteed a place in the Wembley final. Sheffield United had shown an interest in my future and came in for me on the Tuesday prior to the final with Tottenham Hotspur.

"Obviously I was disappointed at not playing, but the fact that it was a single Ralph Coates goal that took the trophy to White Hart Lane seriously softened the blow."

The stainless steel environs of Sheffield's Bramhall Lane ground only saw Jimmy perform for the best part of a season, with Celtic luring him back to the heather climes, possibly remembering his contribution in that memorable League Cup debacle - in Parkhead eyes, that is!

One one paltry goal in five league outings plus a couple on the bench didn't set the Parkhead fans' pulse racing. And Jimmy soon raced to the east coast to join Arbroath. The Gayfield club had his services for three seasons and he yielding 41 league strikes from 97 appearances.

Check out core period of Bone's playing career and life with St Mirren and 32 goals from 161 appearances in black and white are the vital stats. It was manager Jim Clunie who required a bit of push up front and Bone certainly satisfied the need.

That football is a minefield of popular opinion is never more emphasised that when quantifying St Mirren's greatest ever goal.

Alex Linwood's 1943 Summer Cup goal has its admirers, as do Davie Lapsley's array of net-bursting drives, while Ian Ferguson's 1987 cup final strike is held in high esteem by the younger generation.

But what about Jimmy's goal against Aberdeen at Love Street on October 14, 1978?

After collecting the ball midway in his own half, he raced the length of the park before piloting a superb finish past a bemused Bobby Clark in the

Dons goal.

Two overseas stints saw Jimmy perform on loan for a few months with Toronto Blizzards in the North American Soccer League, before he headed eastwards, leaving St Mirren for Hong Kong Rangers.

Hearts signed him on his return from the Orient in 1983, playing him as an out and out striker for an 18-month period.

But there comes a time when the spirit is willing but the flesh heads graphically downwards on the ageing process curve. That time for Jimmy was 1986.

Then player-manager back at Gayfield with Arbroath, his last league game saw him on the bench, no doubt exuding high decibel instructions to his troops in a match with Ayr United at the Smokie production town. He was now 36.

With that wealth of playing experience behind him, it wasn't surprising it would be put to a variety of management uses.

As assistant to Alex Smith at Love Street, Jimmy was a vital component in overseeing the 1987 Scottish Cup returning to St Mirren Park.

Assistant manager at Dundee United preceded taking over the fortunes of Airdrie. But there has always been something of the wanderlust bug in the Bone make up. It was therefore no surprise to find him installed as manager of Power Dynamos in Zambia, followed by a period conducting the affairs of the black township team of Lynesia in Johannesburg.

Time with the Power Dynamo lads is firmly entrenched in the Bone CV, the club being the most successful team in Zambia's history.

Jimmy said: "It was an emotional time for the club. No team from south of the equator had ever won the African Cup Winners Cup and when I came back to Scotland I would have loved to have brought over a number of the Dynamo players. However, the amount of red tape to be sifted through made it impossible."

Subsequent management appointments at Dunfermline, Dundee and Stenhousemuir - all spaced out with unemployment intervals - kept the Bone soccer brain on high alert. And Jimmy renewed his former association with Smith at Ross County at the start of the 2003-04 season.

Bone was a man who led from the front. Never unprincipled, his charismatic character shone through when he took an acrimonious stance on the occasion of Kenny McDowall being deemed surplus to St Mirren requirements - Jimmy promptly resigned.

His level of fitness saw him active on most post-playing weekends in a series of charity games for the Dukla Pumpherson team, organised by the ubiquitous Chic Young. Dukla were renowned as a "drinking team" with a football problem and drew large turnouts to see a galaxy of former greats.

Certainly outstanding in St Mirren's 100 post war greats, who would argue that Jimmy Bone would make the top ten?

WALTER BORTHWICK

VERSATILITY can be either helpful or a hindrance in establishing a career in football. Fortunately for Walter Borthwick, the former prevailed.

He explained: "St Mirren used me in a variety of positions but mainly in what was categorised as an inside-forward role. However, on one occasion under Alex Ferguson, in a match against Partick Thistle, he went for three at the back. It was the first time he'd ever used the formation.

"He played myself, John Young and Bobby Reid as the three centre-backs. It was a success in that game, but eventually I was shunted back up front again."

An Edinburgh lad with academic leanings towards Liberton Primary School, Walter's main teenage soccer tutelage came from his time at the Tynecastle Boys' Club.

His early post-school nine to five activities embraced working with a printing firm, repairing malfunctioning TV sets and serving two years as an apprentice plasterer.

The first Borthwick intrusion into the Senior soccer scene posed the question – how does an east coast lad come to sign for Morton?

Walter explained: "Morton had a scout in the Lothians at the time and took a few players to Cappielow. Hal Stewart, the football impresario, was the man who signed me for Morton. He'll be best remembered for introducing so many Scandinavian players such as Erik and Jorn Sorensen and Preben Arentoft to the Scottish game.

"I was full-time during my time in Greenock but the travelling for training was horrendous. But I did leave my mark at Cappielow – I scored a hat-trick in my last game for the club."

Possibilities of a career progression with Brighton & Hove Albion and Dundee United followed, before Jimmy Bonthrone took the Borthwick talents to Bayview Park. The East Fife boss initiated a degree of positive man management to the move by giving Walter a six-game pack to prove himself.

Prove himself he did in what resulted in a seven-year stay with the Fifers.

During that time the club won promotion to Division One with Partick Thistle in 70-71, followed by relegation three years later.

There was media speculation that St Mirren, Hamilton and Raith Rovers were keen to secure the Borthwick signature.

Walter recalled: "The reason I signed for St Mirren was simply the charisma of manager Willie Cunningham. He had been very successful at Falkirk and had been touted for the Scotland job. I thought, he must be quality, he must be good to work with, so I signed for St Mirren at the start of the 74-75 season."

Walter's first wearing of the black and white stripes saw Saints take on Stirling Albion at Love Street on August 10, 1974. Messrs Morrison, Ian Reid, Beckett, Young, Bobby Reid,, Johnston, McKean, Walker, Biggar, Borthwick and Lawson all contributed to a 3-2 win over Alex Smith's side.

Love Street highlights for Borthwick were varied.

He said: "We were in Division Two when Alex Ferguson took over. League reconstruction was about to kick in with the establishment of the new Premier League and two other divisions. The top 10 teams would qualify for the new Premier League while the remainder would be apportioned into two leagues, each with 12 clubs.

"We had to make the top six to qualify for Division One. We just made it – in sixth place! That was my main domestic highlight.

"One other major memorable occasion occurred on the St Mirren pre-season tour of the West Indies in 1976. The tour was organised through the auspices of former chairman Harold Currie's contacts in the whisky exporting business.

"We played Barbados, Surinam, Trinidad & Tobago and Guyana, and the whole tour contributed to a tremendous team bonding exercise. But the match against Guyana was clouded in controversy.

"Our management duo of Davie Provan and Fergie had stripped as many possible substitutes for most of the games. Against Guyana, some of their tackles were more than generous and the diminutive Robert Torrance took more than his fair share.

"One particular challenge was enough to energise Fergie into coming off the bench to enact a degree of retribution. He managed it but to an extent that saw Fergie receive a straight red card for his eye for an eye and tooth for a tooth doctrine!

"That tour was my major memory of life with St Mirren."

Some 74 appearances for Saints preceded a move to Perth to join St Johnstone as a player/coach – the move being effectively triggered by Jackie Copland's impending arrival from Dundee United.

The Borthwick transfer to the then Muirton Park side was a salvage operation to save the Perth Saints from Division Two oblivion. With

Walter's help, it was mission accomplished as Raith Rovers and Falkirk took the drop.

Ferguson was keen to have Walter back with Saints and he returned as a substitute at the start of season 77-78 against Clydebank at Love Street for St Mirren's first ever Premier League game. But Walter had a problem.

He explained: "I was now 29 and didn't sign an extended contract as I asked myself how am I going to get a regular game in a fairly young team? I'd also enjoyed my coaching time at St Johnstone and the door opened up for me to join Dunfermline in another player-coaching capacity."

The four seasons at East End Park brought an end to the Borthwick playing activities and his coaching expertise was subsequently put to good use when Tony Ford brought him to Hearts. A boyhood dream had now been fulfilled in joining up with the residents of Tynecastle.

Perhaps Walter's worst nightmare in the industry occurred on the last day of the 85-86 season. Hearts were at Dens Park and only had to avoid defeat to clinch the Premier League title.

He recalled: "I was first in at Tynecastle on the morning of the game. Craig Levein had phoned in and had to call off with sickness and diarrhoea. Kenny Black, Roddy McDonald and Brian Whittaker all checked in with similar symptoms. We made a decision over lunch to play Brian Whittaker in the first half with Kenny taking over in the second period.

"Regretfully, we ran out of steam, lost two goals in the last 10 minutes thanks to Brian Kidd and the title went to Celtic, who returned a 5-0 scoreline against St Mirren, of all teams, at Love Street."

With a full alphabet of coaching certificates in his locker and a 10-year spell at Hearts as a coach, Walter was tempted to expose his experience on the management circuit, taking over Arbroath from former Saint John Young.

Management wasn't over palatable to Walter and community coaching proved more satisfying to his taste buds. He went on to join the SFA when Jim Farry was the top man at Park Gardens.

Walter said: "I started at Dunfermline as their community coach and was later interested in a similar job in Galashiels. In effect, I was forced to go as Farry was going to stop my salary if I didn't agree to take up the appointment in the Borders."

Almost three years in this posting preceded a much more amicable move to take over as Football Development Officer for East Lothian, based at the Meadowmill Sports Centre, near Tranent.

Away from football, Walter is still ball co-ordinated, with golf at the Prestonfield course a favourite pastime. He also enjoys indoor and outdoor bowling with his former playing colleague John Young.

TOMMY BRYCELAND

IT was the elder statesman at St Mirren Park, the venerable Davie Lapsley, who summed up Tommy Bryceland to a "T".

Davie said: "Tommy was a cheeky player. He didn't carry a great deal of weight, so all his trickery was achieved through sheer skill. He was a master at nutmegging you and then, just to rub it in, he would come back and poke the ball through you legs again. I reckon Tommy was a better player than wee Tam Gemmell, just because he was that bit cheekier."

That the Bryceland boy could provide such entertainment was all down to an excessive load of self confidence. As one tabloid journalist described Tommy, "He had a guid conceit o' his self."

The Bryceland birth certificate was posted on March 1, 1939 in Greenock, with Tommy attending St Mungo's Primary followed by St Columba's Secondary.

The youngest of a family of nine, his playing exploits at school earned him a call up for both the national Under-14 and Under- 15 sides. Already the local scouting mafia were on red alert, earmarking him for great things.

Tommy recalled: "I signed for Gourock Juniors when I was 16, but spent only six to nine months with them before Willie Reid signed me for St Mirren on my 17th birthday.

"Willie told me he would give me all the time in the world to develop and mature. It didn't quite work out that way. I signed on the Wednesday, played against Celtic Reserves on the Saturday and found myself playing against the Celtic first team the following Wednesday."

Tommy went on to make exactly 150 appearances for St Mirren, netting 66 goals. As is the norm in playing for Paisley's finest, there were numerous high days and generally an equal collection of down days.

April 25, 1959, was one such heyday in the Bryceland annals, beating Aberdeen at Hampden and earning him a Scottish Cup winners badge. And while Tommy was a marksman in that 3-1 win, many would argue his finest hour occurred at the semi-final stage when Saints mesmerised the residents of Celtic Park with a brilliant 4-0 turnover.

Tommy also scored in this game, as he did in the second round against Peebles Rovers, the Bryceland hat-trick greatly enhancing the win bonus payment.

He said: "We had a good side at that time, a good blend of experience, and Gerry Baker made us tick. We had signed Gerry from Motherwell for peanuts and he was ultra fast. Tommy Gemmell and myself fed him a strong diet of through balls and Gerry did the rest."

And then there was that other Scottish Cup final of 1962. Having won the cup three years earlier, the euphoric expectations of the Paisley public went into frenetic overdrive. From the 1959 side only "Cockles" Wilson and Tommy remained, with TB now a mature performer in this Saints side.

It was definitely a low day in the Bryceland diary as Saints succumbed to Rangers thanks to goals from Ralph Brand and Davie Wilson.

It took a fractured leg in the 61-62 League Cup campaign against Hearts to put a brake on the burgeoning Bryceland career. To say he was missed was reflected in St Mirren teetering down the league, only to miss out on relegation on goal difference. St Johnstone were the fall guys for Division Two.

A measure of the Bryceland rapport with the Love Street fans was vividly brought home on his return after that leg break. In a reserve match against Partick Thistle, over 4,000 turned out to see a return of the Brycelend magic. And it worked - Saints won 4-3.

Tommy was stripped to play against Motherwell on September 24, 1962, when an offer for his services was tabled by Norwich City. It was former manager Willie Reid, now with The Canaries, who had recommended Bryceland to the Carrow Road authorities.

Stripped he might have been to face the Fir Park side, but in accepting the deal and fearing any possible injury to Love Street's prized asset, Tommy was mothballed. He didn't play against The Steelmen and headed for East Anglia. The £20,000 transfer fee was a record for Norwich.

Life in the rural domain of the Norfolk club was good for Tommy and his wife Maureen. Norwich weren't doing too badly either, beating a Manchester United side in the FA Cup that boasted Denis Law. But it was a move to Oldham Athletic that stamped the accolade approval on the English segment of the Bryceland CV.

The Boundary Park side galloped up the English leagues, moving from fourth to second division in the space of four seasons. Not surprisingly, Tommy scooped numerous Player of the Year awards for his contributions.

Tommy explained: "I came back to St Mirren as a player for a fortnight. The manager was Wilson Humphries. He never saw me play - I was signed by the directors!

"Wilson left and I was offered the job as player-manager. I'd have to confess that this was one of my more major mistakes in life - it was a disillusioning process.

"The bank were after the club for money and I had to sell players. I sold Gordon McQueen to Leeds, Ally McLeod to Southampton, Iain Munro to Hibs and Jim Blair to Norwich. If you try to build a team for promotion you can't go on selling players."

However, Tommy did broker one prime addition to the St Mirren pay roll - he signed Tony Fitzpatrick.

Tony remembers him fondly: "Tommy was a players' man, he spoke their language. Every manager requires respect from his players and Tommy earned high esteem from all his lads, based on many of his playing exploits and his no nonsense approach in dealing with players."

A step down from the managerial throne in May 1973 meant a crust still had to be earned and it came initially over a six-year period from the proceeds of a newsagent's shop just up the road from Ibrox. Tommy revealed: "I won £4,800 on the Rangers Pools when I was there."

Still keen to be his own man in business, Tommy and Maureen bought a hotel in Ayr in 1983 and sold it 13 years later. It was a family business with Tommy as manager, Maureen doing the cooking and one of his two sons manning the bar.

Well received by the St Mirren faithful on his occasional visits to Love Street, Tommy opted for latter life in Ayr,.

GERRY BURRELL

CONDUCTING an interview with Gerry Burrell can seriously damage your health. Life is a breeze for the wee man from Portadown, in Northern Ireland such that his laugh a minute responses and humorous anecdotes all combine to create life-threatening pressure on the rib cage.

Gerry had already sampled soccer life on the Irish senior stage but rumblings over a settled wage deal and unpaid bonuses saw him step down a rung to the lower divisions to ply his trade with Dundela.

Also featuring in the side was a likely centre-half, Ronnie McFaul by name. McFaul's pedigree had been flashed across the Irish Sea to manager Bobby Rankine at Love Street.

An overnight sea crossing from the Glasgow Broomielaw saw Rankine move to take in Dundela's next game and run his professional eye over what was on offer.

But it wasn't McFaul who caught the Saints chief's eye. What was on offer was something akin to an Irish leprechaun whose touchline cantrips were enough for Rankine to bring Burrell over to Love Street in 1946.

Virtually an outside right in all his playing days, Gerry chuckled at one game where he was arguably played out of position.

He recalled: "It was just before the Second World War. I was picked to play for the Irish Schools side at the Oval, which was Glentoran's ground.

I don't know how they justified their selection but I found myself playing at left-back! Now, come on, I'm only 5'-3", can you imagine me playing in defence with my lack of inches. In truth, I never grew up!"

Gerry's initial outings in a black and white jersey are firmly entrenched in his Irish memory banks.

He went on: "My first ever game was a reserve match against Queen of the South at Love Street. I was on the right wing and Alfie Lesz was on the other. Alfie was a Polish lad who had been involved in the army during the war and stayed to fight St Mirren's battles. Can you imagine it? Two foreigners on the wings and not one over 5'-3"!"

Saints won 2-0 but the Burrell performance was sufficient to earn him his first-team spurs, confirmed a few weeks later in a match against Rangers at Love Street.

The Ibrox captain, the stuffy Jock "Tiger" Shaw - he of Annathill mining stock - never had it so bad as he tried to put a dampener on the Burrell will o' the wisp touchline antics. Saints took both points in this game, Willie Jack scoring twice in the Buddies' 2-1 win.

Gerry's quest for international recognition saw a communication failure on the part of the Northern Ireland FA, whose myopic meanderings failed to become aware of the scintillating wing play on offer.

Although he made the Northern Ireland side in a representative match against the British Army, Gerry's thirst for football fame became media orientated.

He said: "My youthful ambitions were always triggered to be either a Willie Waddell or a Jimmy Delaney. In 1948, The Daily Record ran a survey to select the best wingers in Scotland. Waddell was named number one, Gordon Smith was placed second and I was number three.

"For me, the wee lad from County Armagh, that was absolutely brilliant to be compared with these players. Maybe I wasn't too bad a player after all."

Gerry, for one match, did achieve a minor degree of Inter League selection.

He never actually played but was named as reserve to Smith.

He asked: "Doesn't that just take the biscuit? Me, born and bred in Northern Ireland, playing in Scotland and being nearly selected to play against the League of Ireland at Dalymount Park in Dublin. Talk about a soccer league of nations."

After six years with St Mirren, it was time to move on. George Anderson was the man who made things tick at Dens Park. The combined Dundee chairman and manager needed a winger with flair, and money was the motivating factor for Gerry's switch to Tayside.

He admitted: "I was getting £8 a week at Love Street and when Dundee offered me £14 a week, there was no contest, I just had to go. I felt like a millionaire."

Three years with the Dark Blues preceded a move to Huddersfield Town, where Andy Beattie, the former Scotland manager, was in charge. However, a broken leg in an FA Cup match with Tranmere Rovers put the Burrell career on hold, six months being spent on his rehabilitation.

He did, in fact, finish his UK playing career with Chesterfield but as Gerry recalled: "Around about that time I was getting a bit dull in the beard!"

By this time he had celebrated blowing out 36 candles on his birthday cake and still wouldn't hang up his boots.

A move back to his native heath saw him complete a further six seasons with Portadown, although Gerry would freely admit the same sparkle from his early days wasn't quite so prominent.

An electrician to trade, working on domestic housing and factory installations, one of Northern Ireland's brightest sparks certainly made his mark on the St Mirren scoring records. Credited with around seven hat-tricks, he also gained further immortality by netting four against Morton in the 1948 Renfrewshire Cup final.

Ask his wife Pat how he relaxes at home and she'll tell you there is no apparent cure for perpetual motion. He's never still but did manage time in the past to act as a scout for both Manchester City and Linfield.

He was dubbed "A Belfast Buddie" - a moniker well deserved.

IAN CAMERON

IT was a major dilemma. You are a student at Glasgow University and the academic Dons scheduld a final exam for a Saturday. Not any Saturday, but May 16, 1987, to be exact. It's the day of the Cup Final and you are in the St Mirren player pool. Such was the predicament that confronted Ian Cameron.

Ian said: "I hadn't told the manager Alex Smith that my exams were coming up. In truth, I was shattered to find my exam on Financial Institutions had been programmed for that particular day. The university authorities couldn't change the date and this was an important exam for my MA degree course.

"Fortunately, they did show some compassion by rescheduling a personal exam for me starting at 8.30am and finishing three hours later."

No exam is ever easy but the adrenalin Ian so generated was sufficient to gain a creditable pass. And he went on to be named as a substitute against Dundee United.

Ian explained: "Alex put me on the bench and I came on to replace Kenny McDowall. St Mirren weren't quoted to win, we were clearly labelled as the underdogs. It wasn't the greatest of games in footballing terms but the Tannadice team were still embroiled with their no win cup final hoodoo. That monkey on their backs certainly didn't help them."

The Sunday after that Cup success, Ian didn't make the St Mirren trip to Singapore and the winning of the Epson Trophy. Further examinations were on the nearby Cameron horizon.

A player with an educated left peg, Ian always knew he would be a pro footballer. The kick-start came from his days at North Kelvinside School and The Boys' Brigade.

He recalled: "I was playing in a BB five-a-side tournament at Clydebank. John Wilson was a St Mirren scout at the time. He saw me play and invited me to go for a trial. So I went and joined the St Mirren Boys' Club when I was 13.

"Jim Clunie and Rikki McFarlane signed me on an S Form but it was Rikki who arranged for my autograph to appear on a professional form.

"I had the greatest respect for these guys and I particularly had a lot of time for Eddie McDonald, who was a coach at that time. He taught me a lot."

The autumn of 1983 spawned some memorable times for the young Mr Cameron. He made his St Mirren first-team debut on September 10 against Dundee at Love Street. In Ian's words: "Not a particularly brilliant game. It finished goalless but I hit the post and should have scored."

That debut was a pre runner of St Mirren's UEFA Cup campaign. Drawn against Feyenoord and only one down from the first leg at Love Street, hopes of a reversal on the continent were high.

Cameron said: "My abiding memory of that game was standing in the tunnel beside Johann Cruyff. He was 35 at the time and I'm standing there thinking I'm standing beside a God. As a player, he was simply fantastic.

"We were 2-0 down and Rikki McFarlane wanted to give me the experience of playing at that level. I was told to warm up and was about to go on for the last 15 minutes when Frank McDougall was sent off. Rikki told me he couldn't put me on.

"While I was disappointed, I did get my European chance four years later in the Cup Winners' Cup competition when St Mirren played Tromso and Mechelen.

"What sticks in my mind was the criticism of the press in the Mechelen game. Drawing 0-0 in Belgium and losing 0-2 at Love Street wasn't acceptable to the media on the basis that this was Mechelen's first season in European competition. However, they were a quality side who went on to win that 87-88 competition without losing a game home or away."

Six seasons at Love Street and Tony Fitzpatrick had now taken over.

Ian said: "He wanted a playing makeover. He wanted a more physical approach to the game. I fell down the pecking order when he brought Peter Weir in from Leicester City to play on the left. I decided to leave and that's when Alex Smith, my former mentor, rolled out the Aberdeen welcome mat for me."

Three seasons were spent at Pittodrie before the enigmatic John Lambie signed Ian for Partick Thistle – effectively Ian's home town team.

Considered more as a playmaker than a goal scorer, there were a couple of golden moments in the goal getting department.

August 11, 1993 saw Partick take on Albion Rovers at Fir Park in the League Cup. The final score was 11-1 to the Maryhill Magyars and Ian netted four.

He recalled: "That was one of the strangest games I've ever been involved in. The law of probability is you'll only take a percentage of the chances on offer. In that game every time we attacked we scored. I've never played in a similar game since."

One other scoring nugget for the Cameron CV saw a goal for Thistle against Hearts at Tynecastle.

Ian added: "It was March 23, 1996. We won 5-2 but the personal satisfaction was my ability to delicately chip big Gilles Rousset. Remember the big French keeper was all of 6'-5''"

From Firhill and over 150 outings for the Maryhill side, it was on to Hibernian, followed by a spell with Raith Rovers

Clydebank then had Ian's services for a year but he was then a part-time player. With a developing career in accountancy, marshalling the financial management of a number of companies, the fitting in of training schedules was becoming difficult.

The Cameron career finally finished with one last year with Partick, his 18-year playing spread registering over 400 first-team appearances with six clubs.

Perhaps a legacy of such an extensive playing programme was emphasised with Ian having to undergo a hip replacement operation when he was only in his late thirties.

Still the appetite for the game hasn't in any way been assuaged. The holder of the SFA's "A" Coaching Licence, Ian was involved in youth coaching at Rangers' Murray Park until the George Adams regime took over.

Still determined to be involved in a post-playing coaching operation, Ian, in the short term, was content to monitor the progress of son Ian.

In addition to outings with the Scottish Schools team and the national Under-17 squad, Ian jnr was at one time a youth player with his dad's old club at Firhill. A clear case of like father, like son!

BOBBY CARROLL

THERE are many unsung heroes in the lower reaches of the great game. Many are one-man bands in attending to player recruitment, match secretary duties, the strip laundering, match catering and every other facet of club life.

Bobby Carroll would agree that the nomination for one such hero must be Gerry Marley. Gerry was the manager of Campsie Black Watch when Bobby played for them in 1956, and 50 years later Gerry was still at the helm of the Juvenile side. Clearly a lifespan of dedication destined for possible inclusion in the Guinness Book of Records.

Bobby, fleet of foot in his playing days, owes further thanks to another Campsie stalwart in one Charlie Stewart. A sports coach and physical fitness guru, it was Charlie who contributed in adding another yard to the blistering pace of the young Mr Carroll.

But to the beginning. May 13, 1938 was the day Bobby arrived in Glasgow's Possilpark district and he went on to develop and create interest in his football future with some sterling displays on the left wing with his school side.

Bobby's route to the Senior scene was triggered by former school pals enlisting his services for the St George's Road former pupils' side – not one of Bobby's earlier learning establishments.

Then came Campsie Black Watch before, as a 19-year-old, he set foot on the Junior scene with Irvine Meadow. It was a profitable move, Bobby winning a Scottish Junior Cup medal in 1959 when the Meadow Park side defeated Shettleston Juniors 2-1 at Hampden Park. The 62,000 crowd that day was the second largest ever for a Junior cup final.

Celtic's Jimmy McGrory had provisionally signed Bobby a year before that cup final but his entry to first-team duty at Parkhead was a frustrating experience.

Bobby explained: "This was the era when the Celtic side was collectively known as 'Kelly's Kids'. Frankly there were too many youngsters in the side. I came from Irvine Meadow straight into the first team.

"It was very much a limited learning process when an initial spell in the Reserves would have enabled you to cope better. As for tactics, they were non existent – you just went onto the park and did your own thing!"

Doing his own thing earned Bobby a niche in the Celtic scoring archives. He scored Celtic's first goals in European competition, netting a brace in the 1962 Fairs Cities cup first round tie against Valencia.

He was also the scorer of Celtic's first ever goal under the Parkhead floodlights in a friendly encounter with Everton. This was Celtic's second match under the lights, having previously lost 2-0 to Wolves.

Bobby's move to St Mirren in February 1963 came out of the blue.

He recalled: "I didn't know anything about it until Jimmy McGrory and St Mirren director Willie Waters arrived on my doorstep at the time when 'Bunty' Lamb was the Love Street chairman. I was in and out of the Celtic side and just wanted to play regular football so I agreed to sign for Saints.

"That was on the Friday night and the next day St Mirren were playing Aberdeen in the league at Pittodrie. The St Mirren lads had travelled up on the train on the Friday but by the time I arrived the game was off – it had been snowing heavily."

A fee of £7,000 to the Parkhead exchequer had helped to lubricate the move. Another facet that prompted Bobby's move to Love Street occurred in the previous season.

He said: "Celtic had played St Mirren midweek in a league match at Love Street before the two sides met in the Scottish Cup semi-final at Ibrox.

"In the league game, even if I say it myself, I played a blinder at centre-forward and scored two in a 5-0 win. However, I had been told that no matter how well I played I wouldn't be in the semi-final team."

What was Celtic's loss was clearly St Mirren's gain, the Buddies winning 3-1, but not before the local constabulary had quelled a mini riot.

Carroll said: "The semi-final scoreline wasn't to the liking of the Celtic fans. They invaded the park to try to get the game stopped. The referee took the players off and Bob Kelly, the Celtic chairman, came into the dressing room to tell us that if the match wasn't resumed he would concede the tie to St Mirren in order not to establish a precedent.

"Jim Clunie had played in both games for St Mirren. He was amazed that I had been left out of the team and made the point, 'Your absence was worth a goal of a start to us.'"

Bobby's goal-getting ability wasn't confined to Celtic Park. Two memorable hat-tricks are logged on to his St Mirren CV.

Bobby added: "Perhaps the most memorable was the treble against Partick Thistle at Love Street on December 5, 1964. You see deep down I'm a Partick supporter – I used to get lifted over the Firhill turnstiles when I was a boy."

Bobby's first hat-trick was against Hearts, again at Love Street, in an April 1963 league game. His total scoring return was 19 from 70 black and white outings.

Jerry Kerr needed to spice up Dundee United's endeavours and took Bobby to Tannadice. But his tangerine appearances were limited due to the major influx of Scandinavian players such as Finn Dossing and Orjan Persson.

Bobby explained: "I didn't take to Jerry Kerr. United were due to meet Barcelona in the 66-67 Fairs Cup and Jerry went over to watch them in action. But we were never told anything about their strengths and weaknesses. Fortunately for him, we won 4-1 on aggregate over the two ties."

After life on Tayside, Bobby had short spells with Coleraine and Queen of the South. He returned to Irvine Meadow, where he almost made another Junior cup final only to sustain a severe leg gash courtesy of a frayed aluminium stud. Meadow went on to take the honours in that final in 1973 on the back of a 1-0 win over Cambuslang Rangers after two draws.

Bobby never played again but did some coaching with Yoker Athletic – the coaching sessions being substantially abbreviated due to the Holm Park playing personnel showing a marked reluctance to train.

Always full-time as a player, Bobby's part-time occupation was initially as a wagon repairer with British Rail at Cowlairs, before he became a sales representative with a company specialising in hydraulic fittings.

Indoor bowling at East Kilbride is his post-playing pastime, with the St Leonards club satisfying his outdoor bowling deeds. Records also highlight Bobby as a one-time club champion.

STEVE CLARKE

SOME might classify him as a dour Scot but his self determination blends well with the strengths of his Caledonian character. Such distinctive features allied to Steve Clarke's roots from downtown Saltcoats have provided a platform for charismatic success in the wider football world.

Born on the Ayrshire coast on August 29, 1963, football was all important in the Clarke family. Steve's brother Paul played for Kilmarnock while Saltcoats Victoria were brother Michael's modus operandi on the Junior scene.

Prominent in his school side, Steve immediately caught the eye of the Beith Juniors officials, going on to join the Bellsdale Park club as a 15-year-old.

The St Mirren scouting network provided glowing reports of this emerging talent and manager Rikki McFarlane was quick to have Steve append his autograph to a Saints registration form.

It was as an 18-year-old that Steve made his first appearance in black and white. Partnering Tommy Wilson at full-back, Saints had Ayr United as visitors in a sectionalised League Cup tie. The Buddies logged in a 3-1 win thanks to a Lex Richardson hat-trick.

High on Steve's listing of memorable St Mirren games must be a 3-0 turnover of Rangers at Love Street in October '83, while Hearts at home in the second league game of the 85-86 season saw a 6-2 win registered in St Mirren's favour. The goals that day came from Messrs Rooney, Godfrey, Fitzpatrick, McGarvey, Speirs and a certain Mr Clarke.

Not so pleasing was the 1984 Scottish Cup semi-final against Celtic, the Hoops grinding out a 2-1 win and going on to lose out in the final to Aberdeen by the same scoreline.

The 1980s saw not quite a mass exodus to the English leagues but certainly a steady trickle of football potential opting for life south of Hadrian's Wall.

John Hollins was the Chelsea manager who added to the trickle. Clarke's 150 quality league appearances for Saints had energised the Stamford Bridge boss to bring the Saltcoats man down to London in the middle of the 86-87 season. A fee of £400,000 is reported to have been deposited in the St

Mirren bank account.

"To Infinity and Beyond" might well have been attributed to Buzz Lightyear – but it was also an applicable summary of Steve's Chelsea career.

Initially, his time at The Bridge wasn't without the occasional setback. Relegated in his first full season at the club, a chronic back injury sent him on a downward spiral that resulted in a transfer request being rejected out of hand by boss Bobby Campbell.

Things could only get better – and they did!

A total of 421 appearances for the Blues encompassed a gallery of outstanding success for the Ayrshireman.

In 1988, he trod the international boards for the first time, winning the first of his six caps against Hungary in a 2-0 Scotland win at Hampden Park.

A visit to Wembley for the 1994 FA Cup final against Manchester United wasn't quite so fruitful, the Old Trafford side registering a 4-0 win.

By now, in May 1996, Ruud Gullit had taken over at Stamford Bridge from Glenn Hoddle. Gullit was an old adversary of Steve's, having faced him in St Mirren's halcyon UEFA Cup days in the early 1980s.

Gullit's Feyenoord side had completed a first round double over St Mirren but Steve's performance wasn't lost on Gullit, the Chelsea player/manager awarding the club captaincy to the ever improving full-back..

The FA Cup was secured by Chelsea in 1997 with a 2-0 win over Middlesbrough. That gave the London club automatic entry to the European Cup Winners' Cup – and the competition would provide some additional baubles for the Stamford Bridge trophy room on the back of a tournament win over VfB Stuttgart.

With Gullit subsequently moving to Newcastle United in 1998, the bond between the Dutchman and the Scot continued, with Steve going up to St James' Park as first-team coach.

The Clarke coaching talent was retained by Sir Bobby Robson at Newcastle until Steve was offered the chance to return to London as a replacement for Jim Duffy at the Chelsea Youth Academy.

The placid deep-thinking nature of the Scot was soon recognised by the new Stamford Bridge boss Claudio Ranieri in giving him a major coaching post at the club. While Steve was not totally multi-lingual, he was nevertheless able to fully communicate with the range of foreign tongues in the home dressing room.

From the Italian dialect of Ranieri to the more perfunctory Portuguese outpourings of Jose Mourinho, Steve was never in any way fazed by the change in managerial direction when Mourinho was recruited to Stamford Bridge for the start of the 2004-05 season – and Steve was appointed assistant manager in July 2004.

Buoyed by the apparent bottomless financial pit of Russian oil tycoon Roman Abramovich, potential talent was identified and recruited to the Morinho-Clarke combination with outstanding success.

The English Premiership was secured in 2005 for the first time since 1954-55 and success on the European club front was within touching distance.

A successful passage in the 04-05 UEFA Champions League embraced wins over Paris St Germain, Porto and CSKA Moscow to reach the knockout stages.

Barcelona were narrowly beaten at this stage but some outspoken indiscretions by Mourinho saw him in receipt of a touchline ban for the quarter-final joust with Bayern Munich, leaving Clarke in charge of the Chelsea technical area. A 6-5 aggregate win over the Bundesliga side was a tremendous accolade for the man from Saltcoats.

Could Chelsea go all the way? Regretfully, a single goal from Liverpool's Luis Garcia put paid to the London club's semi-final hopes.

But Clarke's input to these European and domestic occasions demonstrated he had now reached "Infinity". The uncharted territories of "Beyond" now beckon.

JIM CLUNIE

TO be brought up in the coal mining communities of east Fife where muscle and brawn were the necessary working attributes, a strong going centre-half from the area would, in the line of duty, render considerable physical clout on the playing pitch.

That such a clout factor never over stepped the boundaries of football legality, denying some over enthusiastic whistler the opportunity of brandishing red plastic, would be a remarkable achievement.

Such an achievement is firmly logged into Jim Clunie's soccer CV. He was never once sent off in 18 years!

A provisional schoolboy signing for Raith Rovers in 1950, when he was just 17, Jim had yet to determine his most productive modus operandi in being selected for centre-half, right-half and inside right duties by the Stark's Park club.

Arguably, teenage over enthusiasm created a number of injury problems and after a lengthy rehabilitation he was recalled for a match against Dundee.

Jim was in awe at the prospect. He said: "The Dens Park side were going great guns at the time. They were a team of superstars to me, with the likes of Bobby Flavell, Billy Steel and Doug Cowie in their line up. I was injured again in that game and couldn't get back into the side, big Harry Colville had made the centre-half beat his own."

A move to Aberdeen was confirmed on Hogmannay 1953 and later that season the Dons reached the final of the Scottish Cup.

Jim recalled: "There were four of us in contention for one place in the cup final line up - Joe O'Neill, Billy Smith, Ivor Smith and me. I got the nod and played at inside left. We lost 2-1 to Celtic but playing in front of a crowd of almost 130,000 was a fantastic experience."

It was after that game that the St Mirren-Aberdeen relationship developed.

Three seasons later, St Mirren met the Pittodrie side in the final of the League Cup. Saints' one and only appearance at the ultimate stage of the League Cup competition generated heartbreak for the Buddies and a winners medal for Clunie, his defensive performance blunting the Saints strike force of Laird, Brown and Gemmell.

The Love Street brigade sought a modicum of cup final revenge. It came in the 1959 Scottish Cup and Clunie this time picked up a runners up gong after failing to master the attacking effervescence of Messrs Brycelend, Baker and Gemmell.

If you can't beat 'em, join 'em! It might have been the Clunie maxim when Willie Reid signed him for Saints in 1960, and he would spend six years at Love Street.

Considered to be the best uncapped centre-half in the country, the Clunie St Mirren debut saw Saints take on Hearts. His leadership qualities were unique, having guided the fortunes of Aberdeen for some time after taking over from Archie Glen. As a consequence, he was handed the St Mirren skipper's role in first game.

Yet another cup final beckoned for Jim, his fourth, with St Mirren arriving at Hampden in 1962 to test the mettle of Rangers in the Scottish Cup. The mental fatigue was all St Mirren's as goals from Ralph Brand and Davie Wilson gave the Ibrox side a 2-0 win.

Jim provided an insight of what happened next.

He said: "Alex Wright came in as manager. I was getting on a bit, having trouble with my knee and was eventually given a free.

"I went over to Ballymena on a month's trial but the knee didn't respond and I came back to see what was happening at St Mirren, to find the club had gone part-time. I managed to get a job in Rolls Royce and started up a works team who went on to win their Welfare Cup."

Conceivably, that sampling of football organisation was the catalyst that propelled Jim into the world of coaching and management.

He added: "I was all set to take on the job of trainer-coach with Renfrew Juniors when a former playing colleague at Aberdeen, Ian McFarlane, put me in touch with Lawrie McMenemy, who was the manager at Grimsby Town.

"I was really impressed with my first English game. Doncaster against Grimsby wasn't showcase material but I was sufficiently hooked and was offered the job of first-team coach. We went on to win the Fourth Division championship in 1971-72.

"Lawrie went south to manage Southampton and I was invited to move to The Dell initially as second team coach, going on to take over the first team needs.

"We had a major celebration in 1976 when a single goal from Bobby Stokes won the FA Cup for the English Saints against Manchester United at Wembley."

The year 1978 was the Argentine World Cup year. It also heralded

Clunie's managerial arrival at Love Street, to succeed Alex Ferguson. The new boss went on to oversee a sparkling array of St Mirren success.

Clunie was instrumental in taking the Saints to their highest ever Premier League placement - third in season 1979-80. He also steered them to become the only Scottish club to win the Anglo-Scottish Cup and he took St Mirren on their initial expeditions into European competition.

Clunie left St Mirren Park in November 1980 to be succeeded by Rikki McFarlane. He transferred his management affection to Kilmarnock and remained at Rugby Park for a further three years. Jim was always extremely forceful in making the point that he was sacked as St Mirren's boss but resigned from the Killie job.

In his later years, Jim had a leaning for an occasional round of golf over his local Kilmarnock course but his ageing knees were constantly in a rebellious mode, thus having him regularly manage only 12 of the 18 holes.

The local Kilmarnock Fire Service provided the outlook for Jim's working life, with service as a civilian driver in the service's motor pool.

Jim was 69 when he died on May 12, 2003. At his funeral service, former boss Lawrie McMenemy travelled north to provide a glowing eulogy.

In one particular game, a contentious goal caused Southampton to lose the game 1-0. Jim vigourously remonstrated with the two linesmen at the apparent refereeing gaffe. He was told by McMenemy to cool it and back off.

Southampton later received a letter from the FA demanding an explanation as to the unacceptable behaviour of the Southampton manager!

As Lawrie McMenemy made the point: "To be mistaken for Jim Clunie, I take as the supreme compliment in my football life."

DENNIS CONNACHAN

THOSE who take up residency as a club's last line of defence are a breed apart. In days when team formations were less arithmetically orientated – 4-4-2, 3-5-2 and all that – the tongue in cheek team format comprised nine players, a goalkeeper and an outside left. The net minder and the winger were considered the eccentric components of the side bordering on having head-banging status.

Dennis Connachan was a keeper and one would hasten to add he was never in danger of requiring occupational therapy from the men in white coats.

He was a Gorbals boy, born in 1945 and educated at St John's Primary before moving to the higher learning strata of Holyrood Secondary. If nothing else was ever academically implanted in the Connachan brain cells, his history studies would surely have earned him a Higher grade – his tutor being the "Brain of Britain" and soccer pundit Bob Crampsey.

An outfield player in his early days, it was Davie Doig, a former Arbroath player and a teacher at Holyrood, who recognised the Connachan future playing forte was to be domiciled between the proverbial sticks.

The route path from school saw limited stopovers at Giffnock North and Glasgow United.

Dennis recalled: "I was training at Third Lanark's Cathkin Park and managed to get a game with the Queen's Park fourth team. Queen's had a variety of names for their sides – the Strollers, the Hampden XI with their fourth team were the Victoria XI.

"This was all heady stuff. I was still at school and was eventually selected to play a game at Parkhead for a representative schools side. Somebody at Parkhead must have been impressed with my performance because I was approached and asked to sign an "S" Form for Celtic. I was only 17."

However, the magnetism of the Glasgow giants upset the Connachan compass. His career path wasn't sign posted and with the proliferation of goalkeepers on Celtic's books, Dennis found himself way down the pecking order. He was P45'd out of Paradise and headed for the Junior kingdom and Yoker Athletic. His stay at Holm Park was limited as Renfrew Juniors were next to be incorporated into his career equation.

Connachan recalled: "Doug Millward was the St Mirren manager who signed me in 1964. He eventually moved to America and was responsible for me playing for Baltimore Bays for a year. It was an interesting time but my heart was back in Scotland in general and Paisley in particular."

Dennis's heart won and he returned to St Mirren with Alex Wright as manager to become Saints' last line of defence for three seasons.

But Dennis explained: "By the time Wilson Humphries took over the managerial reins, it was clear my future at Love Street was going to provide little or no opportunities. I moved back to Celtic and what really clinched the deal were the ramifications of that League Cup final with Partick Thistle at Hampden on October 23, 1971.

"Losing four goals in a final is not an accepted goalkeeping standard at Celtic Park. Evan Williams was the unlucky Parkhead keeper on the day. That was on the Saturday and I was signed the following Monday."

Playing at Dunfermline's East End Park is firmly etched in the Connachan memory banks. His last game for St Mirren was a friendly at the Pars' ground while his first for Celtic was also at the Fifers' home.

His pinnacle playing experience was never realised in a black and white shirt. The colours had changed to green and white when, in 1974, Dennis was the recipient of a Scottish Cup winners medal courtesy of a 3-0 win (note the clean sheet!) over Dundee United.

And while Dennis won league championship medals with Celtic and subsequently at Cappielow with Morton, he makes the point the winning euphoria couldn't match the camaraderie of his playing companions while at St Mirren Park.

He then left the pearly gates of Celtic Park in 1977 to join Clydebank as cover for the legendary Jim Gallacher.

Life at Kilbowie Park lacked fulfillment and lasted for only three months. The Connachan scruples were stretched to the limit, rendering Dennis to say: "Being stuck on the bench wasn't for me – I didn't like being a paid supporter!"

Dennis took some playing solace with Ayr United prior to Benny Rooney appearing on the scene and signing him for Morton. The association worked well, Morton winning the First Division title in 1978 and climbing into the Premier League.

A year at Clyde followed before Dennis completed the soccer cycle and returned to the Junior game.

It could have been a spectacular curtain call – a Neilston-based goalkeeper playing for Arthurlie. Maybe an unlikely combination but it was a partially successful one. However, it was Pollok who rewrote the script, Arthurlie losing out to the Newlandsfield side by a 1-0 scoreline in the 1981 Junior Cup final.

Outfield players are always keen to brag about scoring a blockbuster goal but it's a bit more difficult for keepers. For them, a memorable save is perhaps their cameo to be considered.

Dennis said of his top moment: "I think it would have to be a save in that Scottish Cup final. Andy Gray, who is not unknown now on Sky TV, whacked in a pile driver. It was an instinctive save and even the Celtic supporters were arguing that it had crossed the line. It didn't and I've got photographs to prove the point. But it was nice to be described as a bird in flight in making that save."

The older generation tend to be somewhat uncomplimentary regarding the current quality of play. Dennis Connachan is no different.

He reasoned: "There isn't the same entertainment value and there's too much stalemate, too defensive. In my St Mirren days, the policy was always to go forward. Nowadays it's all about not losing, which is to the detriment of the fans. Five defenders across the back spells negative football. Players aren't allowed to express themselves."

The Connachan soccer interests have not been totally laid to rest. Son Dennis, not one to follow in his father's goalkeeping footsteps, was a left-sided defender and found favour with Benburb, Queen's Park and Partick Thistle

Dennis senior was latterly a hard-working committee member with Neilston Juniors, with his colleagues at Brig-o-Lea no doubt grateful for his experience.

Always a money man, Dennis was a wages clerk with the civil engineering firm Rockfall prior to going full-time soccer wise.

Once the playing days were finished, finance still played a big part in augmenting the family income with Mr Connachan the company credit controller with Joseph Dunn, the soft drinks, beer and cider specialists.

With his financial career overlapping his playing career, Dennis has always had high credit ratings for all things St Mirren – both then and now.

TONY CONNELL

PLAYER identification in the heat of the on-field battle has always been difficult. Pre-war, it was hairdos of black, red, blonde or bald, together with the physical dimensions of height and/or girth that provided the identifying characteristics.

Numbered jerseys helped the identification process, although as all Saints fans know only too well, finding a colour that stood out rather than merged with their traditional black and white could create considerable eye strain.

Celtic thought they'd snuffed the problem, their numbers appearing on their players' shorts. It was a kosher enough arrangement until UEFA regulations demanded numbers on backs for those engaged in European competition.

However, Tony Connell had no difficulty in being recognised. He was always honest and always a quality full-back. His hirsute appearance did no favours for any Gillette share dealings, although the Connell beard no doubt provided moderate insulation in the colder climes of winter.

Tony was initially recognised as a future player during his time at Holyrood Secondary, where like a few other aspiring footballers he was taught history by the knowledgeable Bob Crampsey.

Tony said: "I was fortunate to join Glasgow United, the well known amateur side. They played at Strathclyde Juniors' ground but regretfully the Junior side are no more. United's roll of honour included a number of prominent players that reached the top, not the least Kenny Dalglish and Alex MacDonald.

"Not surprisingly, many of the United team went on to play for the Strathclyde side and that's when I was signed by George Young for the late lamented Third Lanark."

George - Monarch of the Scottish game and nicknamed "Corky" because of his penchant for sequestrating all the champagne corks used in the celebration process at the Ibrox club's various successes - was having trouble in keeping the good ship Third Lanark afloat. George resigned in 1962 and Connell experienced a succession of new managers. Willie Steel was one, next was Bobby Evans, followed by Frank Joyner and, lastly, former Ranger Bobby Shearer.

Severe financial mismanagement at Cathkin Park brought about the Third Lanark downfall at the end of season 1966-67. It was a regretful demise after a 95-year contribution to the Scottish game.

Connell was still a registered Third's player at the death and we are indebted to Cathkin historian Bert Bell in highlighting one dramatic financial occasion.

He said: "It was following a match against Clydebank in April 1967. Bobby Shearer had replaced Frank Joyner as manager. After the game, the Third's players, as usual, had gathered to collect their wages. Shearer found to his great consternation that they were not available so he took instant remedial action.

"He got hold of the gate monies and prepared the individual dues himself. Truth to tell, one of the envelopes handed over surrendered to the sheer weight of the coins, burst open and an unidentified player was left to scoop up his wages from the floor!"

We have it on good authority that it wasn't Tony Connell who scrambled for the scattered coinage, but he did play in Third Lanark's last ever match - a 5-1 drubbing from Dumbarton at Boghead.

A momentous season was 66-67. Third Lanark folded, the SFA fell heir to all the Cathkin players' contracts and St Mirren were relegated.

A makeover at Love Street was required and Alex Wright was tasked with the job of revitalising Saints' fortunes. He needed a left-back and sought out Connell's signature.

Both Motherwell and St Mirren had offered Tony terms but Wright's deal of £200 was deemed to be more acceptable.

The tide turned for Tony and in his first season in Paisley, Saints scooped the Division Two title, conceding only 23 goals in 36 games. Tony's contribution in the promotion success was to miss out on only one game in the league campaign.

While details of Tony's St Mirren debut are somewhat hazy in the football mists of time, the events of November 16, 1968, spring readily to his mind.

Rangers were the Love Street visitors and returned to Ibrox nursing a single goal defeat thanks to a superb goal from Hugh Gilshan. Some might ungraciously add that the enveloping fog and frosty pitch were prime contributors to Saints' success.

Tony spent four seasons with St Mirren and found favour with Saints fans in 69-70 when they crowned him as their Player if the Year.

A move to join Queen of the South followed and he spent three campaigns at Palmerston Park, followed by reinstatement to the Juniors and service with Pollok for three years.

A desk job with Glasgow District Housing Department meant a need for recreational activity was required at the weekend. And for the full-back, born in Govan, one could still see Tony Connell going through the motions when he was 50 with a Sunday afternoon kick around with the Giffnock North Old Crocks. And, yes, the beard still lives!

NEIL COOPER

IT'S always a convincing dialogue. Any soccer conversation with Neil Cooper leaves you in no doubt that here is a football aficionado steeped in the game with a 100 per cent plus rating in commitment and compassion for the industry.

Perhaps not in the major metropolises of Glasgow and Edinburgh, but most players derive a great feel good factor in signing for their home town team. Cooper was over the moon in putting pen to an "S" Form for manager Jimmy Bonthrone when he joined Aberdeen back in July 1974.

Neil recalled: "I started as a centre-forward at Hilton Academy, managing to bang in a fair collection of goals both for the school and at boys' club level.

"I'd have to admit my academic endeavours weren't great with no Highers to speak of. I never really stuck in at school – sport and football were my passions. I simply wanted to be a football player and luckily I managed to achieve that ambition."

Neil would freely admit to lacking a modicum of pace as a striker but he always had the ability to hold the ball and regularly deposit it in the opposition net.

The Pittodrie legend that is Teddy Scott was the reserve team coach at the time of Neil's arrival on the senior scene. On one occasion the team were short of players at the back. Neil was seconded to a defensive role, performed well, and went on to play his entire career there.

A young player can become frustrated if playing opportunities are conspicuous by their absence. After six years with the Granite City side, Cooper was possibly embalmed in disillusionment.

Willie Miller was never injured and Alex McLeish was playing out of his skin. Collectively, the pair went on to net 142 international caps, so the chances of a game for Neil were extremely limited.

A career switch was a necessity and Alan Clarke took Neil to Barnsley on the back of a £35,000 transfer fee. Even there, defensive roles were thin on the ground as Welsh international Ian Evans and the renowned Mick McCarthy the resident defensive king pins.

Three seasons with the Oakwell Ground club, a change of manager and a move to Grimsby Town followed as Barnsley lad Dave Booth signed the Scot for the Cleethorpes-based club.

By now the St Mirren management team comprised Alex Miller, assisted by Drew Jarvie and Martin Ferguson.

The Love Street defensive line up was in need of refurbishment and with Jarvie highly-knowledgeable of the Cooper skill factors during their time at Aberdeen, Miller was persuaded to bring the Aberdonian to Paisley.

Neil's introduction to the St Mirren way of life was pure theatre. The date was November 19, 1983.

Cooper explained: "My first game for Saints was a league match against Celtic at Love Street. We were two down after 15 minutes but fought back to win 4-2 thanks to goals from Stevie Clarke, John McCormack, Ian Scanlon and Frank McDougall."

Like so many St Mirren players of that era, the 1987 Scottish Cup final looms large in their memory banks. Cooper in particular caught the eye of the attending Press corps, winning the Man-of-the-Match accolade, brazenly entitled "Mr Superfit".

Neil admitted: "It was good to receive the honour, but you must remember that this was a team effort for Paisley. You never want to think about individual performances – it's the team blend that counts.

"We were always confident of getting a result against Dundee United as we always had a good record against them in Paisley.

"We had a good Saturday night, then toured Paisley in an open top bus on the Sunday afternoon before flying down to Heathrow. We were off to Singapore to play in the Epson Trophy tournament and had fellow competitors Southampton on the same flight. The winning of that competition in Singapore completed a superb week for St Mirren."

Dundee United figured largely in Cooper's Love Street memoirs. He didn't score many league goals, two in fact, with the first against the Tangerines in the 86-87 season.

Season 1984-85 nearly brought Neil's St Mirren career to an abrupt halt. Only 10 games into the league campaign Saints travelled up to Dens Park to take on Dundee.

Neil takes up the story. He said: "I was marking the lanky Colin Harris when I twisted and damaged my medial ligament. We didn't have the technology know-how at that time by comparison to today in accelerating the recovery period.

"I was living in Aberdeen and went into Pittodrie to see the Dons physio. He didn't like what he saw and immediately sent me down to Love Street to see Bobby Holmes. Bobby put me in touch with a specialist but I was out for five months."

The core of Neil's overall playing career of over 300 league appearances was served in Paisley, with 160 outings to his credit.

Gaffer Miller had moved on to take charge of Hibernian, but the Easter Road side had a problem. Gordon Rae was badly injured and Alex required a ready-made replacement. What followed was a £25,000 transfer fee for Neil to appear in an Edinburgh green and white top.

After two seasons at Easter Road, Neil had by now obtained his full alphabet of coaching certificates, which certainly interested former boss Alex Smith, by now in charge at Aberdeen. His need was a quality coach for his reserve side. Neil responded in what was a great move for him, with wife Alison and his two daughters, who were all reunited in their allegiance with the Granite City.

The Cooper coaching catalogue was further expanded with a six-month coaching term at Carlisle United before going on to replace Ian McPhee as manager of Forfar Athletic for the start of the 2000-01 season.

Two years at Station Park saw Neil taking The Loons through to the 2002 quarter-finals of the Scottish Cup, only to come unstuck in losing 6-0 at home to Rangers.

The Cooper talents again returned to Aberdeen, where he has a major input in overseeing the club's youth development programme.

Don't ever ask Neil Cooper how he relaxes away from football.

He said: "I don't relax. Occasionally I manage a frame of snooker, a round of golf or listen to some music. I'm not a TV man apart from football.

"Football coaching is an ongoing activity. I eat, sleep and drink football – I always have and always will, much to the suffering of my wife and two girls. I don't suffer losing a game particularly well." Commitment, compassion – we told you!

JACK COPLAND

A ST MIRREN team picture hangs in the Love Street boardroom. It features the 1967-68 squad who won promotion to the First Division. Surrounding the smiling countenances is the comprehensive statistical count of the season.

Near the bottom of the frame, the name Jack Copland appears, a provisional signing from Beith Juniors credited with a couple of league appearances.

This was the era of the first Copland calling to Love Street.

To provide an overview of Jack's career, it would be fair to describe it as starting innocuously. He was given a free transfer after that championship win, before a circuitous route via Stranraer and Dundee United finished in a blaze of glory as a St Mirren legend.

It all began at Williamsburgh Primary School, with the developing Copland skills being selected as captain of the Paisley & District Schools side.

On to pursue a secondary course with Paisley Grammar and here a conflict of interests had to be rationalised.

Jack explained: "Paisley Grammar was a rugby playing school and for a while I played rugby in the morning and football in the afternoon. I enjoyed playing for the FPs for a year before the oval ball politics soured any continuation in the game for me. It was then I became fully soccer orientated."

That orientation was in part due to Jack's brother Jim.

He went on: "Jimmy Whiteside, a representative of the Renfrew side Kirklandneuk Juveniles, came to the door to see my brother. The team were looking for a goalkeeper, but Jim orchestrated a smart bit of PR work and sweet-talked us both into getting a trial. I was only 19 at the time."

From the Juveniles it was on to the Juniors with Beith - a major force in the Junior game at the time, winning everything but the Scottish Cup.

Jack revealed: "I always regarded myself as a defensive player, but it was Beith who moved me up front and I started to score goals. Word must have got around and I was eventually signed by Stranraer as a striker. I understand they paid the Bellsdale Park side £250 - high finance indeed in those days!"

The little ferry port town took Jack in on a part-time basis, which gave him the opportunity of progressing an outside career in civil engineering.

However, the BSc degree course failed to stimulate Copland's thirst for knowledge, the course being abandoned in the second college year.

Jerry Kerr was recruiting for his Dundee United side when Jack received a call from the Stranraer secretary advising him he'd been transferred to the Tannadice club, with Kerr en route to the Copland home with the relevant transfer documentation.

Jack's value was rising - £10,000 was the exchange rate between the Tannadice and Stair Park treasurers.

Life in Arab country provided something of a domestic shock. In his own inimitable way, Jim McLean, who had succeeded Kerr, laid down something of a seclusion rule whereby all his players had to live in the Dundee area.

That meant all those who had yet to wander down the marriage aisle were ensconced in a hostel in Broughty Ferry, where Walter Smith and Hamish McAlpine were fellow Copland residents.

While much of McLean's style was dictatorial in the extreme, Jack had a high regard for him.

He said: "Jim was a perfectionist, constantly striving to record a 100 per cent rating in everything he tackled at the club. McLean was a great coach, his record speaks for itself. He saw me as more of a defensive player, which I had always thought of as being my personal comfort zone.

"I spent seven years on Tayside but never really settled in the area. I thought about a possible career move outside the game and got a job as a representative for the Nestles organisation. This meant going part-time at Tannadice, which wasn't to McLean's liking and undoubtedly led to my move back to St Mirren in 1976."

If the latter days with United were somewhat contentious, they can't hide two outstanding highlights during Jack's time in the City of Discovery. The 1974 Scottish Cup final heralded United's first appearance at the ultimate stage. But despite sterling performances from the Tannadice rearguard, they failed to prevent a trio of Celtic goals, Harry Hood, Steve Murray and Dixie Deans doing the damage.

A second feather in the Copland cap saw his selection for the Scottish League against their English counterparts at Maine Road in 1974.

He said: "It might have been a memorable experience but it wasn't an enjoyable one. We got cuffed 5-0 and I've never worked so hard in all my life in any match. Denis Tueart, Stan Bowles and Colin Todd saw to that."

Jack's second coming to his hometown team was effectively a contractual arrangement between the directors of both clubs. With United in the

Premier League and Saints domiciled in the First Division, there was no immediate prospect of a former player coming back to haunt the Tangerines, and the funding of the deal was generously donated in part by one of the St Mirren supporters' clubs.

To seal the transfer deal, Jack's market value had risen to the astronomical heights of £17,000 - a figure that caused funding problems for Alex Ferguson.

Fortunately, Saints chairman Willie Todd knew the St Mirren Supporters' Association at Knox Street had a healthy bank balance and the club greatly appreciated the fans' input in coming up with a substantial portion of the readies.

In his second spell in black and white Jack made an important contribution in sealing St Mirren's first promotion to the Premier League in season 1976-77.

In his seven-year spell back, Jack demonstrated powers of leadership that established Saints as one of the most powerful adversaries in the top flight. So much so that a tasting of European competition was achieved in 1980, with Jack leading out St Mirren in their initial UEFA encounter with Elfsberg in Sweden.

Jimmy Bone, team captain in the early 1980s, paid a special tribute to the Copland prowess.

He said: "Jack was a member of the St Mirren side that won the Anglo-Scottish Cup in 1980. His drive and commitment were instrumental in St Mirren being the only Scottish club to win that trophy. I was hoisted onto Jack's shoulders when we received the trophy. In truth, he should have been up there."

The Copland administrative expertise came to the fore in his immediate post playing days, when he was invited to oversee additional commercial ideas,including the setting up of various lotteries to generate much needed income for the club.

In place as general manager at the start of the 1992-93 season, he went on to become club secretary and, after the abortive takeover bid by Englishman Reg Brearley, Jack moved to take over the running of the successful St Mirren Sports & Leisure Complex, making him arguably the longest ever serving employee at St Mirren Park.

ALEX CROWE

THE Paisley weather was behaving well and a mature couple were strolling towards the Main Stand at Love Street.

The lady spoke first: "My name is May Crowe and this is my husband Alex. He used to play here and we wondered, seeing it was his 70th birthday, if we could have a wee nostalgic look around St Mirren Park".

The club were delighted to oblige, such was Alex Crowe's goal scoring efforts in the immediate post-war years at St Mirren.

Born in Motherwell, brought up in the then steel town and living in the Lanarkshire metropolis all his days, Alex wasn't unhappy at not playing for his hometown team.

He said: "It wasn't a particularly bright thing to do. To play for your hometown team and live locally was a big risk, especially if you've had a bad game. Some of the comments on offer weren't at all family friendly!"

That decision was, of course, after his early learning days at Muir Street Primary, before moving up to Central School, which later became an annex of the Dalziel High campus.

Alex explained: "At Central I was selected to play with the Motherwell Schools side and eventually was given a trial for the national schoolboys side.

"I gave up football for a while and started working as an oxyacetylene burner with Motherwell Bridgeworks.

"They had a team and asked me if I would be interested in playing for them. I must have done reasonably well as the now defunct Polkemmet Juniors came in and signed me."

It was the Crowe expertise as an inside right that interested Saints manager Bobby Rankine – a man rated by Alex as an outstanding gentleman.

Bobby was in need of a replacement for Alex Linwood, who had departed for Middlesbrough, with Alex Crowe nominated as the immediate successor. He arrived at Love Street in time for the 1946-47 season.

His first game in St Mirren colours was on a tour of Ireland, but the Crowe competitive debut was against Hamilton at Douglas Park, when Saints lined up in that August game with Newlands, Smith, Lindsay, Stenhouse, Drinkwater, Scott, Telford, Crowe, Aikman, McLaren and Deakin.

Alex said: "I was up against the former Celtic centre-half Joe McLaughlin. Joe was one of those players you might want to call robust – he certainly didn't take any prisoners. We won 4-1 and Archie Aikman scored all four. It was the first time my father had been to see me play.

"He didn't get much time off on a Saturday as he was the manager of a bar in Motherwell. When I came home, his first words were, 'Who told you you could play football?' With such parental appreciation I must have performed not too badly!"

And was there a favourite Alex Crowe goal ?

He said: "The one I remember most was against Third Lanark at Cathkin. Willie Davie was the St Mirren inside left. He had a great left foot but couldn't kick the ball a yard with his right peg. I'd have to confess that I had a similar disposition – only it was my left foot!

"The ball came over and I shouted at him, 'My left foot's better than your right – leave it'. He did and I scored with a rocket. It was one of those once in a lifetime shots. We had a lot of fun in the game in those days".

The description of that Cathkin goal clouds a haze of modesty in the Crowe character.

Picture Love Street in August 1951 and a sectional League Cup tie against Hearts. The final score was a mind-boggling 5-5 draw. Alex Crowe's four-goal contribution would surely earn him the weekend headlines. It didn't – because Willie Bauld scored all five Jambos goals !

If there was a period of downtime in the Crowe career it was down to the fact that he was prone to serious injury.

He escaped the possible shortening of his moderate stature in a game against Raith Rovers at Stark's Park. Big Harry Colville, a dominant centre-half and, as a miner, with all the physical characteristics to complement his defensive style, was in direct opposition to our Mr Crowe. And one bone-crunching challenge left Alex draped over the boundary wall in a semi-comatose condition, providing painful memories of a day out in Kirkcaldy.

But further serious physio attention was yet to come. Rangers at Ibrox in November 1949 and wing-half Ian McColl ensured that any immediate Crowe contribution was promptly terminated with an over exuberant challenge that left Alex with a broken leg.

Subsequent visits to Love Street by the Govan side, with McColl on board, gave the North Bank the opportunity of reminding the former Queen's Park man of his defection from their Christmas Card listings.

Alex progressed to full fitness and a year later, while trackside on a training session, tripped over a raised turf at the edge of the pitch and broke another bone a few inches above his "Ibrox" fracture.

1953 saw Alex leave St Mirren Park but not before his mentor Bobby Bell, a referee, had tried to entice him to Bramhall Lane and Sheffield United. However, Alex's roots were firmly planted in Paisley at that time, the big attraction being wife-to-be May.

Once they were married, Alex and May headed for Ipswich Town and Portman Road. The East Anglian climate and quality of life were particularly attractive to the Crowe family and it showed in Alex's play. Ipswich won the Third Division (South) championship with considerable input from the Crowe boots. But nothing is forever, as the next year they were relegated.

Non-league football then beckoned and Alex finishing his playing days with Stow Market.

Asked for his opinion on the differences in standards and technique from his playing days and the current climate, Alex said: "It's a different game entirely.

"It's now possession football. It's all rush. We had more individual skills in my day. We could take on an opponent and beat him, now it takes two to beat a man."

Those with bus pass credentials would probably endorse the Crowe viewpoint.

WILLIE CUNNINGHAM

IN terms of Northern Ireland tourism, the township of Mallusk might not figure too prominently as a top rated holiday attraction. A few miles up the Irish M2, just north of Belfast and close to Newtonabbey, conceivably Mallusk's main claim to fame is its popular nine-hole golf course.

From a football point of view, a more positive Mallusk distinction was recorded with the arrival of the iconic Willie Cunningham on the town's register of births on February 20, 1930.

Willie's early football meanderings were programmed for the school playground before his father, William, whisked the family across the Irish Sea to take a job in the Royal Ordnance Factory at Bishopton.

Young Willie was only nine at the time but his football development blossomed firstly at Camphill Secondary School and then with the now defunct Secondary Juvenile side Renfrew Waverley, before joining Ardrossan Winton Rovers.

Saints manager Bobby Rankin received glowing reports from his scouting team regaling the talents of an athletic and stylish defender at the ferry port town. And Willie, as an 18-year-old, signing for St Mirren on October 12, 1948.

Willie's entry into senior soccer bordered on the extreme. His debut game saw East Fife visiting Love Street in October 1950, the Bayview side upsetting the pools forecasts with a 2-1 win and Willie clad in the No.3 shirt.

He had to wait a further six weeks before being called up again. The St Mirren goal-getting ability had been offering starvation rations to their supporters and Willie was asked to don the No.9 shirt and try to remedy the deficiency.

That match against Third Lanark registered another failure to score stat and the Hi-Hi's netted four, convincing the St Mirren hierarchy that Cunningham's forte was one of the defensive kind.

Five seasons at Love Street generated 76 appearances and only one goal to the Cunningham credit – that in a 3-0 win over Stirling Albion in January 1952. The peerless Alfie Lesz bagged the other two.

The St Mirren full-back supply line was prolific in its outpourings, with Davie Lapsley, Davie Lindsay, Jimmy Drinkwater and Jimmy Mallan all to the fore.

Cunningham, however, did enough to sustain an interest from the Northern Ireland international selection panel.

The Ulstermen were scheduled to play Wales at Windsor Park, Belfast, on March 7, 1951.

Alf McMichael, of Newcastle United fame, was the resident left-back at the time but called off only 24 hours before the match. Enter Cunningham for the first of his 30 caps, four of which were earned while with St Mirren.

The regular north to south footballing exodus of the time continued when Leicester City's Norman Bullock paid Saints £4,750 to take Cunningham to Filbert Street.

The Cunningham medal collection was greatly enhanced when Leicester topped the Second Division standings in 1956-57, with the Foxes returning to Division One after a two-year absence.

Former Sports Editor of the Belfast Telegraph, Malcolm Brodie, eulogised at length on the Cunningham international career.

Brodie said: "Willie was unique – he was immense. He was a solid defender who was almost a permanent fixture in the Irish side for 10 years. He played primarily at full-back but took over at centre-half from Jackie Blanchflower after Jackie was seriously injured in the Munich air disaster in 1958.

"Willie was one of Northern Ireland's 1958 World Cup heroes in Sweden, when Brazil beat the host country 5-2 in the final. Four caps with St Mirren, a further 23 with Leicester City plus three when he was at Dunfermline was quite a record."

The move from Leicester City to Dunfermline was triggered by the inimitable Jock Stein in September 1960, and the return north proved value for money. Willie was a lynchpin in the Pars side when they defeated Celtic 2-0 in the 1961 Scottish Cup final after a 0-0 draw. The financial return from that replay was reported as being sufficient to rebuild the East End Park main stand, too.

Willie could have opted for a career switch after his playing days as he was a time-served machine tool fitter. But he opted to accept a coaching appointment with Dunfermline, before going on to succeed Stein as manager.

He was in charge of the Pars when they lost 3-2 to Celtic in the 1964-65 Scottish Cup final, and three years later transferred his managerial affection to Falkirk, where under his charge was a certain Alex Ferguson.

It was while at Brockville that Bobby Brown was sacked as the Scotland manager and Willie touted as his possible replacement. It was reported that he turned down the £7,500 national appointment. proclaiming that it wasn't for him. Tommy Docherty was next in line to fill the tartan hotseat.

The Cunningham charisma at Falkirk saw the Bairns being relegated to Division Two in the 68-69 campaign, only to bounce back up the following year.

Around the early 1970s, financial stability was rocking the St Mirren playing endeavours. Manager Tommy Bryceland was under boardroom orders to reduce the cash deficit by off-loading some of the more prominent players. Such an edict did nothing to enhance the Bryceland job satisfaction and Tommy subsequently resigned on May 28, 1973.

The popular choice of a replacement fell to Cunningham, who set up shop at Love Street on June 20.

Willie's two years in charge of the Buddies saw St Mirren as middle of the table tenants of the Second Division, which was not deemed favourable to the Paisley public.

Personal reasons were cited as to why Willie left Love Street but he did fire one positive parting shot. He was instrumental in advising the board on a managerial replacement.

He had known of Ferguson's leadership potential during their time at Falkirk and with Alex currently cutting his management teeth with East Stirlingshire, he became the accepted St Mirren nominee on the Cunningham say so.

After his days of football involvement, Willie was reported to have set up the running of a sports shop in Dunfermline, where he now resides.

Only occasionally taking in a game, he is now more active as a walker, maintaining a level of fitness deemed necessary to cope with the energetic demands of his grandchildren.

BILLY DAVIES

IN the Motherwell publication "The Men Who Made Motherwell Football Club", Billy Davies' playing attributes are described as "A workman-like midfielder whose busy style and neat play, allied to an attacking bent, made him a useful player."

St Mirren aficionados would fully endorse the Fir Park eulogy – but their memories of Billy are much more focussed.

In particular, October 29, 1988, springs readily to mind. St Mirren are at Ibrox taking on the Light Blue residents on league business. It's a no scoring game until Davies collects the ball in midfield, storms forward and unleashes a pile driver that simply screams past Chris Woods in the Rangers goal.

Such was the supreme quality of the goal, BBC's Sportscene went on to portray the strike in their opening programme shots. Additionally, Billy's virtual net-buster earned him the accolade of Goal of the Season, his modest comment being it was "a really great delight for me."

It was a frank admission by Billy that any future career path would see him veering to the playing of football rather than be saddled with any occupation with pure academic tendencies. As such, his first jump on the football ladder saw him in action with the Pollok United Boys' Club.

The potential on show was soon harnessed by Rangers, Billy going on to make his Light Blue debut in a pre-season tournament in Canada just before his 16th birthday.

As always, it is difficult for a young player at Ibrox to make inroads on a permanent basis into the Rangers first-team squad, so after six seasons Sweden beckoned for Billy.

Jonkoping were his first port of call and when he stepped up a division to join IF Elfsborg, an amazing case of sibling rivalry virtually took over.

Billy explained: "When I was leaving Jonkoping, I recommended that my young brother John would make an ideal replacement for me.

"The deal went through and, as luck would have it, Jonkoping drew Elfsborg in the Swedish Cup. It must be something of a record for two Scots brothers to face each other in another country's national cup competition.

"Something had to give and, regretfully for me, it was John's Jonkoping side who won.

"What was interesting from a St Mirren point of view during my time over there, was the fact that the folks at Elfsborg's Ryavallen Stadium always spoke highly of their 1980 UEFA Cup recollections of St Mirren.

"I spent three seasons over in Sweden. I was there with my girlfriend Martha, now my wife, and found the football a fantastic learning experience. It generated great job satisfaction to have the opportunity to play in a different culture and learn a new language."

Saints management maestro, Alex Smith, heard of Billy's impending return to the Caledonian climes and sold the St Mirren idea to him. Billy made his Saints league debut against Hibs at Love Street on October 24, 1987.

Davies recalled: "I had three wonderful years at Love Street and I can honestly say it was a major contributory part of my playing career."

The time came to seek pastures new but Billy's move to Leicester City created a considerable problem for him, particularly on the domestic front.

He said: "I had signed a three-year contract with Leicester but on the home front, my wife Martha had endured a series of threatened miscarriages. My first son William was actually born in Glasgow but after due family considerations and only five games for Leicester we decided not to go back down south to Filbert Street."

Fortunately for Billy, Dunfermline came in for him, the Davies style suiting the Fifers. His four-year spell at East End Park yielded 90 league games and a nomination for a national Player of the Year award.

However, the Pars became somewhat strained financially and had to look to move players on. As a top earner, Billy had to go – and he switched to Motherwell.

Five full playing seasons at Fir Park and a goal against Hanver, the Faroe Islands side, in the 1994 UEFA Cup, generated a chance for Billy to climb the coaching ladder.

He explained: "I took the Under-15 side twice a week at Motherwell before graduating to handle the Under-21 team. Then I got the call to replace Harri Kampman as manager. To be truthful, it wasn't an easy transition. It was an appointment I thought had come a bit too early for me.

"Hindsight is a precise science and in effect, I think I gave up playing too early. I could have played on for another four or five years but when you get the offer to be one of only 12 managers in Scotland's top football tier at only 33 years of age, you simply go for it. It was another wonderful learning experience."

Billy went on to pick up a sizeable collection of Manager of the Month awards and that assortment was in all probability instrumental in attracting the attention of a number of English league clubs.

Over the years Preston North End have enjoyed the services of a number of Scottish managers – Scot Symon, Tommy Docherty, Davie Moyes and Craig Brown, to name but four – and Davies followed in their footsteps in August 2004.

What followed at Preston's Deepdale Park clearly provided a two-season period of utter frustration in the advancement of the club.

Billy's inaugural attack on the English Football League Championship in 2004-05 saw the Lilywhites finish fifth. The promotion play-offs beckoned and after disposing of Derby County in the semi-final, Preston took on West Ham at the Millennium Stadium for the right to a place in the Premiership. Sadly for Billy and his team, the Hammers triumphed thanks to a single Bobby Zamora goal.

On to 2005-06 and a possible need for additional valium medication. This time, North End finished fourth and were consigned to yet another venture into the intimidating play-offs. With nails perhaps bitten down to the cuticles, Preston lost out 3-1 to Leeds United over the two-leg semi.

There was never any doubt in the quality of the Davies management performance. But conceivably, the nagging thought at the back of Billy's mind was that this was as far as he could possibly take the club. And, during the 2006 close season, he accepted an offer to manage Derby County.

Billy's career was gifted with many facets but that St Mirren goal at Ibrox remains the abiding memory.

JIMMY DRINKWATER

IN the 1920 United States Federal Census, 102 families accredited with the surname Drinkwater lived in America. Two years earlier, on February 10, the latest addition to the Drinkwater clan arrived in the UK, with the Cheshire township of Northwich heralding the birth.

James Arthur were the Christian names appearing on his birth certificate, but to those in the football industry he was Jimmy or, more affectionately to his playing colleagues, he was simply Drinkie.

In the football playing environment where the odd half gallon of the amber nectar was regularly consumed, having the surname Drinkwater lent itself to numerous jibes of a teetotal nature.

The name originates from the Middle Ages when weak ale was the universal beverage among the working proletariat and so cheap as to be drunk like water. However, the water purification of the era was such that the aqua on offer was of the doubtfully drinkable classification.

Drinkwater, it is thus alleged, became the joking nickname given to a miserly one unwilling or unable to afford beer.

Jimmy Drinkwater was a miserly one but not in a liquid consuming capacity – in providing limited scoring opportunities for the opposition in the football industry

Like so many of his era, the Second World War played a significant part in the development (or lack of it) in the Drinkwater football career.

Born on February 10, 1918, Jimmy was an army conscript who, having played for a number of years at amateur level, found himself posted north of the border.

During the war years, servicemen were conditioned to minimal travel, with the need to pursue their soccer aspirations being satisfied by playing for the local team in the close proximity of their base camp.

Morton were a classic case in this arrangement, with wing wizard Stanley Matthews and the sharp shooting Tommy Lawton – with 77 pre-war and post-war England caps between them – guesting for the Cappielow club in that famed 1943 Summer Cup competition.

Rumour has it Drinkwater wandered into St Mirren Park in 1942 for a kick about. What was on view so impressed manager Willie Fotheringham that Drinkie was immediately signed and catapulted into the Saints first team. This was clearly a step up from his days with Northwich Amateurs down south.

Without doubt the outstanding Drinkwater memory during his military service days in khaki was as St Mirren's right-back in the 1943 Summer Cup final.

Over 100,000 at Hampden and taking on Rangers, most black and white recollections will centre round the Buddies' single winning goal. The record books will single out Alex Linwood as Saints' hero but Alex's goal, generously described by Rangers full-back Dougie Gray as the best he had ever seen at Hampden, owes its construction to some sterling work from Housam and Johnny Deakin.

And Alex wasn't the sole contributor to Saints' success – Drinkwater was immense. With Drinkie at his imperious best, he severely curtailed the cantrips of the Ibrox balding winger, the diminutive Charlie Johnstone.

With Dick McLatchie bottling the efforts of the rampaging Willie Waddell on the other wing, the Rangers supply line to the St Mirren goal was conditioned to accepting starvation rations.

The St Mirren efforts on the day are well remembered and the silverware is on permanent display in the Love Street trophy cabinet.

With wartime league construction splitting the country into two, a challenge match was arranged between St Mirren and the northern champions Aberdeen a couple of weeks after the cup triumph. Boss Fotheringham revealed a story about Jimmy that speaks volumes of the player's commitment.

Willie said: "Drinkie was due to play in the game but was still in the forces and stationed at Inveraray, from where he had to thumb a lift to the match.

"He was dropped off in Glasgow about a mile from Hampden Park and ran the rest of the way to arrive a mere 15 minutes from kick-off. Dripping in perspiration, he managed a quick shower before nonchalantly taking his place in the team."

A vintage case of personified dedication.

That doyen of sports journalists, Willie Hunter, in his dissertation in the St Mirren centenary brochure, also recalls an apparent rearrangement of the Drinkwater good looks in that match.

Hunter wrote: "During the game it was noticed that Jimmy was sporting a couple of black eyes. It transpired he had been late in leaving Inverary as the night before the Hampden game he had taken part in a services boxing tournament. Not surprisingly, the referee held up Drinkie's hand at the final bell. As Jimmy wisecracked, 'Never mind me, you should see the other guy!'"

As Fotheringham maintained, Jimmy was just about the toughest portion of manhood St Mirren ever had on their books. He wasn't in any way the rough diamond, it was his enthusiasm and commitment that proved the point of teak-like toughness.

Two former playing colleagues were fulsome in their praise of the Drinkwater talents.

Jackie Neilson, Saints' immediate post-war powerhouse wing-half said: "Jimmy was a whole hearted player. He was always fully committed but you could never classify him as dirty. He was a bubbly character and always a good laugh."

Davie Lapsley, who followed Drinkie into the right-back slot, eulogised at length in his rich Camelon accent: "In my opinion like, Drinkie was a great player. He used to play at right-half in front of me. He used to kill them before I got to them! "He was a hard player to play against – not dirty but strong in the tackle."

The perfect host and captain, Jimmy was on occasion called upon to introduce the St Mirren team to political dignitaries.

One such time saw The Right Honourable Herbert Morrison on a mission visit to Glasgow. Morrison found wartime fame lending his name to the design of brick built air raid shelters.

He took in the Rangers-St Mirren League Cup tie at Ibrox on September 21, 1946. Regretfully, some of the Morrison bricks might have been useful in boarding up Saints' goal – they lost 4-0!

A versatile player, Jimmy spent six post-war seasons in St Mirren colours. He played in both full-back positions, was occasionally in the right-half and centre-half berths and, in addition, operated with success in three of the forward positions.

Jimmy formed a tremendous partnership at full-back with Davie Lindsay. In truth, the rumour mill had it on good authority that many a winger found immediate and mysterious hamstring problems that generated a high degree of unfitness on hearing they would be up against the no-nonsense Saints full-backs.

Some 111 post-war St Mirren outings for Jimmy generated a mere five goals, three of which were scored against Kilmarnock at Rugby Park in 1947. But his Paisley career would have been considerably supplemented with the addition of all his wartime appearances.

After Saints, Jimmy moved back to England and joined Torquay United, where he played for two seasons.

A tremendous ambassador for football, he died in 1996.

TONY FITZPATRICK

THERE are a variety of lies and statistics in the football industry and many are pigeon holed in the utter rubbish bin. However, one stat that is irrefutable, certainly not rubbish but more pure gold, is the number of league appearances racked up by one Anthony Charles Fitzpatrick.

Tony to the football fraternity, his total of 351 outings in black and white in pursuit of league prominence covering the period 1973 to 1988 is a tally not likely to be superceded in the modern game. Short-term contracts ranging from one month to one year will certainly contribute to that St Mirren statistic being cast in stone.

One of a family of eight, Tony's early learning days were spent at St Joseph's and St Columba's Schools in downtown Maryhill - the latter establishment having the honour of spawning the football talents of not only Mr Fitzpatrick but also those of Charlie Nicholas and Jim Duffy, both of whom were destined to make their soccer mark in later life.

The teenage football progression saw Tony parading his emerging skills with Dundas Vale - his father's team - before moving on to Dykemuir Star and Possill YM. All three sides acquired the Fitzpatrick contributions while the lad was still at school.

Tony would be the first to admit his future career was not going to depend on a attaining a university degree. He would be happy to lock horns with the academic requirements of life but only if they led to a career in football.

He was training at St Mirren Park on Tuesday and Thursday evenings and his developing potential was such that he was invited to join the St Mirren ground staff straight from his Alma Mater.

He recalled: "I used to cut the park, perhaps not as expertly as the resident groundsman, but I thought it was a job well done."

Saints chairman Willie Todd went on to recruit Fitzpatrick for his Paisley painting firm, with that association lasting four years. As Willie reminisced, the Fitzpatrick football bug had in no way been assuaged.

He said: "Working on site, when the lunch break arrived the painters enjoyed some down tools time, some food and relaxation. As far as Tony was concerned, it was a break not for any sustenance - he simply applied his lunch break to the honing of his soccer skills."

These foodless breaks came good when manager Tommy Bryceland secured the Fitzpatrick autograph on a full-time pro contract. Tony was a mere 17 at the time when Stenhousemuir arrived at Love Street and the former Possill player then played as a right winger, celebrating his debut on the back of a 4-1 win.

When Tony beamed in on Love Street, Saints had just missed out on promotion in the 71-72 campaign. Dumbarton and Arbroath were the promoted pair, with St Mirren only two points away on fourth place - Stirling Albion just having a better goal difference than Saints.

If that season generated some abject disappointment in the lack of league success, the full cycle of emotions resurfaced five years later. Under Alex Ferguson's direction and Fitzpatrick as captain, St Mirren zoomed to the Division One pole position with a four-point winning margin over second placed Clydebank. Tony missed out on only two games in the 39-game format, contributing a couple of goals in the process.

If that was one Fitzpatrick high spot, clearly a league game at Motherwell's Fir Park provided Tony with his playing nadir. It was an innocuous challenge, not one to maim but one that pole-axed Tony.

He explained: "I actually broke my jaw. It was an injury I wouldn't wish even on my worst enemy. I was wired up, couldn't move my jaw muscles, was fed on a liquid diet mainly through straws and over the eight-week recuperation period I lost two stones."

Subsequent seasons saw Saints failing to stamp their undoubted authority on the game. Frank McGarvey and Robert Torrance left, with Tony engulfed in some disillusionment. He joined Bristol City in 1979 and spent almost 18 months at Ashton Gate. It was a learning experience for the ever eager former Saints man.

He returned refreshed to St Mirren with another playing high coming in 1987 when he came off the bench to help Saints win that Scottish Cup final against the men from Tannadice.

Although Alex Smith had been the Buddies mentor in that cup success, the board deemed a change of management was necessary to further Saints' fortunes. Fitzpatrick had become a St Mirren icon, finishing his playing activities in 1988 and then settling into the managerial throne.

He said: "I was only 32 at the time and in retrospect, perhaps I should have waited. It's difficult to move from being one of the boys to accepting the full responsibilities of management.

"I didn't think too deeply about the problems at the time but one point made it easier for me in that I didn't socialise with the players. Hindsight is a great gift and I suppose if I'd left and cut my managerial teeth elsewhere and then came back later as the manager it might have worked differently."

It did work but only for a three-year period and Tony was replaced by the enigmatic David Hay.

The Fitzpatrick experience rating was exceptional and too good to be binned. Eight months unemployed, Tony had to provide for his wife Elizabeth and a family of three boys and a girl.

He said: "I bought a newsagents in Paisley which kept us going. This was at the time when club community coaches were seen to be the way forward in improving the game in Scotland. I applied for the job at Motherwell and was on the final shortlist, but didn't make it and was hugely disappointed."

The disappointment didn't last long. If Tony wasn't destined for darkest Lanarkshire, there was clearly only one other location to suit his iconic past - a return to St Mirren Park, the appointment coming one month after purchasing his shop.

Tony added: "Foreign clubs have their community appointments. Here in Scotland the need is perhaps a reflection of the teachers' strike a number of years ago. With fewer youngsters around, the promotion of the game is all important.

"Lack of street football due to traffic density is a contributory factor to the game's demise at youth level. I'd just love to get the kids away from their home computers at primary school age. It's a challenge but we've got to market the game, got to get people working at it."

Tony did have the opportunity of working at it, until the acrimonious departure of Jimmy Bone as manager at the start of the 1997-98 season. In difficult circumstances, St Mirren turned to their former boss in what was seen to be a stand-in or temporary appointment.

Saints' league performance was complete under achievement and the Fitzpatrick fevered brow was mopped in grateful thanks when only a superb goal from Hugh Murray at Forthbank Stadium in May 1998 kept Saints in the First Division and condemned the Binos to life at a lower level.

The temporary status of Tony's second spell in charge terminated at the time of the 1998 Yuletide celebrations when Tom Hendrie was unveiled as the new Saints gaffer.

Life after community coaching and problem solving at management level would have floored many. Not Tony Fitzpatrick. He is a born survivor, with the survival package being the establishment of his Total Soccer Experience coaching courses in and around the Paisley environs.

Livingston didn't quite want a new manager but the ambitious West Lothian club did require a quality coach to oversee their expanding youth programme. Anthony Charles Fitzpatrick was the man to fill the bill.

Tony left Livingston in 2004 and now runs a sports training and development company.

BOBBY FLAVELL

THE surname is of Flemish origin, from continental Flanders, and it prompted historian Douglas Lamming in his Scottish Soccer Internationalists Who's Who to portray Robert Flavell, better known as Bobby, as a "Stocky leader with a larger acquaintance of senior Scottish clubs than most. Aggressive and dangerous and made a name in war time football."

One of a family of four, Bobby was born in Airdrie on September 1, 1921, before the family moved to nearby Annathill. The mining community of Annathill was a remarkable football breeding ground, with three rows of houses yielding six internationalists at this time – including the former Rangers skipper Jock "Tiger" Shaw.

Some teenage frustration was in order when, as a pupil at Coatbridge High School, Bobby was selected for a trial with the Scottish Schoolboys side. The emotional reaction was predictable: "My side won 3-1 and I scored two of the goals but it was the other centre-forward who was picked!"

The Flavell talent had been closely monitored by Airdrie and the former Broomfield club provided training facilities from the day Bobby blew out 13 birthday cake candles. In addition to Saturday morning scholastic soccer, Bobby also performed in the afternoon with the quaintly named Eastwood Heatherbell.

If that team title generated a less than dynamic appreciation of the beautiful game, the Flavell career soon veered back on track when he signed for Airdrie as a 16-year-old in 1937. The career toughening up process was moved along courtesy of a loan spell on the Junior scene with Kirkintilloch Rob Roy.

With Adolf Hitler causing substantial Second World War mayhem to many playing careers, Bobby found himself seconded to the Royal Navy. However, being posted to any south coast port didn't stop him strutting his stuff with Brentford and Arsenal and there were strong rumours that Tottenham Hotspur wanted to sign him.

With active service demobilisation eventually in place, Bobby returned to Airdrie and his first post-war season yielded a remarkable 37 goals from 26 league games.

He became shop window material and manager David McLean of Hearts was first in the queue to transport the goal-getting talents to Tynecastle in December 1947, courtesy of a £11,000 price tag. This was the highest transfer fee between Scottish clubs at that time.

Bobby spent two and a half seasons with Hearts but the job satisfaction was deteriorating at a fast rate of knots.

He said: "I wasn't happy at Tynecastle. During the war years I had played with big Jock Dodds of Blackpool, the Scotland wartime centre-forward. Jock became an agent for the Millionerios club in the Colombian capital Bogota and he was the motivator in my move to South America.

"At that time there were restrictions in place in terms of players going abroad. But that didn't apply to Colombia as they weren't affiliated to FIFA so I bucked the trend and went over with a couple of prominent English players, Neil Franklin and Charlie Mitten.

"We went over to play for the Santa Fe club. We had two Peruvians and four Argentineans, all internationalists, in our side. One of these was Alfredo di Stefano, who went on to perform with the great Real Madrid side that dominated the early European Cup competitions.

"Folk thought I was leaving Scotland to play in a jungle environment. Not so. It was extremely cosmopolitan with high rise flats having swimming pools on the roofs. My wife and daughter enjoyed living in a lovely flat there, complete with maid service."

The South American experience only lasted a year when Bobby returned to his Caledonian roots and joined Dundee in September 1951.

The Flavell time at Dens Park saw him merge with such Tayside notables as Doug Cowie, Alfie Boyd and Billy Steel. With such accredited accomplices to hand, the Flavell fortunes in amassing medals went on overdrive.

A runners-up gong in the 1952 Scottish Cup against Motherwell was superseded with two successive winning League Cup medals, Bobby scoring in both games against Rangers and Kilmarnock respectively in 1951 and '52.

Itchy feet then required scratching, the Flavell boots going on to tread the turf at Rugby Park for a couple of seasons. There, he generated a haul of 13 goals from 38 league appearances.

By now Bobby was on track to celebrate his 35th birthday. St Mirren manager Willie Reid was ever anxious to bolster his strike force and even though the diminutive frontman– he was only 5'-6" – was less spring heeled than of yore, Bobby signed on at Love Street in July 1956.

Bobby made his St Mirren debut against Hearts at Tynecastle on September 15, 1956, and scored in a 2-2 draw, Billy Dallas netting the other.

Keeper Campbell Forsyth was the Saints custodian on that debut day and spoke highly of the little striker.

Forsyth said: "When Bobby came to St Mirren, he had performed well at Bogota as well as at Dundee and Kilmarnock, but he was now in his twilight soccer days. He had slowed but was still adept at holding the ball up and spreading the play. He was simply a great professional and a wee gentleman."

The Flavell files will reveal a minimal total of 29 St Mirren games and a collection of only six goals, small by comparison with his early scoring feats. One of these goals was incorporated into a mammoth 7-1 whacking of Queen of the South in Paisley in October 1956.

Keen to stay in the game, Reid appointed Bobby as the Saints first team coach – a position he held when St Mirren won the Scottish Cup in 1959.

A management future beckoned and Bobby went on to boss Ayr United. However, he only lasted in the Somerset Park job for a mere 17 days!

Reid had opted for a career progression post in joining Norwich City and Bobby was invited to return to Love Street in a managerial capacity in December 1961.

The Flavell Paisley tenure lasted only a year, Jackie Cox succeeding him as boss. Bobby reverted back to Somerset and was subsequently involved as manager and director of Albion Rovers.

The curtain finally came down on the Flavell active football involvement when he took on the post as chief scout for Berwick Rangers.

The wartime shenanigans of Germany clearly denied Bobby many international honours but he was capped post-war while with Airdrie against Belgium and Luxembourg. Also, in one Scottish League appearance while at Dens Park he scored five in a match against the Irish League in Belfast, the Scots winning 7-4.

Bobby continued to live in Airdrie in his latter days but passed away in a care home on March 18, 2005.

CAMPBELL FORSYTH

FOR those adolescents in and around the Stirlingshire mining village of Plean, the prospects of organised football in the 1940s were somewhat limited. For Campbell Forsyth in his early teenage days, there was no cinema, no television and the dissipation of their overflowing energy banks being dependent on street football and the Boys' Brigade.

Campbell recalled: "There was no football team at our primary school and it was always playground stuff, with my mother raising the roof at the state of my shoes. The Boys' Brigade was a big thing in my life and as everybody played the game, I had to wait some time before I got my chance."

If there was no structured soccer at the early learning level, there was even less at Stirling High School. Campbell's Stirlingshire Alma Mater was a confirmed rugby playing establishment as Jimmy Bone was also to find out in later days.

Forsyth said: "I had always been a goalkeeper, but had to wait until I was 16 before I got my chance with the BB.

"There followed a local contact that told me I was wanted to play for a local Secondary Juvenile side. I turned up to play but I was the wrong guy, it was a case of mistaken identity. However, because I had turned up they gave me a game.

"That was Gairdoch United. They seemed to like my form and I eventually signed for them and spent nine months at the club."

Although the Second World War hostilities had finished in 1945, the need for an armed forces top up was paramount in the immediate post-war years.

At 18 in 1952, Campbell was one of the many conscripts to the colours, with a two-year spell being endured, initially with the Royal Signals at Catterick, a translation primarily due to Campbell having worked as a technician with the Post Office.

He said: "I managed to graduate to the Battalion team once we were posted to Germany. Some German sides wanted me to turn out for them but the army authorities laid down the strict no fraternisation rule and I wasn't allowed to play for any of them."

One or two glowing Press cuttings spread the word back home of a developing talent between the sticks.

Campbell went on: "When I was demobbed, my former BB captain contacted Duncan Ogilvie, a Falkirk director, and I received an invitation to play a couple of trials. Bob Shankly, the Brockville manager, said I needed toughening up and required some Junior experience, so I was farmed out to Kirkintilloch Rob Roy."

However life at Adamslie Park wasn't all sweetness and light. A serious bang on the Forsyth cranium left him concussed and out of the game for a while, but not before representatives from Shettleston Juniors persuaded him that football life in Glasgow's east end was a better bet.

It was only a part season until the St Mirren scouting duo of Jack Gilmour and Fraser MacKintosh asked him along to Saints.

But Campbell admitted: "I felt I still had an obligation to Falkirk. They had suggested that a possible move to Birmingham City was on the cards. But in all honesty, the England keeper Gilbert Merrick was the man in charge at St Andrews and there was little likelihood of me breaking into the team.

"I was greatly impressed by the two gentlemen from St Mirren and joined up at Love Street in 1955."

Campbell still cherishes his Saints signing on documents which earned him the princely sum of £12 a week for first-team duty, £6 if in the reserves and £6 during the close season.

However, his debut in a St Mirren jersey was a semi disaster, to say the least.

He explained: "I was now living in the Falkirk area and after having had some pretensions of joining them, my nerves were on red alert. We were thumped 5-1 at Brockville and that was November 1955."

Being a part-time player and working full-time on the nine to five shift imposes a strict limitation of your life style.

Forsyth said: "I'm sure today's players haven't a clue about being part-time. For me it was a dash after work to Larbert to catch a train to the old Buchanan Street Station. Then a run to get the subway to Cessnock and board a bus to Paisley town centre. It was hard going."

Clearly the Forsyth St Mirren nadir surfaced in early 1959. Saints' league results were less than impressive immediately prior to the Scottish Cup, with only two games having been won in an eight-game run.

A run in the Scottish Cup seemed unlikely, so with Saints down to play Peebles Rovers at home in the second round, at least a win against the non-leaguers was predicted.

The prediction came true - a 10-0 win - but it wasn't Campbell who provided Saints' custodial needs.

A muscle twinge had reared its head and although Campbell admits he could have played, his assessment of being only 98 per cent fit meant a call up for Davie Walker, recently signed from Airdrie.

Campbell never played again in that successful cup run. He did play for a further season and a half with Saints, logging in a total of exactly 150 games, 19 of which were registered as shutouts.

Early in the 1960-61 season, an exchange deal was agreed with Campbell heading for Rugby Park and Jimmy Brown, the thunder thighs of the goalkeeping union, leaving Kilmarnock for Paisley.

Measured on the basis of sheer success, this was a turning point in the Forsyth fortunes. He went on to win four Scotland caps against England, Northern Ireland, Wales and Finland.

He said: "Ask me regarding a career high spot and it would have to be playing England at Hampden. To play in front of 135,000, keep a cleansheet and win 1-0 thanks to an Alan Gilzean goal takes some beating.."

On the domestic front, it did take some beating, Kilmarnock going on to take the 1964-65 League title. Few will ever forget their last game of the season, winning 2-0 at Tynecastle with TV clips featuring an ecstatic Willie Waddell cavorting around the Gorgie Road arena embracing his team.

From the wilds of Ayrshire and six seasons at Rugby Park, it was onwards to Southampton in December 1965 to join Ted Bates' Saints, who won promotion to their First Division in 1965-66.

Now aged 33, Campbell sustained a bad leg break in a match against Liverpool, an injury that sent him back to Scotland never to play again.

Sustained throughout his playing career by the encouragement of his wife Cathie and daughters Kirsty and Linsey, a career change was in the offing.

The days of Post Office engineering were behind him, with the Drybrough organisation in Edinburgh liking what they saw and offering a secure management position.

Golf had always been a major leisure time pursuit and once the Forsyth commitment with Drybrough had been completed, Dalmahoy Hotel & Country Club enrolled the charismatic Campbell as co-ordinator for their corporate golf packages - two alcoholic appointments and Campbell a teetotaler!

One postscript to this Forsyth saga... Campbell was a mite apprehensive at leaving St Mirren. He was conscious Davie Lapsley was the most ferocious striker of a dead ball in the country. Any shot of up to 40 yards was net bound. Campbell was always safe at Love Street but after leaving he was in the firing line with Kilmarnock and on occasion facing the redoubtable Mr Lapsley.

LES FRIDGE

THERE he was, he'd just left school in Inverness with three 'O' levels and had joined up with the local Thistle team as a 15-year-old. The year was 1983, Les Fridge had a football future in front of him.

His goalkeeping performances in the Highland capital had not been lost on the national Under-16 selection team, with Les receiving his initial Under-16 call up to face Finland in a Scandinavian away game.

The football horizons were extensively widened when local Highland League scout Rod Clyne sent a glowing report to the hierarchy at Stamford Bridge.

John Neal was Chelsea manager at the time with Scotsman Ian McNeill as his assistant. McNeill regularly kept tabs on the range of Caledonian talent and with the Stamford Bridge policy of bringing talented Scottish youngsters down south, Les was invited to join up with the big boys as a stripling 16-year-old.

Not surprisingly, his immaturity weighed heavily against an immediate tasting of first-team football. He was called to perform in a handful of pre-season games and made only one senior team appearance in an end of season game against Watford – he was now 17.

Alex Smith, who had arrived at Love Street to take over from Alex Miller, found himself in some complex transfer negotiations as Les recalled.

He explained: "It was at the time when Chelsea were involved in the transfer of Steve Clarke from St Mirren to Stamford Bridge. Steve was heading south and Doug Rougvie and myself were the make weights in balancing the transfer. Eventually Doug pulled out of the deal and I came back up north on my own as the back-up keeper to Campbell Money. In fact, I was Alex Smith's first St Mirren signing."

The question was posed to Les that the London Press must have had a field day with his surname.

He replied: "Sure, I've heard all the puns. In fact my surname has been invaluable in providing some positive PR – always subject, of course, on me turning in some career enhancing performances."

Les Fridge's St Mirren debut is firmly etched in his memory banks.

He recalled: "We were due to play Rangers at Ibrox on May 9, 1987 – the week before the cup final. They were on a high having just clinched the Premier League title the previous Saturday up at Aberdeen.

"Campbell Money came into Love Street the day of the game for a bit of a warm-up and then we would go off at around mid day for a pre-match meal. It must have` been something he'd eaten but Campbell became unwell and Alex Smith told me, 'You're in!'

"Alex told me it was our last league game of the season so to go and enjoy it.

"Robert Fleck scored for Rangers after only three minutes and I remember looking up at the scoreboard thinking – this could be a long day. I enjoyed it more so for containing them and only losing 1-0."

Les' appearance on the senior goalkeeping scene was at a time when substitute goalies were not part of the domestic team selections. However, they were a mandatory requirement in European competition.

Although he never played in the 87-88 European Cup Winners' Cup, being involved as back-up keeper in the games against Tromso and Mechelen were particularly satisfying experiences.

With Money securely ensconced between the Love Street sticks, it was inevitable Les would seek a goalkeeping challenge elsewhere. That need was satisfied by Smith who, after orchestrating Scottish Cup wins for both St Mirren and Aberdeen, had arrived to handle Clyde's affairs at Broadwood. Les spent a couple of seasons with the Bully Wee.

So after Clyde, what were the reasons that persuaded Les to move to Raith Rovers ?

He explained: "Participation in the 95-96 UEFA Cup. I had a phone call from Jimmy Nicholl who wanted me as back-up for Scott Thomson.

"We went on to beat a team from the Faroe Islands in a preliminary round, then knocked out Akranes from Iceland in the first round proper. The big occasion was taking on Bayern Munich in the next round but to be in their stadium with the scoreboard at one point showing 1-0 to Raith was an unforgettable experience. Okay, we lost 2-1, but what a night."

Former Aberdeen and Celtic winger John Hewitt had been a playing colleague at Love Street and with John taking over Dundalk in the Irish League, he invited Les over for a short stay.

The Fridge career came full cycle when he joined Inverness Caledonian Thistle in the 1997 close season, going on to spend almost six seasons with Caley.

A confirmed Highlander, Les went on to move further up the A9 for the best part of three seasons with Ross County.

Interspersed in his travels with a pair of goalkeeping gloves, Les's association with national youth coach Smith produced two Under-21 caps.

He said: "The first was against France in 1989 and the second the following year against Yugoslavia. Playing Yugoslavia away was a different ball game. They were an immensely talented team and if I remember correctly we lost 4-0. What was really satisfying about these games was being able to train with the full Scotland side."

A 20-year professional career including six clubs and over 250 starts has earned Les a tidy collection of baubles for his mantelpiece. Young Player of the Year plus a 1987 Epson Cup winners medal in Singapore while with St Mirren, Player of the Year with Clyde and a massive Goalkeeper of the Tournament trophy from a four nations tournament in Italy all need regular dusting.

In his post playing days, Les made a tentative footing onto the management stairway with Nairn County. And with some poetic Fridge encouragement the Station Park side won the North of Scotland Cup in 2005 – the first piece of silverware landed by Nairn in the last 40 years.

The goalkeeping fraternity regularly appear to have extended shelf lives and as Les proclaims: "Old goalkeepers never die – they just get better looking!"

MARK FULTON

THE adherents of Clan Fulton made a lasting impression in the defensive fortunes of St Mirren over the period 1967 to 1985. Neither were blood related, with Willie Fulton patrolling the rearguard beat from 1967 to 1972 and Mark Fulton taking over in season 1978-79.

Born in Johnstone on September 16, 1951, Mark made a big impression as a gifted player in schools football. The feedback to manager Alex Ferguson was so positive that the teenager was recruited to the Love Street cause from the St Mirren Boys Club in 1977.

Mark was toughened at Johnstone Burgh before being called up for first-team duty as a substitute for the last league game of the 78-79 season. Celtic were the visitors, Saints' starting line up being Thomson, Young, Munro, Fitzpatrick, Dunlop, Copland, Stark, Richardson, Torrance, Abercrombie and Docherty.

However, the joys in celebrating his St Mirren debut were conceivably diluted with the Parkhead side recording a 2-0 win and clinching the Premier League title.

The following season saw Mark consolidated his hold on the No.5 shirt and he really turned it on in St Mirren's encounters with the residents of the Govan citadel called Ibrox.

On the four league occasions Saints met the Light Blues, Mark was on a winning St Mirren side three times. The scores were 2-1, 2-1 and 4-1, Dougie Somner helping himself to five of the goals, Jimmy Bone had two with Frank McDougall netting one.

Season 80-81 saw Celtic have reason to rue the Fulton-inspired side as Mark and his team-mates celebrated the Alex Beckett "Most memorable St Mirren goal at Celtic Park" game.

Equally pleasurable to Mark was season 1980-81. Jousts with our county neighbours from the Tail of the Bank were always spicy and there was a special atmosphere to the derby games. That particular season saw Saints win three of the league encounters, the fourth match ending in a 0-0 draw.

Billy Stark was a playing contemporary of Mark's and well remembers his strengths.

Billy recalled: "Mark came into the side at a very young age. I think he was 19, which is not an easy start for a young centre-half. He acquitted himself well and had a great left foot. He wasn't perhaps the fastest centre-back but was a good competitor

"His strength in being able to hold his own at the back gave the team a nice balance. I'm sure it was his powerful ability to attack the ball that led to his time with the Scotland Under-21 squad."

It was during Jock Stein's time as the national supremo that Mark received his first Under-21 call-up to play Belgium in 1980. West Germany and England followed before he took on Sweden and Denmark the following year, the latter game from the bench.

Tony Fitzpatrick remembers playing both with Mark and against him.

Tony said: "It was at the time of the Anglo-Scottish Cup competition and Bristol City were the common denominator in our games. I played with Mark against City side in the 78-79 competition when we beat them at the quarter-final stage.

"But I was then transferred to the Robins and the following year, in the two-leg final, I played against St Mirren at Ashton Gate. But I was injured and didn't make the return leg in Paisley.

"I think I derived more pleasure for St Mirren winning the cup than if Bristol had won.

"As for Mark, he was a great reader of the game, great on the ball and his distribution was superb. He was a tough character in terms of going in and winning the ball. A quiet lad by nature, he was a classy centre-back who could play football and was more like a European centre-back."

A taste for European football was sampled by Mark in the early 1980s with St Mirren's incursions in the UEFA Cup, Mark enjoying the jousts with Elfsborg, St Etienne and Feyenoord.

By the time Campbell Money had been given a regular run between the sticks, Fulton was a well established resident in his centre-half role.

Campbell made the point: "I was on the bench in that Anglo-Scottish Cup win, one of the substitutes having to be a goalkeeper.

"The team who won were Thomson, Young, Munro, Fulton, Copland, Curran, Bone, Stark, Logan, Somner, Abercrombie, Weir, and Mark's contribution was immense. He was an excellent footballer first and foremost but also had a well educated left foot and was good in the air. A particular strength of his was his timing. It was superb and it had to be as he wasn't the tallest of players."

Seven seasons with Saints produced over 200 appearances, including 20 as a sub. However, after the 1984 close season the Fulton St Mirren career became a mite pearshaped. Some ill-advised comments in the press were attributed to Messrs McDougall, Thomson and Fulton, which led to all three being fined £200 for breach of contract.

As a result, Thomson moved to Dundee United for a reported £82,500 and Frank McDougall opted for life in Aberdeen on the back of a £106,000 transfer fee.

Fulton was stripped of the Saints captaincy and the clash of personalities between manager Alex Miller and Mark was further stoked up when Mark was red-carded against Dundee United at Tannadice in November 1984.

Not surprisingly a new career path for Mark became essential and he was transferred to Hibernian for a fee of £52,000 in time for the 1985-86 season.

Clearly relationships with St Mirren management had degenerated and one wonders as to Mark's position when Miller moved to manage the Easter Road club in 1986.

However, Mark made 30 Premier League appearances for the Hibees before finishing his playing carer with Hamilton Accies.

A stickler for law and order, Mark embarked on a post-playing career with the local constabulary, going on to establish a permanent niche with the Lothian & Borders Division at Bathgate.

WILLIE FULTON

THE pattern is well known as a football idiosyncrasy. You play up front, the ageing process descends, you step back to midfield and when the ravages of senile decay loom on the playing horizon, a central defensive beat or sweeper role becomes your forte.

Willie Fulton would probably endorse the theory but would definitely take issue with the suggestion that he has a Zimmer in his garage.

An Ayrshireman born and bred, his scholastic days were initially spent at a Glenburn school. But those with a Paisley persuasion should note Glenburn Primary is located in downtown Prestwick.

Secondary school life at Prestwick High School followed and Willie's inside forward ploys were sufficiently endemic to attract the interest of the local Juniors Irvine Victoria, who were the next rung on the Fulton career ladder.

It might be considered almost heretic at times to label the SFA hierarchy as being dictatorial, but in George Graham and Willie Allan, the SFA had sufficient secretarial clout to discourage any deviation from their straight and narrow.

To consider postponing a match in the 50s and 60s was tantamount to a football rebellion, irrespective of the reason.

Ayr United had one such major problem. A 'flu epidemic" had ravaged the Somerset Park team selections. They wanted to postpone a game but could feel the heat from the SFA stronghold in pursuing such a course.

It was Fulton who provided Ayr with a get out. He helped with their player shortfall and scored a couple of goals on his trial run.

In five years with The Honest Men, the Fulton goal input helped Ayr win the Division Two title in the 1965-66 season.

A move to Falkirk followed in the days when high finance was practical, as opposed to salaries being measured in telephone number proportions. The Fulton transfer to Brockville generated a fee of £4,000 and Willie was the grateful recipient of a £500 signing on fee.

John Prentice arrived to guide the Falkirk fortunes and Willie provided a

"What happened next" picture.

He explained: "Initially, I played in every forward position when I was at Ayr. Falkirk had seen me play as a striker. Certainly, I'd scored a few goals but I was far too slow, so I was converted into an attacking left-half.

"The playing practice at Falkirk was simple, after five years you either received a Testimonial or you got the boot."

Sufficient to say, Willie's bank account wasn't over endowed with the income from any Testimonial.

On the other hand, there was one practical outcome from Willie's time with the Bairns. Not full-time at Brockville, he had some free time in the afternoons which he converted into attending chiropody classes. After graduating as a qualified foot man, he body swerved the NHS to take private patients on board.

Regretfully the Fulton business acumen wasn't on a par with his on field ability. He was over generous to his many friends with their perambulation problems and wasn't sufficiently shrewd to establish a successful chiropody practice. In short, he simply didn't charge enough.

However, a clutch of clubs were anxious to resurrect his playing career. Dunfermline, Queen of the South, East Stirling and St Mirren were in for him and Alex Wright's persuasive ways won the day signing the 30-year-old for Saints.

By the time the Fulton talents were paraded at Love Street, the game's playing pattern was changing. The old "W" attacking formation was heading for oblivion and only at the best two strikers operated up front.

Willie vividly recalls the transition.

He said: "I reckon Alex Wright was the best manager I played under. After one lengthy injury he pulled me back to operate in a central defensive role.

"I was lucky playing young centre-halves and with the help we had at the time. Andy McFadden was the first followed by Gordon McQueen. By this time I was well into my 30s so with their help it suited me to become a sweeper.

"Gordon was a great guy. I was involved in raising funds for a charity for a while. I tried to get an autographed Manchester United ball from Gordon when he went down to Old Trafford and found out it would cost £25, so I sent off the requisite cheque. Back came both the ball and the cheque with Gordon's compliments, saying it was a small appreciation of my help to him at Love Street. It was a nice wee touch."

Willie's arrival to play in black and white wasn't a particularly rose tinted spectacle occasion. Saints were relegated, but the Paisley faithful proffered future support with a standing ovation for a hopeful immediate return to the top flight.

The Fulton contribution was, of course, on hand for the following season.

That 67-68 campaign was memorable for that Division Two championship title when only one game against East Fife was lost, with Willie pulling on a Saints strip in 34 of the 36 league outings.

He recalled: "The St Mirren fans were superb, although the standing ovations didn't last long.   When we won that Division Two title we were on target to score 100 league goals. We only drew 1-1 in an April game with Arbroath and the fans booed us off the pitch. Fortunately we managed to beat Berwick Rangers 4-0 in the final game, Jim Blair netting the 100th goal. We won the league and I had my cherished medal."

There are an abundance of memories from Fulton's playing days, but one in particular has a gold plated hallmark.

He explained: "We were back in Division One but the fans seemed sure we wouldn't achieve much in the top league. They were wrong. In fact, we even went 11 games undefeated - second to Celtic and just above Rangers. The Ibrox side came to Love Street just after signing Colin Stein from Hibernian for £100,000 - the first six figure transfer between Scottish clubs. There was a huge crowd at the game and we beat them 1-0 thanks to a Hugh Gilshan goal."

A visit to Willie's Motherwell bungalow and he'll regale with yards of newspaper cuttings chronicling the Fulton way of life at Ayr, Falkirk and St Mirren.

One particular keepsake takes pride of place in his trophy cabinet. At 32, he was presented with the Player of the Year trophy in season 1968-69.

Titled St Mirren's Most Valuable Player, it was presented by the Toronto Branch of the St Mirren Supporters' Association - a clear indication of St Mirren's worldwide support.

TOMMY GEMMELL

IT was a response of unprecedented humility and understatement. Tommy Gemmell, who laboured under the label of the Saints "Quiet Man", was asked for thoughts on his most memorable goal.

He pondered for a moment and replied: "I didn't score many goals!"

It was typical of the man. Modest, unassuming, never seeking the limelight.

Tommy is, in fact, rated St Mirren's top post-war goal scorer. His inside forward role was instrumental in netting 67 goals in league competition, nine in the Scottish Cup plus a further 18 in the sectionalised League Cup campaigns. His tally of 94 places him three in front of Frank McGarvey and 19 ahead of Billy Stark

Slight of build and fleet of foot, Tommy withstood a barrage of limb-crunching tackles, never retaliating. And his football frame on a Monday morning was generously fluorescent with hues of black, blue, yellow and green, a physical receipt from the Saturday encounter.

An Ayrshireman, he was born in Mossblown, near Annbank, and lived all his life in the village until the ravages of dementia necessitated full-time care in his latter life at the County Care Nursing Home at Burnfoot House in Patna.

A pupil at Annbank Primary School, the quiet spoken Tommy's full-time education continued until he was 14. Guided and influenced by his father who played at Junior level, he was always an inside forward playing for his school side before joining the local Under-18 team Tarbolton Juveniles, who operated some three miles up the road from Annbank.

Saints boss Bobby Rankin was well versed in the Gemmell attributes and kept tabs on his progress when his learning curve took an upward sweep with Irvine Meadow. He spent two seasons with the Meadow Park side.

Pursued by a clutch of clubs keen to avail themselves of the Gemmell finesse, Rankin achieved something of a coup when he arranged for the Gemmell autograph to appear on a St Mirren recruitment form on June 12, 1951.

Recalling his first match for Saints, Tommy was mindful of a tough game at Bayview Park.

He said: "East Fife were a strong going side at that time. Many of their players earned a living from the local coal mining operations. They weren't in any way muscle bound but, boy, they were strong.

"They had players like George Aitken, Charlie 'Legs' Fleming and Henry Morris, so I was more than happy we managed a 3-3 draw.

"The date? I think it was in late October 1951 and I was even more pleased to score on my debut."

Tommy was a one club man, leaving St Mirren on a free transfer in 1962 after 11 years in black and white. Blessed with a turn of pace, he was ever considerate of those operating in the team's boiler house.

He added: "Only four players ever ran about - the two wing-halves and the two inside men. I was one of the workers!"

Just up the road from Mossblown is ICI's Nobel Division at Ardeer. Famed for its development and manufacture of all things explosive, many a covert explosion was accidentally triggered off, resulting in extensive overtime for the local glaziers as countless suburban windows achieved fragmentation status.

Tommy was not a party to the wayward pyrotechnics - he was employed at the Ardeer plant, but only in his capacity of applying his clerking skills in the Organic Section.

However, leaving home to clock in at 8am with subsequent night training at Love Street on Tuesdays and Thursdays meant a late arrival home around the 10pm. Clearly a tiring day.

Never a car owner, Tommy was a confirmed bus and train man, and Rankin and later Willie Reid and Bobby Flavell provided much needed travelling respite, as well as allowing him to train locally at Ayr United's Somerset Park.

At a time when the Scottish game had an abundance of creative inside forwards, the gateway to the national side was of chicane proportions. But the Gemmell class managed to break down the admission barrier and he appeared in the national side on two occasions.

Tommy explained: "Scotland played a friendly against Portugal at Hampden in 1960 and I was over the moon with my first cap, although the 3-2 defeat was never in the pre-match script.

"I was also selected for the Scotland touring party in the summer of 1955 to play Austria, Hungary and Yugoslavia. I didn't play in the games against Austria and Hungary but was selected for the 2-2 draw with Yugoslavia in Belgrade.

"That was a tour where we flew around the continent. I'd never been on a plane before, so for me the excitement was really something."

If those Scotland games claimed pride of place on the national front, clearly the 1959 Scottish Cup final was top of the pops for Tommy on the domestic vista.

He went on: "I was a part-time player with a job during the week so I couldn't get away for long to join in the pre-match build up."

Few would argue against the Gemmell input in both the semi-final against Celtic and Aberdeen in the final being the creative difference between Saints and their opponents.

Tommy never married, with his leisure time pursuits utilising his local Kyle & Carrick leisure pass. No, not a bus pass, but certification that permitted him to enjoy rounds of golf at least three days a week over the numerous county courses.

Reminiscing on the differences between his playing days and the current football climate, Tommy was scathing on what was now on offer.

He said: "I watch very few games. I get fed up with the standard of games on TV and invariably switch it off at half-time.

"I would think the main difference now is the weight of the ball. You could knock today's lightweight balls the length of the park. The heavy ball we had made you play it on the ground with close ball control and dribbling being more entertaining factors."

"I didn't score many goals..." Another season with Saints and he could have been a ton up!

ARCHIE GEMMILL

THE epithets rained in thick and fast. The downpour of acclaim heralded the appearance of a precocious talent on the Scottish soccer scene. Archie Gemmill had arrived!

Football historian Douglas Lamming, in his Scottish Soccer Internationalists Who's Who, portrays the diminutive newcomer – after all he was only 5'-5" – as a "persistent durable midfielder, his stocky figure, full of hard running, contributing greatly to the scoring of memorable goals."

Ken Gallacher, of the Daily Record, was more descriptive in his personalisation. He said: "Archie, that tough tiny tot, the kid whose career has so often been threatened by injury."

The Paisley Daily Express went wild on the occasion of his Senior debut.

Archie, having been signed by Jackie Cox for St Mirren as a 17-year-old from Stanely Green School, first appeared wearing the No.10 shirt against Dundee United at Love Street in October 1964. The PDE waxed lyrical at the teenage Gemmill's work rate, his assertiveness and general dynamism.

Archie tried hard to relive the occasion.

He said: "It's been so long and there have been so many games, it's difficult to recall much of the detail. What I do remember was Bobby Ross and Tottie Beck scoring in the 2-1 win. But the result was greatly helped by Pat Liney saving two penalties."

While Paisley born – Archie signed for Saints straight from school – his football development had been substantially enhanced with an almost three-year term at Drumchapel Amateurs. But with such a latent talent up for grabs, why St Mirren?

He explained: "To be honest, both Rangers and Celtic were chasing me but my dad said that, in his opinion, I should go to a smaller club, and that's without belittling St Mirren in any way. He thought I'd have a much better chance of breaking into the first team and I made it after only six weeks. Clearly my dad's advice had paid off."

More of a goal provider than a scorer – Archie only ever netted nine goals in is 75 St Mirren appearances – Gemmill did provide the Saints faithful with a Christmas Eve present in 1966 in the shape of a superb hat-trick in a

3-1 win over Ayr United at Love Street.

Archie's transition to the St Mirren senior stage encompassed the introduction of substitutes into the game. The prevailing practice at the time was for any injured player to hirple along on the wing in the forlorn hope of snatching an unlikely goal. Undoubtedly, the paying public rightly demanded to view a match with 22 fit players on call – hence the introduction of one substitute at the start of the 1966-67 season.

St Mirren had been drawn in the sectionalised League Cup tournament with Hearts, Celtic and Clyde. The first game of the season saw Saints face Clyde at their former Shawfield Stadium. It was big Jim Clunie who picked up an injury that necessitated the first ever substitute in Scottish football, Gemmill making history in replacing the centre-half Clunie, who failed to recover for the rest of the League Cup games.

Clearly Archie's relatively small stature replacing the substantial physique of Clunie only served to emphasise the versatility of his playing potential.

Archie explained: "I nearly always played wide left and I remember standing in at left-back when 'Cockles' Wilson was injured. That gave me the opportunity of matching my wits against the likes of wee Jimmy Johnstone and Willie Henderson."

So after three seasons at Love Street, what were the circumstances that led to Archie signing for Bobby Seith at Preston North End in 1967?

He recalled: "St Mirren were a side in the lower reaches of the Scottish First Division, whereas Preston, who spawned the great Tom Finney, were in the top league in England.

"The move presented a new challenge to me and it also provided £13,000 for the St Mirren coffers. I was still only 20 at the time, it was a step up and my parents were great in helping me. As an only child, they maybe expected me to stay in the parental home. But they said go for it, broaden your horizons – so I did!"

It was around this time that Brian Clough entered the Gemmill soccer equation. The then Derby County manager invested £66,000 to bring Archie to the Baseball Ground in September 1970, and the fusion of two strong personalities provided Derby with their first league championship in 1972.

With Archie now captain of Derby and Clough moving on to further the fortunes of Nottingham Forest, Dave Mackay took over at the Baseball Ground and went on to win a second title for the club two years later.

The records will show the Clough-Gemmill charisma had worked wonders at Derby and Cloughie hoped the developed charm would also come good at Nottingham. He forked out £25,000 plus another player to enlist the Gemmill services for the City Ground.

The magic was still on tap, Forest winning their first championship in 1978 by a seven-point margin over Liverpool.

In all Archie's recollections of his time with Clough, it is significant that he always addressed his former mentor as Mr Clough – a clear indication of the respect he had for him.

A move to Birmingham City in August 1979 for a reported fee of £150,000 materialised after Archie had appeared on the bench for the Nottingham club's first European win over Malmo of Sweden in 1974.

A devoted family man and one fiercely nationalistic, Archie ensured that, despite living in Derby, his son Scott would be born in Scotland.

He revealed: "It was at the time when you had to be born in Scotland to play for your country. We found out we were expecting a boy so I arranged for Betty to come back to Paisley for Scott's birth on January 2, 1971. It was certainly a very happy New Year."

And right well did the flit north work as Scott went on to collect four Under-21 caps and 26 at full Scotland level.

Father Archie had a rather traumatic introduction to the international fold. Selected initially to play for the national Under-23 side against England at Sunderland's Roker Park, the Scots were 3-0 down at half-time when the game was abandoned due to an excessive fall of snow. It was a decision that was happily endorsed by the entire squad!

With 43 full caps to his credit, many would expect the game against Holland in Argentina in 1978 – incorporating Archie's super strike – to perhaps be his most memorable international outing. But they would be wrong!

He explained: "It was always going to be a wonderful experience for me to represent my country and I gained that pleasure with my first cap in 1971 when I was at Derby. We played Belgium in Liege but it was a bit of a dampener to lose 3-0."

However, further pleasure must have been generated from that World Cup goal against Holland, when Archie virtually took on the entire Dutch defence to score what has been acclaimed as Scotland's finest ever strike.

Archie said: "A taxi driver buttonholed me the other day about that goal. Remember that was back in 1978 – it's amazing how it has stood the test of time. But in reality, we were only famous for about one minute.

"We were in with a chance of qualifying for the knockout stages when Johnny Rep thundered in a rocket to make it 3-2 in our favour but not enough to change the goal difference arithmetic."

Archie may not modestly place that Argentina goal on high, but the Scottish Football Museum at Hampden Park have. They've brought the goal into virtual reality with life size figures portraying the strike. Conceivably, many have taken the opportunity to shake the inert Mr Gemmill's hand for a most memorable experience.

From Birmingham, it was off to join the quaintly named Jacksonville Teamen over in the States.

Archie admitted: "I went over there basically as a break for the family. The Florida climate is fabulous, the people are friendly and I had a good six to seven months there. The kids, Scott and Stacey, went to school there. In the USA the educational pattern is you go to school early and finish around 1pm, with the afternoon being entirely devoted to sport."

Wigan Athletic and a return to Derby were drop off points when Archie and family returned to the UK. Since the end of his playing days, he has always been involved in the game in a variety of appointments.

Administration at Nottingham Forest, a southern spy for Scotland manager Berti Vogts, both at home and abroad, Archie went on to guide the Scotland Under-19 squad, in tandem with former St Mirren full-back Tommy Wilson, to the European Championship final, where they just missed out on glory.

But if just one of these talented youngsters can emulate that Gemmill goal, immortality is assured!

RICKY GILLIES

A CALLOW youth who conceivably hadn't as yet faced the need to sample the products of the Gillette organisation, Ricky Gillies was a mite nervous when he found himself in Jimmy Bone's favoured squad for a league fixture against Cowdenbeath. Ricky was initially handed a seat on the bench.

He takes up the story: "I was immensely pleased with myself at my achievement, but then shock horror took as I realised this was now senior football on a much higher stage.

"We were four up when Jimmy Bone sent me on. Campbell Money had scored with a penalty, Barry Lavety netted two with a further goal coming from Garry McVie. Not surprisingly, I was over the moon to get the fifth. The feeling was unbelievable when I managed to ping one into the top corner.

"Cowdenbeath's cause wasn't helped when their keeper Alan Combe was sent off. However, he must have enhanced his standing when he later signed for St Mirren."

To score on your debut enters Ricky into a select St Mirren club, but one further statistical record emerged from that December day in 1992.

Ricky's age of 16 years and 100 days made him the youngest ever St Mirren debutant – a record that stood until Scott Gemmill came off the bench in August 2003 in a match with Raith Rovers at Kirkcaldy, Scott's time on planet earth being 16 years and 60 days.

Former St Mirren Youth Development Officer Joe Hughes takes the credit in persuading midfield playmaker Ricky to sign a St Mirren "S" Form.

Joe had tracked Ricky's career from his Eastwood High School days via the Barrhead Boys' Club and onto the Highbury Boys' Club, before David Hay initiated the signing of a professional form in December 1992.

The incentive to sign on at Love Street was enhanced by elder sibling Kenny.

Ricky explained: "Kenny joined St Mirren in September 1992. At the time I was told that Celtic and Liam Brady were interested in me but I quite fancied St Mirren. It was local to my home and my brother was there."

Kenny and Ricky never played together in the same St Mirren youth teams but they did manage 16 first-team games together, which poses the question – when did brothers before Clan Gillies last don a black and white strip in the same match?

An early high spot in the Gillies career was the 1993 B&Q Cup Final against Falkirk at Fir Park when he came off the bench to replace Alex Bone.

He said: "I remember it well, not so much for the football but more for the weather. The conditions were vile with hail, sleet, rain and high winds making football a lottery.

"Our captain that day was Neil Orr and he was the biggest moaner I've ever come across. I think we were all on edge when the kick-off was delayed due to traffic congestion on the M74. The number of vehicles coming from Paisley was the root cause of the problem. The delay certainly didn't help to placate Neil – and it certainly didn't help when we lost 3-0!"

Much more pleasurable in the Gillies career catalogue was his selection for seven Under-21 Scotland caps.

He went on: "These were pretty special occasions and I think I played my best football when I was involved in the Scotland set up. Prior to the Under-21s, I played with the national Under-17 side. And when I was moved up to play with the Under-18s, it provided a great boost to my confidence."

Tommy Craig, the former Newcastle United man and Scotland youth coach, was then employed by Aberdeen. Conceivably, Tommy had a big input into Ricky's move to join the Dons in August 1997.

Ricky recalled: "I've often been asked if I was fed up with St Mirren at the time. But no, it was simply a possible career progression. I wanted to see if I could make it in the Premier League.

"It was Alex Miller who signed me for Aberdeen. He thought I was doing okay but when Ebbe Skovdahl arrived as manager he thought otherwise. My face and style didn't fit and he banished me to train with the reserves."

A return to St Mirren was on the cards and with Saints hot favourites to land the millennium First Division title, Ricky returned to play in the last four games and join in the celebrations.

He said: "I even managed to get a medal! It was good to play in a team high in confidence after being involved with Aberdeen in a relegation battle. But while it was good to win the championship, I have to put my contribution into perspective. It was pretty minimal and all credit should go to the rest of the team."

With 56 goals from 327 appearances under his belt, Ricky is in no doubt as to his most memorable goal. There were, in fact, two and both came in what Ricky rates as his playing high spot.

He went on: "It was all about the game against Dundee United at Love Street near the end of our 2000-01 SPL season. We were both looking to beat the drop.

"We were one down and really needed all three points to stay up. Jim Lauchlan handled the ball in the box. He refuted the fact that it was a penalty but referee Hugh Dallas was adamant.

"There was a wee bit of a scuffle before I took the kick to put me off but I was focused enough to fire in the equaliser.

"To net the winner on the day all combined to give me a momentous game, plus two more than satisfying goals. Wee Jose Quitongo was involved with a pass to Stephen McPhee, who laid it off for me to score the winner in the last minute."

A St Mirren career that started in 1992 and ended 13 years later with a Testimonial against Celtic at Love Street was further endorsed when Ricky was inducted along with Tony Fitzpatrick, Campbell Money and Hugh Murray into the newly established St Mirren Hall of Fame.

Ricky said: "That was a surprise – a very pleasant surprise. To think I'll always be linked to St Mirren once I'm long gone is especially meaningful for my wife Kate and sons Ronan and Max."

Leaving St Mirren at just 28 years old meant his Love Street associations were almost certainly over. After being released by St Mirren, Ricky enjoyed a short spell with Partick Thistle before emigrating to New Zealand with his family.

PETER GODFREY

IT was a summit meeting of considerable financial importance. Peter Godfrey and his wife Rhona sat down to mull over the possibility of a major career switch. Peter had been a part-time player with Meadowbank Thistle and the family income had been supplemented from the returns of a painting and decorating business.

Peter explained: "I was 27 and didn't really know what to do. St Mirren wanted me to go full-time. I looked at Rhona and she looked at me. She made me make the decision. 'Well, don't ask me - you're the bread winner, you do what you want' - and that was it. I signed on at St Mirren Park."

Peter arrived at Love Street in January 1985 but the catalyst that triggered St Mirren's interest in the six-foot central defender originated from the previous season's Scottish Cup run.

St Mirren had been drawn to play Meadowbank in the third round. The untenanted acres that constitute Meadowbank Stadium are never conducive enough to generate a rousing cup tie atmosphere, but Saints weren't too unhappy with the 0-0 scoreline.

Back to Love Street for the replay and again St Mirren's Premier League status failed to overcome the First Division opposition. Another draw, 2-2 this time, with Neil Cooper netting a brace for Saints. The Meadowbank counters came from Aidrian Sprott and a certain Tom Hendrie - a name not unknown in and around the Paisley environs.

This particular era was pre penalty shootouts and the Edinburgh side won the toss to take the second replay back to Meadowbank.

Godfrey and his defensive colleagues again did a pretty good job in shackling the Saints' frontmen and it took a spot-kick from Ian Scanlon plus a Frank McAvennie goal to offset another Sprott counter to ease St Mirren through to the fourth round to meet Hamilton.

Alex Miller eventually secured the Godfrey autograph but it was McAvennie who endorsed the deal.

Peter reminisced: "When I arrived at Love Street, Frank took me aside and told me, 'Just remember it was me that got you here, simply because I couldn't get past you in those cup ties, you s***!'"

Soccer camaraderie at its woeful best.

A staunch supporter of the Junior game, Peter had spent a number of seasons with Linlithgow Rose prior to going senior. More a midfielder in these days, he confided he'd even been a dashing outside left when he was 11.

Terry Christie, the wily headmaster and part-time manager of Meadowbank introduced Peter to the senior game, where he pulled on an orange shirt on 94 league occasions in his three seasons in the capital.

A playing contemporary in Peter's entire sojourn at Meadowbank was former St Mirren boss Hendrie, who spoke volumes of the Godfrey talent.

Tom said: "He was a very athletic centre-back. Very mobile, he moved quickly and was exceptionally good in the air. He was particularly strong in the tackle and his physical attributes were such that he seemed to have telescopic legs in making those vital tackles."

Peter made his St Mirren debut against Dundee United at Love Street. Not surprisingly, the Tangerines failed to score. Saints did - 1-0.

He went on to spend seven seasons wearing black and white, logging in 174 league outings. Surprisingly, he was only ever once listed as a substitute.

Checking the Godfrey appearance record in the 86-87 league campaign, he was almost an ever present, so it was a major disappointment he didn't make the 1987 Scottish Cup final team.

He said: "I was very disappointed. To be fair to Alex Smith, I had at first been suffering from an illness and was then injured. But I think Alex blamed me for giving a goal away in an earlier round and I was dropped - but that's football for you."

A free transfer from Saints and the Brockville manager Jim Jefferies moved quickly to enlist he services of the Falkirk-born defender. It was a dream move. Peter played in the remaining 11 Falkirk league fixtures, the Bairns were unbeaten and went on to lift the First Division pennant.

Capable of nicking the odd goal or two, perhaps Peter's most memorable strike was at Ibrox - an effort that earned Falkirk a 1-1 draw in October '91.

By this time, Peter was fast approaching his 35th birthday - perhaps not quite sprightly enough for Premier League action, but still clearly an asset for a Second Division team. Mickey Lawson was the man that took Peter to Arbroath, although only for a limited whiff of the east coast air.

A Carronvale man by birth, Peter was anxious to return to his roots and his former mentor Christie enrolled him for a three-season spell with Stenhousemuir. Peter's last game on the senior circuit saw the Warriors defeat Brechin City 3-0 at Ochilview.

The end of a satisfactory career? No way. Always keen for a game or two, Peter reverted to the Juniors and turned out once again for Linlithgow Rose before helping out Bathgate Thistle.

With Peter now no longer a full-time player, Rhona Godfrey was ever mindful of the need for food on the table to satisfy the appetites of Steven, Kevin and Jennifer. The Prison Service offered another career switch, with the inmates of Glenochil Prison now being subjected to the Godfrey style of discipline.

Even there, the footballing bug bit. And Peter, in tandem with fellow officers Willie Irvine (ex-Alloa) and Davie Beaton (ex-Falkirk) led the prison warders team regular victories in the prison soccer league.

Off duty, Peter lent his administrative skills to furthering the interests of Sauchie Juniors, where he became assistant manager to the aforementioned Irvine.

Peter's last game at St Mirren Park was to participate in a legends team in support of Norrie McWhirter's Testimonial match.

As ever, the socks were down at his ankles, the gangling gait still in evidence - a gait that reminded the denizens of the North Bank of that Minister of Funny Walks, alias Basil Fawlty.

Peter revealed: "They used to call me Basil. Kind of funny, but it gave me a great feeling of being bonded to the fans. I always tried to give them 100 per cent."

The charisma of Pte Godfrey from Dad's Army? Absolutely no way. It was always 100 per cent Basil and he's well remembered at Love Street.

BRIAN HAMILTON

"I'VE taken so much out of football, the main reason I came into this job was to put something back into the game."

The words of Brian Hamilton, the recently appointed Football Development Officer for East Renfrewshire, whose Council oversee the physical and football well-being of thousands of youngsters in an endeavour to wean them off the current craze for modern technology.

Not many players are born in Paisley and aspire to winning a Scottish Cup badge with their local team. But Brian did, having a prime role in that 1987 St Mirren spectacular at Hampden.

Some might question the youthful involvement in teenage games as being excessive. But the adolescent enthusiasm didn't appear to affect Brian, playing for Craigbank Secondary School in the morning and St Mirren Boys' Club in the afternoon.

The mix didn't appear to provide an overdrawn account at the Hamilton energy bank, with recognition being accorded by both the national Schools Under-16 and Under-18 sides.

Rikki McFarlane initially recruited Hamilton on an "S" Form when he was 14.

A couple of years on and St Mirren were keen to farm him out to Arthurlie in a bid to toughen him up.

Brian recalled: "I was only 16 at the time and went to Dunterlie Park for a week. In truth, I wasn't mature or strong enough for the rough and tumble of the Junior game and opted to play at Juvenile level with Pollok United Boys' Club.

"It was from there that Alex Miller took me on as a full-time YTS lad in the year the YTS project started. I was in good company, joining the likes of Paul Lambert, Norrie McWhirter, George Shaw and wee John Butler."

Taken on a pre-season tour of Northern Ireland at the start of the 85-86 campaign, Brian was honest enough to admit he was seriously raw and played well below par.

He had to wait six months before he made his competitive domestic debut against Dundee at Dens Park. The now 18-year-old arrived off the bench but failed to complement his pocket money with any win bonus, the City of Discovery team winning 3-1, Brian Gallagher being the Saints sole marksman.

The necessary maturity level was eventually achieved by Hamilton, whose comfort zone in a central midfield role saw him firmly entrenched in a Saints side that went on to win that 1987 Scottish Cup.

He said: "That was a magnificent day. People didn't expect St Mirren to be there. What was inspirational was the turn out of the fans, when many appeared out of the woodwork to support the team."

Hamilton went on: "We went down to prepare at Seamill. The facilities, the food and all the training were superb. Dundee United were about to play IFK Gothenburg in the UEFA Cup final a week later so St Mirren were clearly the underdogs in the national final. We proved a point - underdogs can win!"

A four-year stay at Love Street saw 87 league outings logged on to the Hamilton CV, and this was further embellished with four Scotland Under-21 caps, Yugoslavia in 1989 being his first in dark blue.

By now Miller had moved on to mastermind the needs at Hibernian. He well remembered the Hamilton exploits during his three years in charge at Love Street.

A new Saints contract was offered to Brian but that scenario was trumped by the Hibernian offer of a £260,000 transfer fee, which saw the St Mirren treasurer salivate at the thought of reducing the club debt.

In fact, Brian's time at Easter Road encompassed the peak of his playing career.

Almost 200 league appearances for the Hibees saw additional baubles earned to complement that Scottish Cup badge. Dunfermline were beaten in the 91-92 League Cup while Hibs lost out to Rangers two years later in the same tourney.

The Hamilton taste buds also relished European competition, appearing against Mechelen and Slavia Prague while at Love Street, and going on to experience further UEFA activity against Videoton, FC Liege and Anderlecht wearing green and white.

It takes a strong minded player to play for both St Mirren and Morton in the west. Equally, one's personal hide has to be resilient enough to withstand the Edinburgh jibes for those who forsake Hibs for a peg at Tynecastle.

Life as a Jam Tart was of short duration, though. Only 25 games, in fact, before Eamonn Bannon secured the Hamilton services for Falkirk in the 1996 close season. That move to Brockville heralded a downturn in the Hamilton fortunes.

Brian explained: "I broke my leg in the first round of the Scottish Cup on January 25, 1997, against Berwick Rangers. I remember the date well. Of some Paisley interest, it was Scott McKenzie, later to play in black and white, that came on to replace me.

"The following season I won a medal with Falkirk as we won the League Challenge Cup. But that came as a somewhat diluted consolation prize - I was on the bench in the final and didn't even get on."

Ayr United showed a modicum of interest before the emigration bug took over. A short spell in Sweden with the Huskvana club predated a move to Australia and the Canberra Cosmos.

Brian added: "Canberra played in the national league where every second week necessitated a flight to Sydney, Perth, and Adelaide or wherever. The Cosmos had some talented players there, including former Saint Dave Winnie.

"The standard of play would possibly equate to that of the Scottish First Division. It was a fantastic experience and provided the opportunity to explore such a vast and remarkable country."

A return to Scotland saw Brian team up with Ian McCall at Clydebank.

Although homeless, the Bankies played some excellent football at a time when they had seven former internationalists on their books.

And finally... John Lambie, that revered icon down Maryhill way, signed Brian to enhance the Jags' promotion push in 2001. It worked. The Firhill team moved up to the First Division and Brian won another medal - although he was forthright enough to admit his standard of play indicated it was nearly boot hanging up time.

With such a reservoir of experience, it wasn't surprising the SFA, in tandem with the East Renfrewshire Council, came calling to enlist the Hamilton soccer know-how.

Undoubtedly the youngsters who forsook their mobile phones and computers find a talented teacher to further their football interests.

RONNIE HAMILTON

WHAT is intriguing in providing a chronicle on the life and times of Ronnie Hamilton is that he was never really allowed to change his strip stripes from Kilmarnock's blue and white to the black and white of St Mirren.

Kilmarnock born, bred and educated, Ronnie's wife and family were also from the town. Heck, he stayed there, played at golf there - but wait...

A self styled "war baby" whose birth certificate was posted in 1945, Ronnie's life-long association with Kilmarnock saw his attempts at mastering the three "Rs" start at Loanhead Primary School. Early recognition came his way with soccer selection for the Ayrshire & District Under-12 Schools side.

The football blue touch paper had been ignited but was almost extinguished on his arrival at Kilmarnock Academy. This scholastic institution was a rugby playing establishment and Ronnie joined other St Mirren mortals such as Jimmy Bone and Campbell Forsyth whose early affinity to the oval ball game preceded success in the association code.

According to Ronnie, instead of generating a downturn in his athletic progress, the soccer launch pad was created.

He said: "I used to play rugby in the morning and football in the afternoon. I was fortunate that my dad worked in the Saxone Shoe Company which gave me an entry into joining the Saxone Boys' Club.

"They had their own playing fields and it was a great club to learn your trade as it were. My father was an active scout for Kilmarnock and I was recommended to those in authority at Rugby Park. But although I had the opportunity of signing for both Chelsea and Rangers, I chose to join my home town team."

Former Rangers winger, the galloping Willie Waddell, was the Killie manager who secured the Hamilton signature in 1961.

The Waddell-Hamilton association peaked in season 1964-65. The winning of that league championship was pure theatre. Hearts were in pole position, needing one point for the title as Kilmarnock visited Tynecastle on the last day of the season.

Killie won 2-0, taking the pennant on goal difference, and Waddell forsaked his normally stern visage to cavort around the pitch congratulating his ecstatic players.

Ronnie, honest as ever, made the point: "Out of the 34 games in the league programme, I only played in 28, and was dropped towards the end of the season. I was always a part-timer but still finished up with a medal and Kilmarnock's leading scorer."

Waddell retired after winning that championship and Malcolm McDonald arrived as manager.

He tended to chop and change the team round and Ronnie's striking attributes were deemed surplus to requirements.

Doug Millward, the Saints manager, was in the lookout for a ready-made striker. Hamilton was reluctant to make the move but money talks and the wage package on offer from St Mirren was the catalyst that clinched the transfer, the 20-year-old arriving in Paisley in 1966.

It was a makepiece deal, Ronnie moving go Love Street and Gerry Queen plus a £4,000 cheque going to Rugby Park.

With the likes of Jimmy Robertson, Pat Liney, Tommy Kiernan, Peter Kane and Archie Gemmill on hand to greet the new boy, he was clearly at ease in his debut game. And that trip to Pittodrie on January 22, 1966, saw a single goal from Ronnie giving Saints the full points.

Hamilton said: "I thoroughly enjoyed my time at St Mirren Park. They were a great family club and I'd have to say it was a much more friendlier place than Rugby Park.

"I was never quite sure if I was good enough for the top flight. If I was to start my career again I might have considered going full-time, particularly with the amount of money in the game now."

Ronnie was certainly good enough for St Mirren. He spent five years with the Buddies, helping Alex Wright to win promotion in 1968 amd contributing eight goals from 29 league outings.

After St Mirren and still a part-timer, Ronnie moved to Queen of the South, spending five years with the Doonhamers under Jim Easton.

With retiral horizons on the playing pitch looming, and the travelling to and from Dumfries becoming a mite tedious, Ronnie returned to his first love, spending the final two years of his 17-year playing career with Kilmarnock.

If Hamilton's cup was over flowing with league title successes, memories of success in cup competition must conceivably centre on what was initially called The Fairs Cup in Euro competition, later to be rechristened The UEFA Cup.

In Ronnie's first stint in Killie colours, the Rugby Parkers travelled to take on Eintracht Frankfurt in the 1964 Fairs Cup first round. Due to the demands of his CA exams, Ronnie was left at home for the first leg in Germany. Killie lost 3-0. But in the return at Rugby Park, the Ayrshiremen went ballistic, winning 5-1 and Ronnie scoring twice.

Do on-field challenges breed continuing animosity in later life? Ronnie can personally refute such allegations.

He said: "I played in a match at Rugby Park against Celtic and both Billy McNeill and Bobby Murdoch broke their ankles. I was responsible, so after that there were always terracing chants for some form of retribution.

However, that all changed once we'd retired and we became the best of friends."

Once the boots had been binned, Kilmarnock still figured largely in the Hamilton lifestyle. Involved for 12 years on the Rugby Park board of directors, Ronnie eventually achieved his ultimate accolade at his hometown club - he became their chairman.

Once an accountant your financial expertise is in constant demand. Ronnie and his wife Eleanor are both Elders in the Church of Scotland, with Ronnie being just the man to mastermind the Church's Deeds of Covenant Scheme.

While club captaincy on the soccer playing fields escaped him, Ronnie did, in his latter leisure years achieve such prominence at the Kilmarnock Golf Club, his car being parked prettily into the bay marked - CLUB CAPTAIN.

BOBBY HOLMES

FOR someone who was once a bricklayer of some note, Bobby Holmes built a career in football the foundations of which were most certainly structured on solid rock.

Never a natural left footed player, his comfort zone saw him monopolise St Mirren's left-half berth in the 1950s with occasional sorties in the inside left corridor.

A Coatbridge boy with a birth certificate registered in 1933, it was from that township's Central School that Bobby's soccer development was spawned - firstly with the Under-18 amateur side of Lochend Rovers going via the Campsie Black Watch Juveniles side before mounting the Junior stage with Kilsyth Rangers.

As Bobby reminisced: "We had a tremendous side at that time at Duncansfield Park. Kilsyth went on to win almost every trophy on offer, the Scottish Junior Cup being the only one we missed out on."

Like most of his contemporaries, the demands of national service kicked in and Bobby saw out his two-year stint with the colours clad in airforce blue.

He had, in fact, signed a provisional form for St Mirren while he was still in the forces and celebrated his demob on a Wednesday by turning out for Saints on the following Saturday.

Debut day for Bobby saw the high-flying Motherwell side visit Love Street, the occasion being firmly embedded in Holmes' memory bank as the illustrious Willie Kilmarnock, Archie 'Baldy' Shaw and Andy Paton endorsed a physical Fir Park policy of "They shall not pass."

A six-year spell at Love Street created a number of momentous occasions, some high and others exceedingly low.

St Mirren's first incursion into the ultimate stage of the League Cup competition saw the Buddies take on Aberdeen in the 1955 Hampden final.

Although picking up a runners-up medal, the 2-1 defeat was a bitter pill to swallow for Bobby and his Love Street mates.

He said: "We most certainly didn't deserve to lose. OK, I managed to score St Mirren's only goal and that's obviously a pleasing memory. But the two goals that beat us were without doubt manufactured in the fluke factory.

"Jimmy Mallan was unlucky to turn the ball into his own net and then Graham Leggat sent over a speculative ball that was neither shot nor cross and it sailed over keeper Jim Lornie."

That St Mirren felt a little aggrieved at the result was emphasised when Aberdeen manager Davie Shaw arrived in the Saints dressing room. His assertions that St Mirren had been the better side and his Pittodrie team lucky in their two goals was cold comfort to the chastened Saints.

If that was a semi-high on the Holmes CV, an undoubted full blooded low was a broken leg early in 1959 which cost Bobby a place in the 1959 Scottish Cup final team, Tommy Leishman taking his place. It also signified the end of Holmes' playing career.

It was a career that brought international recognition with the Juniors, in taking on the Irish Intermediate League team, in addition to an Under-23 cap and an Inter League call up against England.

As every player will eventually verify, there is life after the boots have been unlaced for the last time.

Bobby explained: "I wanted to stay in the game but coaching wasn't an option. The surgeon told me to give up running around in a coaching capacity or risk being a cripple before my time.

"I decided to take up physiotherapy and took a three-year course at the Victoria Health Centre in Glasgow."

Armed with his Physiotherapy Diploma, Bobby started out manipulating the muscles of Arthurlie Juniors, before going senior and assisting Bobby Flavell at the Cliftonhill Stadium in Coatbridge.

It was Jackie Stewart, having eased into the managerial armchair at "fatal" Boghead, who insisted on Bobby becoming Dumbarton's main muscle man, and that was a vocation that lasted for 15 years.

Life with the Sons generated considerable job satisfaction for Bobby, the Boghead side providing a more than friendly disposition to all their employees.

When Alex Miller took over at Love Street in October 1983, he was in need of a full-time physio and Bobby was the man who responded to the call.

If Bobby had been somewhat vexed at losing out in that 1955 League Cup final in a playing capacity, he certainly made amends in his role as a club physio.

In charge of the Saints massage parlour for the 1987 final against Dundee United, he subsequently moved on to take charge of Motherwell's aches and pains for their 1991 Scottish Cup win, again over the Tannadice men.

Holmes said: "I think I became something of a lucky mascot. St Mirren's success was out of this world. We weren't the flavour of the final, Dundee United were the out and out favourites.

"Motherwell were also the underdogs. They did really well, particularly with the problems we had with their goalkeeper Ally Maxwell.

"We didn't know what was wrong with him. We thought it was a simple case of damaged ribs - if ever such an injury can be classified as simple. He was magnificent and managed to stay on for the whole 120 minutes despite being in great pain. It was only later we learned that he'd ruptured his spleen."

With limited playing resources at most clubs, the demands on a physio are great in returning a player to active football duty, perhaps sooner than would medically be acceptable.

Bobby said: "There are always pressures. The constant query is 'Will he be fit for next week?' A player could be sidelined for two to three weeks but the demands of the game are such that they want him fit for next Saturday.

"It was always the physio's prerogative that he would recommend the requisite course of treatment and exercise for a full recovery. Inevitably, some short cuts took place due to the manager always having the final word."

The compilation of any physiotherapist job description in the football industry will never spell out a nine to five operational week.

After 30 years working on a seven-day week basis, covering a multitude of unsociable hours, Bobby had had enough of coal face soccer.

He had the last word: "I'm not really missing it. I'm more relaxed. There was no animosity when I left Motherwell, but I was simply fed up with the travelling. It was a daily battle in traversing Glasgow's traffic chicane on the Kingston Bridge.

"Now I've a five-yard journey to my garage, which I've fitted out as a treatment room. I work from home and I'm still involved in football injuries. The difference is the walking wounded now come to me!"

DEREK HYSLOP

HE was undoubtedly classified as one of the more pragmatic footballers of his time. Derek Hyslop was well aware that by the time he had reached his mid 20s he wasn't in line to amass a fortune from the soccer industry.

What he was more aware of was the need to clothe and kit the active participants in the wider sporting spheres, his warm dulcet tones being tailor made to provide a selling feature in carving out a post-playing career in the sports and leisure business.

But to the beginning... It was September 6, 1957, when Derek first saw light of day in Girvan on the Ayrshire coast. Derek and younger sibling Brian were both into football, with Brian's playing zenith homing in on the Juvenile side Dunipace Thistle.

Derek's prowess as a striker had been honed on the playing fields of Cumbernauld High School, turning out in the morning for his Alma Mater side and for Dunipace Thistle after Saturday lunch.

The scorer of a barrowload of goals at that level, he was soon attracting the attention of the scouting clans.

Derek recalled: "I was persuaded to sign S Forms for Hibernian when I was only 13. The natural progression was to turn professional when you were 16, which I did, and after that I went on to spend another 18 months at Easter Road, before Eddie Turnbull released me. In all honesty, there were some outstanding players at Hibs at that time and my future playing prospects weren't too bright."

Alex Ferguson had succeeded Willie Cunningham as the Love Street mastermind, his first game in charge being against Clydebank at New Kilbowie Park on the 1974 Boxing Day.

In the spring of the following year, Fergie's scouting team had alerted him that Hibees were releasing a lad with considerable potential. And to boot, a lad with a west of Scotland heritage that might interest St Mirren.

It did and Hyslop signed on at Love Street on May 10, 1975. The teenager with talent made his first black and white appearance in a pre-season warm-up game. Hereford United provided both the opposition and the frustration, with Saints two up at half-time before letting the game slip with a full-time scoreline of 2-2.

Derek had to wait another month for his competitive debut. A League Cup match against East Fife at Bayview saw him on the bench with Jackie McGilvray. The St Mirren starting line up comprised Hunt, Johnston, Beckett, Fitzpatrick, Reid, Young, Ferguson, Stark, Leonard, Campbell and McDowell.

Regretfully, the 90-minute score was a 2-0 win in the Fifers' favour.

The Hyslop teenage appreciation of the St Mirren icons at that time looms large in Derek's memory banks. Tony Fitzpatrick will be forever remembered for his skill, his graft and his paternal encouragement for all the young Saints players.

Full-back Alex Beckett was another who took Derek under his wing, although Alex might just take umbrage at Derek's description of him as the player with the severe centre parting!

In his four-season Love Street career, Derek logged in 22 substitute appearances to compliment his 78 St Mirren starts. And his substitute record seemed to generate a secret St Mirren strategy, with Ferguson regularly bringing him off the bench to net an important goal.

Indeed, Derek's first Saints goal was achieved in such a manner up at Pittodrie in a 1976 League Cup match with Aberdeen. Derek, with his substitute hat, on netted one and Walter Borthwick scored a second. But the Dons found the onion bag on three occasions, securing the section points.

Dens Park, Dundee's ancestral home, was something of a nadir location for the home side in respect of the 1976-77 promotional aspirations of Clydebank and St Mirren.

The Bankies had achieved promotion on Saturday, April 16, and the following Tuesday St Mirren required just a point to register their claim to the First Division championship. Secure it they did, with Derek fully involved in the promotion celebrations.

Derek recalled: "The whole season was unbelievable. We were on a roll.

Fergie had us believing in our own ability. He was a great exponent of mind games with the opposition and always had a playing plan in his head. If he put you on the bench, it wasn't in any way a form of demotion - it was always part of the overall game plan.

"For me, it was simply superb to have linked up with Lex Richardson, Billy Stark and Frank McGarvey and it was pretty special to have contributed 17 goals in the promotion push."

Not withstanding Derek's goal haul in that league campaign, his favourite strike wasn't achieved in domestic competition.

He explained: "At that time, St Mirren were enjoying a lengthy spell of success in the Anglo-Scottish Cup. The 1977-78 season was the club's first sortie in the competition and we lost out to Bristol City in the final 3-2 on aggregate.

"The following season we came up against Bristol again in the second round.

We'd beaten them 2-1 down at Ashton Gate and managed a 2-2 draw at Love Street.

"If I'm asked for a favourite goal it came in that 2-2 draw. I was up against the strong going Norman Hunter, formerly of Leeds United, who had 28 England caps to his credit and was widely known in the game as 'Chopper'.

"I managed to get on the end of a peach of a cross from Iain Munro and bulleted a header into the top corner. Even Hunter was impressed. He came up to me at the end of the game and said, 'Well done son - cracking goal'."

St Mirren went out in the semi-final to Oldham Athletic but, third time lucky and at the expense of Bristol City, they won the trophy in 79-80, and were the only Scottish team ever to do so. However, by this time Derek had been given a free transfer by Jim Clunie - May 5, 1979 to be exact.

Two further Love Street experiences are firmly entrenched in Derek's St Mirren memories. One was a major disappointment when he wasn't selected for the St Mirren 1976 Caribbean tour.

Hyslop recalled: "There was always going to be a limited pool of players going and I wasn't far enough up the pecking order to be considered. Being a mere 18 at the time was a contributory factor as was, I'm sure, the financial outlay from the club."

What was a more memorable occasion was the celebration of the St Mirren centenary. The star-studded Liverpool side came north to taste the delights of St Mirren's 100th birthday cake.

Kenny Dalglish scored for the Merseysiders with Billy Abercrombie bringing parity to the proceedings with a late equaliser.

However, a recipient for the Centenary Silver Salver had to be found and a penalty shootout determined the winners. The Anfield side won 5-4 in the shootout. Frank McGarvey and Bobby Reid miscued their spot-kicks but Derek was delighted to make the point: "I scored mine!"

No further Hyslop football after St Mirren, but a satisfying career in the sports and leisure business followed for Derek. Firstly with Arena Swimwear, after which he had a 10-year spell with Umbro International, where Derek ended up as general manager UK. Berghouse, the outdoor sports company, followed before he moved on to Hi-tech Sports.

As Alistair MacPherson, a confirmed Saints aficionado and with a fellow involvement in sports outfitting, made the point: "Derek was a great player with St Mirren and his personality was tailor made to succeed in the sports and leisure business."

PETER KANE

FOR those with memories of the Saintly deeds from the late 60s, the name Peter Kane conjures up visions of a striker with pace, twinkling feet and a predatory instinct for planting the ball in the opposition net.

Once Peter had started to blow out the birthday cake candles from his own personal 60s era, the relative pace was still there. As were the twinkling feet, as he enjoyed life as a song and dance man, performing as a cabaret artist in the north west English club scene.

Although latterly residing in Blackpool, Kane's arrival on planet earth was destined for Glasgow's Govan district. He went on to play mainly as a striker and occasionally in midfield in his scholastic times at St Constantine's and St Gerard's schools.

The normal teenage football pathway was followed as he played Boys Guild football before joining Petershill as a 17-year-old.

Trials with both Stirling Albion and Hamilton Accies followed before the lure of playing at Hampden with Queen's Park was a temptation that was too good to ignore.

The 1960 Rome Olympics were on the horizon and a fair number of Queen's Park players were on standby for the British team pool, the GB side of the day being strictly amateur. Peter was in the GB pool and registered a stake for permanent inclusion with four goals in a warm-up game against a Caribbean side.

However, a ticket to Italy went on hold as Northampton Town required a goal scorer and manager David Bowen took the Scot to their County Ground for a season.

A 16-goal return from only 28 games with the Cobblers posed a problem for Peter.

He explained: "After only five months with Northampton, I was given the chance of joining Arsenal. It was a big move as it was a jump from Division Four to Division One.

"I thought I might not get my place at Highbury and initially said no. A couple of weeks later, I received my National Service call-up papers, so I changed my mind and signed for the Gunners just to escape my call-up!"

Not that Kane was afraid of performing for Queen and country, but a seemingly reserved occupation as a pro player with the mighty Arsenal was an attractive proposition to a developing player.

If signing for the Highbury club was a treasured memory for Peter, his first day at training was an even bigger highlight for the then 21-year-old.

He recalled: "I was playing against my boyhood hero Tommy Docherty. He was marking me and kept pulling my jersey, holding me back to keep up with me. I must be better than I thought was my immediate reaction!"

The Arsenal sojourn was of limited duration, though, with an eventual return to Northampton, where Peter's two-year stint with the colours finally came home to roost.

There was, however, some disappointment in his time with the Royal Army Medical Corps. Hopes of developing a possible future career in physiotherapy never materialised.

Season 1963-64 saw the Kane talents transferred to Crewe Alexandra – a move that bordered on pantomime proportions for Peter and the then Gresty Road manager Ernie Tagg, a local milkman.

Peter said: "Ernie didn't have much of an idea about the game. I remember him saying to me, 'Pete, we're playing Darlington on Saturday. Who am I going to play at right-back?' I said, 'Dave Whelan's your man.' Tagg responded, 'Dave doesn't want to play – he's got his shop to run and it's a full day trip to Darlington, so who am I going to play?'

"I said then, 'play the boy Ralph Marshall, the lad we got from Rangers'. Ernie then trumped this bizarre team selection process by telling me Marshall couldn't play either as he was dong his milk round!"

The unprofessional set up at Crewe initiated a deep desire to move, thankfully fulfilled by St Mirren manager Alex Wright.

Alex sent former Rangers inside forward Willie Paton to run the rule over Peter's scoring abilities. The resulting measurements were more than acceptable.

Peter arrived at Love Street midway through the 66-67 season, playing his first match against Stirling Albion at home, the Saints winning 4-0.

The St Mirren marksmen were Pinkerton, McLaughlin, Gemmill and Aird – the remarkable point being that this was the only occasion Peter had never scored in a debut match for his clutch of senior clubs.

He had to wait for another four games to record his first St Mirren goal, Hearts going down 3-0 at Love Street.

An integral member of Wright's 67-68 promotion-winning side, Peter's contribution was a 21-goal return from 29 league outings. And the St Mirren "Goals For" column stood at exactly 100. Other double figure inputs came from Jim Blair (21), Bobby Adamson (17) and Bobby Pinkerton (12).

The following season saw Peter appear in every one of the 34 league fixtures, a personal highlight being a 1-0 turnover of Rangers at Love Street.

Peter said: "That game generated a lot of pleasure for me. I was up against John Greig and managed to nutmeg him on three separate occasions. He wasn't particularly chuffed with my cheek. What was probably more important to me and the team was the £100 bonus instead of the usual £4. We felt like millionaires!"

A bad injury saw Peter leave St Mirren at the end of the 69-70 term, with Clydebank signing him for a couple of seasons.

Kane went on: "When I was at Kilbowie Park, Barrow wanted me as their player/manager. I didn't apply for the job but I thought I'd take the chance and Jack Steedman let me go.

"What the Barrow directors didn't tell me was that they only had four signed players. They did tell me they needed a couple of players but that couple quickly became 10 and I was given £3,000 to buy players – such is the manager's lot!"

Peter and his wife Betty had six of a family, with father Peter happy to spend his leisure hours watching the progress of youngest son Peter jnr, who played as a semi pro in the local Blackpool leagues.

Blackpool is still a popular venue for Paisley holidaymakers and with Peter still in the entertainment business, his cabaret act went down well with the Blackpool visitors and St Mirren garbed Buddies in the audience happy to lead the appreciative applause.

DONNIE KERRIGAN

THE arrival of Donnie Kerrigan on planet earth was one of pyrotechnic proportions, although fireworks weren't readily involved. Donnie's mother, heavily pregnant, along with the rest of the family, were wartime evacuees at Seamill on the Ayrshire coast.

At the time Mrs Kerrigan went into labour, the German Luftwaffe were pounding Greenock and Gourock, so much so that the ground tremors reverberating around Seamill caused a metallic bread bin lid in the Kerrigan household to clatter to the floor.

The attending doctor was convinced Seamill had suffered a direct hit. He panicked and quickly vanished into the night air - but not before Donnie had been safely delivered on May 7, 1941.

Educational involvement at Bankhead Primary and Victoria Drive Secondary Schools coupled with membership of the 184th Glasgow Boys' Brigade Company - Donnie going on to win the coveted Queen's Badge - all combined to provide a positive start to teenage life.

Capped by the Scottish Schools, Donnie's football career took off when Douglas Smith, the doyen founder of Drumchapel Amateurs, took Kerrigan on board. Douglas spoke highly of his protege.

He said: "Donnie was a brilliant player with remarkable pace and the ability to turn and take players on. My one regret was that, although he was often in the pool, he never gained a full Scottish Youth cap."

A trial with Duntocher Hibs saw the St Mirren scouting team of Jack Gilmour and Fraser McIntosh take in the game. They were more than impressed with Donnie's performance, harnessing additional Love Street back up in the shape of "Bunty" Lamb and manager Willie Reid to lay siege to the Kerrigan household with a view to a signing for Saints.

The deal didn't go through. At that time a youngster going senior without going through the Junior ranks could never return to the Juniors in later soccer life. The solution was simple. Sign him as a part-time player and farm him out to Johnstone Burgh. A sum of £5 a week as an engineering apprentice with the defence company Barr & Stroud allied to a part-time payment of £16 a week at Love Street was a high financial platform for a 17-year-old.

A winning senior debut against Third Lanark at Cathkin Park on December 12, 1958, saw Donnie wear the No.7 shirt and he went on to appear on the left wing in a further seven league fixtures that season. Cup-winning goalkeeper Davie Walker also celebrated his first Saints outing in that same game.

The latent Kerrigan expertise was more than promising but he was conceivably a touch miffed at not displacing Alistair Miller at outside left and gaining celebrity status in the 1959 St Mirren Scottish Cup win.

His eye for depositing the ball in the opposition net was as sharp as ever as the renowned Billy McNeill of Celtic and Scotland fame would confirm.

Big Billy was the national centre-half at that time when Celtic faced St Mirren in the 1962 Scottish Cup semi-final at Ibrox.

The score was 3-1 in Saints' favour and the confirmed highlight in that encounter was the Kerrigan goal, Donnie taking Billy on for pace, beating him and unleashing a rocket past the bemused Celtic guardian.

One further scoring high spot came with Hearts visiting Love Street on April 2, 1963. Saints logged in a 7-3 return, Donnie scoring four and Bobby Carroll netting the other three.

A more than commendable St Mirren career saw the Kerrigan CV enhanced with a 43-goal return, generated from only 112 outings.

Aberdeen were on the lookout for a scoring frontman - most clubs are - and it was Tommy Pearson who signed Donnie for the Granite City side. The transfer deal equated to Donnie going north with Willie Allan and a makeweight financial top up of £7,000 coming south.

Pearson didn't last long at Pittodrie, Eddie Turnbull, he of the Hibernian "Famous Five" quintet, taking over.

Turnbull pigeon-holed Donnie as an out and out winger, whereas the former St Mirren man had a more positive playing comfort zone in one of the three inside berths. There was considerable Pittodrie discord over this choice of playing position and Donnie was relegated to the Reserves.

He only ever played one Reserve match for the Dons. It was against St Johnstone and Donnie reminded boss Turnbull of his potential with a five-goal return from the centre-forward berth.

Hearts secured the Kerrigan services in 1965, the legendary Tommy Walker signing him for the Tynecastle club, before Donnie moved on to Dunfermline in March 1967, under the managerial jurisdiction of former Scotland keeper George Farm.

A taste of English football beckoned. Former St Mirren manager Jackie Cox was now the chief Scottish scout for Fulham and his positive recommendation brought Craven Cottage manager Bobby Robson north to sign Donnie in a lounge at Glasgow Airport.

Limited appearances for the Cottagers saw Donnie off on loan to Lincoln

City, despite strenuous pleas from Johnny Haynes - the first £100 a week player in England - trying to persuade Robson not to let him go.

He did depart with a further senior career ending sojourn at Portadown with Gibby McKenzie for two years, and a final fling with Shettleston Juniors.

Donnie ended his playing career a trifle early as he was still only in his late 20s when he hung up his boots.

A living had to be earned to sustain the needs of his wife Margaret and their three youngsters. A series of wide-ranging income earners satisfied the need - some good, some not so good.

Donnie and Margaret were the proud proprietors of the Darnley Cafe in Glasgow's Dumbarton Road - a venture that sustained them for around 10 years and the local residents proclaimed the quality of their ice cream the best in the district.

What wasn't so successful was the opening of a small hotel in Saltcoats.

This, in retrospect, was classified by the family as a disaster.

The paramount need to provide an accommodating income saw Donnie return to engineering on the recommendation of a contact from elder sibling Bobby.

The operator of a computer controlled lathe, Donnie lost his life in a tragic industrial accident.

November 9, 1990 was a black day in the life of Clan Kerrigan. But the memories of a precocious football talent laced with goals are still treasured down Love Street way.

ARCHIE KNOX

THE trackside spat at Ibrox between fourth official Willie Young and Rangers assistant boss Archie Knox bore no relation to the academic heritage of either. The match – the 1997 New Year Old Firm encounter – hadn't been flowing particularly sweetly in a Light Blue direction.

A barrage of contentious decisions on the pitch had been hotly debated on the touchline with Mr Young. Archie's demeanour bordered on the incandescent. He fumed: "You don't know what the pressures of this job are like. You don't know what it's like to be in our shoes."

Young's riposte was less than conciliatory: "Archie, if I was in your shoes, your IQ would treble!"

Clearly the touchline verbosity failed to reflect their academic standings – Young a noted Glasgow solicitor and Archie Knox a former surveyor with Dundee Corporation before entering the football portals of playing and management.

Born in Dundee in May 1947, one of three brothers and two sisters, Archie was a joiner to trade before transferring his salary earning potential to the estimating and surveying requirements of the Dundee Corporation.

A minimal increase to the Knox income was achieved by signing for Forfar Athletic from the now defunct Erroll Juniors in time for the 1964-65 season.

Former St Mirren full-back Sam Smith became a kenspeckle figure in the administration of the Station Park side and while Sam wasn't involved in Archie's initial playing career with the Loons, it was Sam who was instrumental in bringing Archie back as a player/coach to succeed Jerry Kerr in 1976.

In current soccer parlance, Archie's early learning days on the football front would see him classified as a striker.

But he said: "I don't honestly think my physical proportions were kind enough to see me described as a striker – I was more likely to be categorised as a forward!"

Saints manager Wright was keen to strengthen his attack and Knox boosted his credentials with a hat-trick in a midweek match for Forfar against Montrose at Links Park.

Ten days later, Archie returned to the City of Discovery in a St Mirren strip. Saints and Dundee drew 2-2 and Knox, to the satisfaction of all at Love Street, scored on his debut. Archie's team-mates on that September day in 1970 were Connaghan, Murray, Connell, Fulton, McFadden, Munro, McKean, Hamilton, Gilshan and Lister.

The sum of £5,000 was the reported transfer fee but how does an east coast lad fulfil his Paisley training requirements?

Archie said: "Five grand! The mind boggles as to my current value on the transfer market! I was part-time when I joined St Mirren and used to travel through to Love Street for training. But the travelling became impossible.

"At this time, John Prentice was manager of Dundee and Jim McLean was the coach. In an arrangement with Alex Wright, I used to train at Dens Park during my lunch breaks."

Knox's time at Love Street could hardly be classified as meritorious, Saints being relegated in his first season.

He said: "It was difficult to take. It happened in the last game of the 70-71 season. Dunfermline were third bottom and we needed both points to overtake them. We only managed one and the Pars pipped us on goal difference."

McLean was now in charge at Tannadice and knew the Knox capabilities well. He forked out £8,000 to ease Archie's travelling difficulties to Paisley.

That move to Dundee United saw Archie in Tangerine colours in the 1974 Scottish Cup final against Celtic. Although in Archie's words it could hardly be classified as a career highlight, the 3-0 defeat was only partly cushioned by the receipt of a runners-up gong.

With Celtic winning both the 1974 Premier League and Scottish Cup, their European aspirations were directed towards the European Cup. United, meanwhile, had their a first taste of continental soccer in the European Cup Winners' Cup.

This welcome diversion saw Archie sample the delights of the European culture in beating Jiul Petrosani from Romania in the first round, only to be tumbled out on a 1-0 aggregate score to Turkey's Bursaspor at the next hurdle.

By now, a recurring pelvic injury was instrumental in triggering Archie's release from Tannadice and he went on to play for a short spell at Montrose. Archie completed a full cycle of clubs in the 76-77 season by returning to Forfar as their player/manager.

If Knox's playing career was of modest proportions – his time at Love Street saw only 49 league appearances and 11 goals being registered – then his contribution to management, both as his own man and in an assistant capacity, has been outrageously prodigious.

Four and a half years at Forfar followed by a similar time as Alex Ferguson's assistant at Pittodrie preceded a three-year spell as the manager at Dundee.

He went back to Aberdeen after the 1986 World Cup finals for a few months before heading down to Old Trafford to link up with Ferguson again, this time at Manchester United. Knox spent five seasons with the Red Devils before joining up with Walter Smith at Rangers for a successful seven-year period, prior to the pair going down to Merseyside to oversee the fortunes of Everton.

Still he hadn't hit the managerial buffers, as he linked up with Richard Gough in an attempt to stabilise the unsteady ship that was Livingston.

We did say it was a prodigious management input, with perhaps the high spots being the winning of the 1983 European Cup Winners' Cup for Aberdeen against Real Madrid in Gothenburg and securing the 1990 FA Cup for Manchester United, the 1-0 win following a 3-3 draw with Crystal Palace.

Clearly here is management potential that is yet available for future clubs' use. Indeed his soccer CV has been further enhanced with his appointment as the SFA's overseer of the national Under-21 squad

Knox was the Guest of Honour at the St Andrew's Sporting Club at the Holiday Inn in Glasgow in April 2006 to recognise his outstanding services to football.

Prodigious is still the buzzword in the football affairs of Mr Knox.

PAUL LAMBERT

TOURS of St Mirren Park are always a treasured moment for many school parties. Once the youngsters enter the Gerry Baker hospitality lounge, their focus is invariably directed to the framed portrait on the wall.

"That's Paul Lambert," the cherubs will chorus in unison. "He played for Celtic!"

What is missing from the football education of these youthful fans is that European Cup winner Lambert – suitably portrayed in a jersey featuring the logo Graham's Buses – learned his soccer trade at Love Street.

To be fair, the football apprenticeship initially started at school, to be followed by a Juvenile leaning towards Linwood Rangers. So where was the Lambert comfort playing position?

He said: "I don't think I ever had one particular playing position at school – you're just happy to get a game. I like to think I was outwardly mobile and versatile and probably played most of my school games as a centre-forward. Football was always my number one priority and I did manage a number of "O" Levels but left school after my fourth year."

It was Rikki McFarlane who had the foresight to appreciate the Lambert potential and persuaded Paul to append a St Mirren "S" Form when he was a mere 13.

Lambert added: "If I am ever asked who was responsible for any football progression I might have made then it would have to be Rikki McFarlane. His all-round knowledge of the game was simply massive, as was all the encouragement he gave me."

Paul had to wait just over three years to make his debut in a game clouded in St Mirren drama. Saints were on league duty in an April '86 game at Fir Park against Motherwell. A crunching tackle on Tony Fitzpatrick left the St Mirren icon with a shattered jaw, consigning him to a liquid diet and sidelining him for weeks. His replacement from the bench was a young stripling named Lambert.

What followed in an eight-year spell at Love Street saw Paul amass 183 St Mirren starts and a further 44 substitute appearances, all spiced with a 14-goal return. It doesn't take much to speculate on Paul's St Mirren most memorable file.

He said: "Making your debut always gives you a great feeling but playing in a cup final beats the lot. Games like the 1987 final don't come along that often and when you're only 17, it is even better.

"It was a particularly poignant day for me. Tony Fitzpatrick was on the bench and I was in the starting line up. By this time, Tony was in the twilight of his career and when he came off the bench to replace me it was a replay in reverse from my debut day."

That defeat of Dundee United earned St Mirren automatic entry to the European Cup Winners' Cup competition and provided Paul with his first taste of continental soccer in the shape of Tromso in Norway and Mechelen in Belgium. Asking Paul for his thoughts on one of his favourite St Mirren goals brings a snort of derision.

He replied: "Oh for goodness sake, they are all important. But if you are to press me, perhaps the goal I scored against Celtic at Celtic Park in April 1990 might top the bill.

"There were only about five games to go and we were flirting with relegation. We managed to beat Celtic 3-0 that day and went on to win a further two games with one drawn. That created a six-point gap between ourselves and Dundee, who were relegated."

Lambert's leadership prowess more than surfaced during his time with St Mirren with the Scotland Under-21 side. Eleven caps, the first against Romania in 1991, saw him appointed as the national team's captain for more than half of his Under-21 outings.

He might appear almost quiet on the field but in the dressing room Paul was the perpetrator of a variety of nicknames – some good, some bad and others seemingly libellous!

Lambo said: "You've always got to have some good banter in the dressing room. Quiet surroundings almost always lead to poor performances on the park and winding up your playing compatriots is good for morale.

"It wasn't just me, Brian Gallagher and Jim Rooney were both pranksters and funny lads. Their style of humour generated good team bonding."

Paul's time at St Mirren Park ended in September 1993 when he joined Motherwell.

He explained: "I was out of contract at the time and you always want to better yourself. Motherwell gave me that opportunity to do just that. Some newspapers quoted a transfer fee of £150,000. I don't know if there was a fee, but in all honesty I wasn't worth that amount at that time. St Mirren were still in the First Division, so playing in the SPL was an advancement."

The move to Fir Park paid off for Paul in the winning of his first full Scotland cap.

He recalled: "The game against Japan in Hiroshima was a real bogey. The pitch was waterlogged and the game should never have been played. Wee John Spencer was ordered off and I was sacrificed to provide an alternative striker for the side. The 0-0 draw provided mixed memories and not many pleasant ones."

One fortunate aspect of Lambert's playing career was his ability to avoid serious injury. In Motherwell's 94-95 campaign, he logged in a 100 per cent record of league appearances.

That consistency factor earned the Steelmen the runner-up spot in the SPL and entry into the UEFA Cup, although losing out to Finland's My-Pa 47 side on the away goals rule in the preliminary round wasn't particularly memorable.

The Lambert name on the international air waves had further exposure when Paul, Monica and the family moved to Germany to join Borussia Dortmund. Paul waxes lyrical about the Westfalenstadion club.

He said: "It was a tremendous opportunity to join a club like Dortmund, who are astronomically big. They had world-class players and were simply a phenomenal club with a phenomenal fan base."

If participation in a Scottish Cup final isn't an outing readily inked into most Caledonian players' diaries, then European Cup finals are the prerogative of a select few.

Paul is one of the few, with the Dortmund club's 3-1 win over Juventus in Munich in 1997 being rated as Paul's career zenith. So entrenched was he in the winning of that trophy that on his departure to join Celtic in November 1997, the chanting of his name by the Westfalenstadion faithful led to moments of high emotion.

Lambert said: "For the crowd to chant my name at what was my last game for Borussia, with with me being effectively an outsider in a foreign country, was very emotional. It was a big German thank you for what I had achieved there and the occasion will always be close to my heart."

But as they say in Irish comic circles, there's more!

Signed by Wim Jansen for Celtic in November 1997, the accumulation of soccer baubles went on overdrive.

As Paul made the point: "The goldfish bowl pressure in playing for Celtic is severe but if you can handle all the personal intrusions, you'll do well."

And didn't he just! Four SPL titles, one League Cup badge, three Scottish Cup medals – two of them from the bench – another European cup final, regretfully losing the 2003 UEFA Cup to Porto, plus a further 31 international caps bringing his cap collection to a prodigious 40.

Such success would essentially be a football commodity in demand and after Paul's farewell match at Love Street, playing for Celtic in Ricky Gillies' Testimonial, he took over Livingston as their player/manager at the start of the 2005-06 season.

In tandem with him at the Almondvale club was long-term friend and associate Norrie McWhirter.

Both had joined St Mirren from Linwood Rangers, each the best man at each others weddings.

And while both stepped down from the Livingston job in early 2006, who would bet against them taking on another managerial appointment in the future?

It was clear Paul's football future wouldn't be in cold storage or long.

He said: "I'm keen to stay in the game. I've been down south on a number of occasions watching teams in training and picking up ideas on fitness routines. Once something comes up on the football market that I consider suitable, then rest assured I'll go for it."

No long after these comments, Paul took over the reigns at English League Two side Wycombe, leading Wanderers to the top of the table after a blistering start. The signs are he could be as good a manager as he was a player…

DAVIE LAPSLEY

IT was the immediate aftermath of the Second World War, Davie Lapsley, now a resident in Civvy Street, was on the lookout for a club. St Mirren were in a recruiting mode but Davie's arrival at Love Street for a recommended trial was pure theatre.

The St Mirren icon explained: "When I came home I got a letter from the St Mirren manager Bobby Rankin asking me through for a chat. I had been playing as a centre-forward and scoring a lot of goals down south and he had apparently heard good reports about me.

"Bobby asked if I'd brought my boots with me. Now these were boots with bars on the soles - no nailed or screw-in studs. The bars were great for putting the brake on but weren't all that good if you had to twist and turn.

"I was taken out onto the park and told to take a penalty against wee Gordon Rennie. I gave it all I had and Gordon never saw the ball."

Rankin had seen enough and promptly signed the 22-year-old in 1946.

But back to the beginning...

Born in Kirkintilloch on April 7, 1924, Davie was one of a family of four and a pupil at Bainsford School. His scholastic days saw him operating in the centre-half and left-half berths, the end product being a trial for the Scottish Schoolboys side. However, the youthful Lapsley playing career was put on hold as a result of a bad ankle injury, which provided him with leave of absence from the algebra chores for 10 weeks.

He had moved forward to operate in the inside right channel when he joined the Juvenile ranks with High Bonnybridge Rose. And there much gnashing of teeth when they lost out 3-1 to Provanmill Hibs in the sixth round of the Scottish Cup at Brockville.

In 1940 Bathgate Thistle enlisted Lapsley before he was called up for active service in the Royal Navy.

Victory in Europe was achieved in the early summer of 1945 but the cessation of hostilities might have been considerably extended had it not been for Able Seaman Lapsley. To see the future Saints captain involved in ferrying ammunition across the Channel on a converted Thames barge, in a combined operations job in support of the Normandy landings, must have generated severe misgivings in the ranks of the Hitler hordes.

Stationed at Birkenhead for most of the war, Davie was playing for the Stork Margarine team when an Everton scout spotted him. The Goodison Park man tried to get him into the Tranmere Rovers team with a veiled promise of a month's trial with Everton after the war. A couple of games with the Prenton Park Rovers followed before a naval posting to Hayling Island.

A period of leave in Grangemouth saw a Falkirk director provide a letter of introduction for Davie to the Bairns manager Tully Craig.

Davie explained: "In essence, it was a note saying, 'Give this boy a game on Saturday'. Craig's response was pretty damming. 'You're no good to me as a serviceman. You'll be here one week and somewhere else the next'. I wasn't over pleased at his attitude and swore I'd never ever play for Falkirk."

Davie's introduction to the St Mirren first-team was spasmodic to say the least. He had been signed as a centre-forward brandishing a ferocious shot.

He recalled: "On one occasion I burst the net and the ref gave a bye-kick!

Eventually someone persuaded him to examine the damaged net and I got my goal!"

It was September 4, 1946, when Davie first pulled on a first-team black and white jersey. Partick Thistle were the opposition at Firhill but even Davie's dynamism couldn't find the net, Saints losing 3-0.

Only three games were logged in for that 46-47 season. The following year, a mere two Lapsley appearances were registered. Ironically, the first was against Partick Thistle again in downtown Maryhill, with right-back Lapsley on target with his first goal and Saints' sole strike in a 1-3 defeat.

1948-49 was the season Davie established himself as St Mirren's first choice full-back, but only because the resident choice failed to turn up for one game. Davie was converted, going on to take up his almost permanent home in the Buddies defence.

First choice for Saints but second choice for Scotland, the Monarch of the Ibrox Glen, big George "Corky" Young, was the player who relegated Davie to being the national side's understudy right-back.

Never capped for Scotland at full international level, Davie did manage to catch the selectorial eye of the Inter League chiefs and represented the Scottish League on two occasions, the Irish and the English being the inter League adversaries.

Lapsley's ability to jet propel a dead ball with pin-point accuracy and blockbusting power saw him top the St Mirren scoring charts in a couple of campaigns, with many of his strikes being penalties.

It's a long run from the right-back beat, so in an energy preservation mode, Davie would enlist the services of a playing colleague to place the ball, the goalkeeper no doubt pondering on the strength of his personal injury policy. The keeper needn't have worried, he invariably never saw the ball as it raged into the net.

With a St Mirren career total of 40 goals, the strike that most people of the day remember was a free-kick against Airdrie in the 1948 League Cup.

Some 35 yards out, the ball was placed, the run up began and the Diamonds keeper sheltered from the slip stream as the howitzer raged past him. A standing ovation followed for what many regarded as Saints' finest ever goal.

For those that played with him, Lapsley was the original Captain Courageous, willing to stand up and be counted in addition to fighting the battles of his team-mates both on and off the park.

The Scottish Cup-winning season of 58-59 was a case in point. Saints were drawn to play Peebles Rovers at Love Street in the second round. Davie had a wee pre-match chat with manager Winnie Reid.

He said: "I just asked him what like the win bonus was going to be. He said he would make it 10 shillings - or 50p in today's currency - for every goal scored. I just told the lads to score as many as they could and 10-0 became a nice little earner, the £5 getting us into the next round to play Motherwell."

That April 25 date at Hampden was the pinnacle of the Lapsley career. He never played again for Saints, but went out in style when the team were given a rapturous reception on the balcony of the Paisley Town Hall.

But just before the cup left Hampden, Davie had to act out one last ritual. Davie McCrae, a survivour from St Mirren's first Scottish Cup win in 1926, had kept his gift of a bottle of whisky intact - only to be opened when Saints next won the Scottish Cup.

STV commentator Arthur Montford supervised the ceremonial rite, with Mr McCrae proffering Mr Lapsley the first celebratory dram.

A resident in the Falkirk area, Davie lived most of his life in Camelon, working in the now defunct Port Downie foundry.

Survived by his wife Dinah, son Alan and grandsons David and Alan, Davie died on January 15, 2001. A number of Saints fans and past players were at his funeral and they spoke volumes for the affection held by one of St Mirren's greatest ever players.

He will not be forgotten, as that winning cup final shirt is now an encased St Mirren memento in the Scottish Football Museum at Hampden Park.

BARRY LAVETY

IT'S the players who bang in the goals that generally inherit iconic soccer status.

The mercurial Davie McCrae had such a stature in the mid 1920s, when he is accredited with a collection of 221 St Mirren goals.

That was in the era of defences having to contend with five rampaging forwards.

However, the current playing climate will no doubt peg back any thoughts of such gargantuan scoring returns in the future.

In the post war period, wee Tommy Gemmell heads the St Mirren scoring charts with a 94-goal tally, so it goes without saying that Barry Lavety's haul of 72 – the fourth highest return since the cessation of Second World War hostilities – demands respect.

Born on August 21st 1974, Barry shares his birthday with a host of celebrities. Country and western singer Kenny Rogers appeared on planet earth in 1941, Olympic athlete Chris Brasher arrived 13 years earlier, while jazz maestro Count Basie was born in 1904.

That football finance has radically changed is mirrored in the First Division admission charges that were in vogue on Barry's birth date.

Main stands were rated at 80p, the ground or terracing at 40p, while youngsters and OAPs checked in at 25p.

Such financial meanderings weren't a worry to the youthful Barry.

Initially, his playing activities revolved around the Junior Section of the 1st Houston Boys' Brigade Company, before moving to Renfrew Waverley when he was 10.

Six years later, Gleniffer Thistle acquired his services and it was while he was still at school that Tony Fitzpatrick signed him on an S-Form for Saints.

A change of St Mirren management saw David Hay and Gordon Smith take over, with former Rangers and Brighton striker Smith taking a special interest in Barry's soccer development. Typically, together they took in a pre-season friendly at the old Boghead Park, Dumbarton's visitors being the Wanderers from Wolverhampton.

The purpose of the Smith/Lavety interest was to appreciate the expertise of Wolves' Steve Bull, whose voracious scoring appetite had seen him amass a century of league and cup goals for the Molyneux club over seasons of 87-88 and 88-89.

Barry's St Mirren debut wasn't one for the memory banks. Off the bench for a home league clash with Celtic on October 26, 1991, the Hoops showed no mercy in administering a 5-0 walloping.

Four games later, on the last day of the 91-92 season, Barry was on from the start against Dunfermline and the Lavety scoring account opened with a superb double.

Lavety's thirst for goals saw Cowdenbeath beaten in the round two of the Skol Cup the following season, Barry's only goal winner being enough to elevate him into collecting the Man-of-the-Match award.

A player who was blessed with superb family backing, the entire Lavety Clan would report on match days to support the new main Saints strike force and he responded wonderfully.

St Mirren's top scorer for four successive seasons enabled Barry to register 46 in league games alone.

The scoring rate of a goal in every third game brought the selectorial posse into focus.

After selection for Scottish Schools, he also made the national Under-16 side, before graduating on two occasions to the Under-18 squad for duty in the European Youth Championship.

The almost automatic step up to the Under-21 team brought a further nine caps, the first against Iceland at Rugby Park in 1993.

However, amid all the praise there a moderately dark cloud on the Lavety horizon.

St Mirren wanted to protect their youngsters from the temptations of modern day living. To this end, the club established a random drug testing procedure, perhaps the only one at club level in Scotland. Regretfully, Barry was found wanting and was immediately involved in a rehabilitation process.

Needless to say, such a misdemeanour from the Saints hitman generated countless column inches in the tabloids.

St Mirren chairman Bob Earlie clamped down on the media hysteria.

He said: "The time is ripe for the melodrama to cease. As and when Barry Lavety is match fit to return playing, we will welcome him back.

"However, the full cycle also requires a substantial input of support from all the fans. I trust and hope you will not fail me in offering that support."

In fact, Barry missed only seven games and was soon back banging in the goals again.

With such a scoring record, it was inevitable other clubs would ponder on a possible transfer, Barry whetting the aspirations of Hibernian and moving to Easter Road during the 1996 close season.

Saints assistant manager in 2004, Andy Millen, was a playing colleague with Barry in their Hibee days.

He recalled: "Barry came to Easter Road after some difficult off the field problems at St Mirren. In terms of his ability as a player, he was a young man with a lot of talent.

"He was perhaps the first one to recognise that once you play in the Premier League, the scoring chances on offer are not so proficient, which is probably why his net finding ability wasn't as high with Hibs as it was with St Mirren.

"The half chances on offer became quarter chances but he did well at Easter Road and for a while was Hibs' top scorer.

"He certainly deserves to be highly regarded at St Mirren, where he had his most enjoyable and profitable spell."

Three seasons with Hibernian embraced both relegation and promotion, but the Lavety strike rate hadn't quite lived up to his Love Street standards.

St Mirren had started the millennium season in style. There were early promises of possible promotion fulfillment, but a striking supplement was required as back up for Mark Yardley and Junior Mendes.

Feelings among the fans and in the town ran high in that the man affectionately nicknamed "Basher" should be brought back into the St Mirren fold.

Even the Paisley Daily Express was about to orchestrate a "Bring Back Basher" campaign when Saints signed Barry on a loan deal from Hibs.

That piece of shrewd business saw St Mirren top the First Division and rejoin the Premier elite after an eight-year absence, Barry's contribution being 16 goals from 21 starts.

As has been widely chronicled, Saints' flirtation with the SPL lasted only a season and Barry's registration was not renewed. He was also released by Hibernian.

A season in the wilderness followed before Derek Ferguson – in a player/manager role and trying to stabilise the fortunes of Clydebank – harnessed the Lavety skills, the robust striker pitching in with a couple of goals.

Regretfully, Clydebank didn't remain afloat and went out of business at the end of the 2001-02 season.

By this time a more stable form of employment became a necessity for the Lavety future. A college course on Coach Education and Sports Performance was on offer at Bath University and Barry was a willing pupil.

His all-action style of play was a major plus point for the Yoonie team, as Team Bath went on to make a splash in the 02-03 English FA Cup.

Barry remembered it well.

He said: "We played around five cup ties before qualifying for the first round proper to play Mansfield Town, the team that Junior Mendes eventually went to.

"The publicity for that game was unbelievable. It was something I hadn't experienced, even when Hibs were top of the league.

"I've never seen so many cameras on call. Even when we were training there were around 20 cameras following your every move."

That FA Cup publicity and nationwide TV coverage prompted St Mirren to re-enlist the Lavety services, Barry signing for Saints for a third time.

One of Barry's major difficulties was always keeping his weight in check. When he first signed on at Love Street, the avoirdupois ratings homed in at 12st 12lbs. In his latter appearances in black and white, the scales had been upped to 14st 10lbs.

One mentor who took particular interest in the Lavety progress was former Saints boss Jimmy Bone. Barry made the point: "You either got an arm round your shoulders or a boot up the backside from him."

Jimmy was more conciliatory. He said: "The biggest thing about Barry is he was always a player who would get a goal for you when you needed one. He had the ability to lift the crowd and excite them, he did the unorthodox thing.

"He was one of the best players I have ever seen when he was knocked to the ground – he'd be like one of these rubber wobblies and be back on his feet immediately.

"He played wholeheartedly and gave you every ounce of energy he had. He had a minor problem in keeping fit but when he was on his game he was a real handful for the opposition."

Once he turned 30, perhaps a degree of disillusionment crept into his life in being unable to hold down a regular first-team place.

But let there be no doubt that there is no disillusionment on the part of the St Mirren faithful. The B-A-R-R-Y L-A-V-E-T-Y verbals from the Love Street North Bank were always a testimony to Barry being a clear favourite in St Mirren's top post-war 100.

TOMMY LEISHMAN

THE Changing Rooms presenters on national TV seemingly seek to destroy accepted homestead layouts with the apprehensive home owners displaying sheer trepidation at their room makeovers.

Conventional lounge arrangements usually provide a couple of focal points with the fireplace and the ubiquitous television set being self-evident. In Tommy Leishman's trim Bannockburn bungalow, there are a couple of such contrasting features in his homely lounge.

In one corner there is a well stocked trophy cabinet while on an adjacent wall a framed St Mirren shirt holds pride of place - the jersey Tommy wore on that momentous 1959 cup final win over Aberdeen. Both speak volumes of a more than successful career in the Beautiful Game.

Leishman's entry into St Mirren folklore saw him head for a teenage holiday to Butlins Holiday Camp on the Heads of Ayr. Sponsored by the Daily Record, a number of comprehensive football coaching sessions were on offer to aspiring youngsters and the Leishman skills particularly impressed one notable coach - Davie Lapsley.

Davie recommended Saints director Jack Gilmour have a look at an emerging talent and the Leishman wing-half performances went under the microscope with Cowie Juveniles.

Born in Stenhousemuir, educated at Larbert Central School and going on to play for Bothkennar Rovers, Tommy was well versed in the soccer shenanigans of the Falkirk & District precinct.

Tommy takes us through his transition to the senior grade.

He said: "I was 16 at the time and was training with Falkirk. Everything seemed to point to a future career with the Bairns. But after Jack Gilmour watched me play for Cowie, I was asked to play a trial in a reserve match for St Mirren against Third Lanark at Cathkin.

"Bob Shankly was the manager at Brockville and he wasn't over pleased at the development of the St Mirren association and virtually shut the door on me.

"After the trial I signed a provisional agreement with St Mirren but they couldn't register me until I was 17, so I was farmed out to Camelon Juniors. Willie Reid officially signed me in 1956."

Like most players of his era, the demands of National Service provided an interruption to the Leishman time at Love Street. But after his two-year square bashing deal with the Argyll & Sutherland Highlanders, he still provided Saints with a five-year term of service.

Not surprising that late April day in 1959 at Hampden and the 3-1 turnover of Aberdeen is firmly entrenched in Tommy's memory banks.

He recalled: "I had popped into Alistair McDonald's pub in Longcroft in the morning - not for any sustenance you understand - it was just the local meeting place.

"Two bus loads of Aberdeen fans had stopped in for breakfast and I was pretty conspicuous with my St Mirren blazer and tie on.

"They were nice enough folk and I took a bit of a ragging but they still gave me some Aberdeen memorabilia in addition to a bottle of whisky."

The practice of shirt exchanging had not become part of the post-match celebration routines. However, there was never any chance of anyone getting their hands on the shirt he wore that day. It now being a framed central attraction at chez Leishman.

At the end of the 1950s, St Mirren were a part time team. Tommy, a driver with Haig's the brewing firm, always had a hankering to try his luck on the full-time stage. His wishes came true when Liverpool's Phil Taylor signed him for the Anfield club in the autumn of 1959. Somewhat ironically, eight months later St Mirren went full-time.

Four seasons on Merseyside saw Liverpool enhance their growing reputation with promotion to the First Division in 1961-62, the gravel voiced Bill Shankly now in full flow with his highly charged rhetoric.

Clan Shankly quite definitely provided a degree of diminishing return on the Leishman career pattern. Bob had spurned him at Falkirk, while elder sibling Bill didn't fancy his style at Anfield, bringing in Billy Stevenson from Rangers as a direct replacement as Tommy headed across country to join Hibernian.

Jock Stein was the central figure at Easter Road before taking up the managerial reins at Celtic Park. And who arrived at Hibs as the Stein successor? A certain Mr Bob Shankly!

Something about oil and water failing to mix... Inevitably, the Shankly-Leishman discordant days led to Mr Leishman crossing the Irish Sea to take up a player/coaching appointment with Linfield.

Linfield were cocks of the Belfast walks, regularly lifting the Northern Ireland championship, which provided automatic entry to European competition.

Leishman said: "I was at Linfield when Celtic won the European Cup in

1967.

We reached the quarter-finals and lost 1-0 to CSK Sofia after drawing 2-2 with them in Belfast. However, finance has a major input in talking you out of success and if we hadn't sold our goalkeeper Ian McFaul to Newcastle United, it could have been us in the semi-finals."

There were many outstanding players around during Leishman's time at Love Street. Aberdeen's George Hamilton was one and lived up to his nickname of 'Gentleman George'.

Tommy said: "Prior to the cup final we had beaten Aberdeen in a league match. I'd managed to display some fancy footwork in that game and at the end George came up to me, congratulated me and clapped me on the back. Not too many players would have done that."

It was a different scenario at the Leishman St Mirren debut.

He remembered: "It was against Rangers at Love Street in a League Cup tie. They had the South African Don Kitchenbrand in their line up and he used to charge around like a demented beast. His nickname of Rhino was well warranted.

"Willie 'Togo' Johnstone was the St Mirren left-back that day. He told me they would try to upset me. Willie Waddell delivered a few choice verbal nasties at me seeing it was my first game but Togo's advice was simply to ignore all the jibes - and I did."

Very little can upset the Leishman demeanour, although golf could have been a major contributor. He was for some 40 years at member of the King's Park course in Stirling.

Despite playing three times a week, Tommy's weekly confrontation to trim his 13 handicap has on occasion sent his blood pressure onto a higher plain. But quiet normality soon returns him to planet earth.

ALFIE LESZ

IN the immediate post-war era, a considerable number of overseas servicemen, many with a favourable football affinity, were attracted to stay on in Scotland in pursuit of professional football.

One such soccer immigrant was Feliks Staroscik, who joined the late lamented Third Lanark in season 1947-48.

"Starry", officially classified as being short in stature but big in heart, is profiled in Bert Bell's History of Third Lanark – Still Seeing Red – as the Polish player being "One who lit up many dark Cathkin moments with a scintillating brand of wing play and a devastating shot."

Staroscik, initially an amateur on the books of Wolverhampton Wanderers, subsequently moved back south to join Northampton Town.

In truth, Alfons Lesz was born out of the same Staroscik pea pod. Another Polish serviceman stationed in the north of Scotland, Alfons played a number of games for Forres Mechanics before being posted to Johnstone, where he was a member of the Polish Forces Resettlement Corps.

Always keen for a game, he was watched by a St Mirren scout in a bounce game between a Polish services side and the Glasgow Tramways team.

What was on show greatly interested Saints manager Bobby Rankin, who immediately signed the pacy winger.

Not surprisingly, the ribald comments from the Love Street terraces couldn't cope with the name Alfons, "Alfie" being a more acceptable nom de plume in the Paisley vernacular.

Alfie made his first St Mirren appearance in a Reserve League Cup tie against Motherwell at Love Street on August 23, 1947. Saints lost that one 2-1 but Alfie had the satisfaction of scoring on his debut.

This was the time when Errol Flynn was swashbuckling his way in The Adventures of Robin Hood at Paisley's Astoria Cinema.

Rankin required a degree more swashbuckle in his first-team attack and satisfied the need by introducing Gerry Burrell, the Belfast Buddie, to the right wing beat, with Alfie slotting into the inside left berth.

The game, three days later on a Tuesday evening against Aberdeen in the league at Love Street, attracted a crowd of 12,000 and St Mirren won 3-0 thanks to a Willie Jack hat-trick. The diminutive forward line on that night comprised Burrell, John Guthrie, Jack, Lesz and Arthur Milne.

The next match – a League Cup encounter, also against the Dons, this time up at Pittodrie – saw St Mirren come unstuck with a 2-0 defeat.

However, the phraseology of the popular Press of the day eulogised at length over the two precocious newcomers, stating: "Burrell and Lesz were the most troublesome of the raiders and it must be said they made a favourable impression on the onlookers."

Burrell well remembers his Polish accomplice. He said: "The local Press took us to heart and pronounced that St Mirren now played with two foreigners on the wings – one Irish, the other Polish!

"Alfie had a tremendously powerful shot for a small man. He had a great left foot and if I had to criticise anything in his make up he maybe lacked a wee bit of devilment at times."

In assessing the respective minimal heights of Messrs Burrell, Lesz and Milne, one wag on the Love Street surrounds was tempted to suggest they were all around the 4'-15" mark!

The fact that they were fondly classified as midgets prompted a tactical need for the ball to be played on the deck.

As Gerry remarked: "We were lucky in having a half-back lineup of Jackie Neilson, Willie Telfer and Willie Reid, who were all superb football players and they helped us out by playing the ball on the ground. We couldn't cope with any high balls."

Alfie's goalscoring prowess saw him net 37 goals from 131 St Mirren outings, his stay stretching from 47-48 to 51-52.

From the club's scoring records, his first strike was against Queen of the South in that remarkable League Cup campaign of 1947. St Mirren had been drawn against Motherwell, Aberdeen and the Doonhamers in their section.

In the first match against the Dumfries men at Palmerston Park, Saints were taken to the cleaners on the back of an 8-1 thumping. In the return at Love Street, St Mirren replicated the goal deluge, registering a 7-1 return. Alfie scored two, Jack netted another hat-trick with singles coming from Jimmy Stenhouse and Burrell.

Shawfield Amateurs had qualified for the first round proper of the 47-48 Scottish Cup. It wasn't their day of glory as they fell foul to a rampant Saints side – 8-0 being the final score, with Lesz netting his one and only St Mirren hat-trick.

Alfie's crowd-pleasing talent eventually caught the eye of the residents of Stamford Bridge. But while the Chelsea officials did make an approach in October 1951, requesting St Mirren to name their price for the Polish winger, subsequent moves on a possible transfer fizzled out.

Alfie made it on to the news pages of the national Press instead of the sports sections. He and Willie Telfer were prosecution witnesses in a trial at the High Court, in Glasgow.

A Joseph McCudden, from Blantyre, in Lanarkshire ended up being found guilty of attempted bribery of professional footballers and was sentenced to nine months in jail.

A locksmith to trade, Alfie left St Mirren in 1952 and is reported to have moved south to play with Worcester City and Kidderminster Harriers before emigrating to Canada.

ALEX LINWOOD

IN producing a publication chronicling the lives and times of St Mirren's post-war greats, some might question the inclusion of Alexander Bryce Linwood.

For the sake of historical accuracy, the Japanese surrender that heralded the end of the Second World War was dated August 14, 1945. Alex Linwood's last game for St Mirren was against Hearts at Love Street in the embryonic days of the League Cup competition on March 30, 1946.

Technically, Alex was a post-war player, although the official leagues and cups did not resume nationwide relationships until 1946-47.

But to deny Alex a place in St Mirren's late 20th century folklore would mean denying acceptance of one of the club's all-time greats never mind post Second World War.

The social economics of the day, with the downturn of trade in the 1930s, meant job availability was at an all time low. Fortunately, if you lived in and around the Ayrshire mining communities, the hewing of coal provided some financial security for the local youngsters.

Linwood was one 14-year-old who earned a crust at the coalface. Born in Drumsmudden, near Drongan, the former mining village has now become miniaturised since the cessation of coal production and is now reminiscent of a mythical modern day Brigadoon.

Keen on football, young Linwood was also a bit of a runner, winning the Scottish Schoolboys' half mile championship – despite his Eric Liddell-style collapse as he hit the tape.

But the local Drongan football team were a secondary juvenile side in a degree of decline.

Alex played with the team until he was 17 but defeats at the ultimate stages of a number of national competitions totally dispirited the Drongan committee and the team, both morally and physically, were heading for disintegration.

Skares were another local Juvenile side – the community comprising four rows of miners' cottages and a football committee of 13 !

The Linwood contribution to the end of season success for Skares was prodigious.

He explained: "They managed to reach two semi-finals of major cup competitions. Skares had an outside left who had been suspended sine die. I was asked to replace him and played in the two semis, both finals and in a league play-off. We won them all."

Alex's entry to the Junior scene was even more spectacular.

He went on: "Muirkirk Athletic had signed a centre forward with previous senior experience in England. He wasn't properly reinstated and that made him ineligible. I was asked to play and was up against the Scottish Junior side's centre-half – he was 6'4" and I broke his nose! But We won 2-1 and I scored both goals.

"The next game was against Largs Thistle at their Barrfields Stadium. We were winning 5-0 at half-time and I'd scored all five. The final score was 7-1 and I managed the other two as well."

Sammy Blythe was the man who mattered at Love Street, with glowing reports coming in of a free scoring centre causing havoc in the Ayrshire Junior Leagues.

And after only five games for Muirkirk, this was translated to Love Street in October 1938.

Alex's scoring contributions for St Mirren were phenomenal, as his appearance and goals records reveal.

A total of 168 goals from 241 appearances is a striking rate of exceptional magnitude.

It was the anticipation of being called up to the armed forces that prompted Alex to sell his mining boots. Life away from the Ayrshire mines, albeit in military apparel, generated a certain appeal. However, a certain Ernest Bevin had other ideas.

So essential was coal production to the war effort that the Government Minister introduced his Bevin Boys Scheme – a project whereby young miners were given reserved occupation status, excused military service and told to dig for victory.

Linwood was in a dilemma. He'd sold his working boots in anticipation of some army square bashing, but just managed to buy them back. And the famed footwear eventually appeared as a prime exhibit in the National Football Museum at Hampden Park.

With 168 goals to choose from, one of them was a bit special, not only in Alex's eyes but also for Rangers' legendary full-back Dougie Gray.

Dougie's playing piece de resistance was having a sixth sense to be on the Ibrox goal line just behind his keeper to make countless net-bound clearances.

Dougie takes up the narrative in his autobiography:

"I think the goal Alex Linwood scored against us in the final of the 1943

Summer Cup during the war will vie with the greatest goals of my career.

"The St Mirren centre forward took the ball on the drop when it came over from the left, and I can picture in my mind that shot raging past Jerry Dawson. It was a goal in a thousand and worthy to win a cup – which it did that day for St Mirren."

If that 1943 final was a high spot in Alex's football life, that same year provided some negativity in his eight-season spell at Love Street.

There was almost a sense of acute annoyance at national team selections during the wartime years. England apparently seemed to cushion their top players, finding homegrown postings for them, while the prominent Scottish players were generally fighting at the fronts.

So the 1943 confrontation between England and Scotland at Maine Road, Manchester, turned into a bit of a mismatch, the Scots losing 8-0. However, the pawky Mr Linwood, the Scots centre on this less than memorable occasion, could still raise a smile.

He said: "I was the one Scottish player that touched the ball more than anyone else – I kicked off nine times !"

With the war over and the Bevin Boy boots finally hung up to dry, Alex did achieve his ambition of full-time football when David Jack of Middlesbrough came north to bring the Linwood talents to Ayresome Park.

But soccer life on Wearside wasn't all sweetness and light and Alex was more than delighted when the Hibernian managerial icon that was Willie McCartney brought him to Easter Road after only a year in the English game.

Alex's first season with the Hibees saw the Edinburgh club win the 1947-48 League Championship – not surprisingly when you could field a forward line of Smith, Combe, Linwood, Turnbull and Ormond.

A season and a half at Easter Road preceded a £10,000 move to Clyde, where Alex finally logged into the official record books, being capped while at Shawfield against Wales in 1950.

The playing career curtain was finally downed with a short fling with local rivals Morton in the early 50s.

A prominent cry in the modern game is the lack of characters providing value for money in the entertainment stakes. Asked to include himself in his team of all time greats from that era, one tends to salivate profusely at Alex's selection.

Jerry Dawson (Rangers), Willie Kilmarnock (Motherwell), Davie Shaw (Hibernian), Adam Little (Rangers), Willie Kelly (St Mirren), Davie Laing (Hearts), Gordon Smith and Bobby Johnstone (Hibernian), Alex Linwood (St Mirren), Alex Venters (Rangers) and Charlie Tully (Celtic).

Those fans that can readily remember Tommy Handley's ITMA radio programmes would surely agree with his choice.

A resident in Renfrew for many years, Alex turned to insurance in his post-playing days. Offered an area manager's job in Manchester, it would have meant some segregation from his devoted family. He stayed home, became an insurance agent, blossoming to inspector and eventually achieving managerial status.

He never lost his eye for a ball as the denizens of the local bowling green would readily confirm.

ALAN LOGAN

IT was wee Archie Gemmill who set the ball rolling. With football embarking on the introduction of substitute players, Archie was the first ever sub in Scotland. He came on to replace Jim Clunie against Clyde at Shawfield for the opening League Cup game of the 66-67 season.

Steven McGarry, in his six years with St Mirren, had a virtual season ticket for the bench, weighing in with 92 appearances as substitute.

However, it was a predecessor of Steven's, Alan Logan, who initially created a new art form in taking the substitute business to a new level with 73 appearances – almost twice the number of his actual starts.

Such a sedentary occupation conceivably implanted numerous wooden skelfs in the Logan posterior!

Logging in only 43 starts and being tarred with the substitute's brush, was Alan ever annoyed with the selection procedures of his various managers?

He said: "Jim Clunie signed me on a pro form when I was 17. He was followed by Rikki McFarlane and Alex Miller. At the time, the substitute business was a bit of a stigma for me. It was frustrating as I always seemed to do well when I came on, although I had to accept there were really good players keeping me out."

Alan wasn't kept out in his early intrusions into competitive football. Initially a midfielder in his scholastic times at Crookston Castle Secondary, he moved onto the Pollok United youth team. before spending two years with the Celtic Boys' Club Under-14 side. Paternal involvement then took over.

Alan explained: "My dad was a taxi driver and it was 'Baldy' Lindsay – another cabbie, a friend of dad's and a St Mirren scout – who arranged for me to join up at Love Street. That's when Alex Ferguson provisionally signed me."

An apprenticeship as a plumber followed but at only 5'-5" and 9st 9lbs, the physique of the young Mr Logan was never in line to repair any defensive leaks. What was on offer was pace.

That speed was fashioned in his school days with a place in the 80 metres final of the Glasgow Schools Championships at Scotstoun Showgrounds.

Not surprisingly, it was as a substitute when Alan made his Senior football entrance, replacing Robert Torrance in a 2-2 draw with Aberdeen at Love Street in October 1979.

Logan recalled: "I played against Willie Miller and Alex McLeish but I was an unknown newcomer who hadn't as yet made any impact on the Senior game. It took the Dons defensive duo a while to suss me out.

"They weren't chasing me all over the park – they were letting me turn and run as they assessed my capabilities. In truth, I wasn't sure myself which way to twist and turn but I finished up content with my contribution."

It took Alan another four months to register his first St Mirren goal, Partick Thistle being the despondent recipients of a 3-0 turnover. Indeed, the Firhill team conceivably became Alan's favourite opposition following a memorable match against them in April 1981.

He explained: "We were two down against the Jags when I came on at half-time to replace Frank McDougall, who had developed a back injury. In the first half Tony Higgins had scored twice and Doug Somner had missed a penalty for us. We dominated the second half and I managed to net a hat-trick.

"Did I get the ball? You bet I did, my dad now has it."

A career goal haul with St Mirren of over 50 in domestic competition masks another scoring highlight which Alan rates as his prime black and white experience.

Hat-tricks are always a pleasurable commodity for strikers and while that threesome against Thistle was a highlight, Alan possibly topped that with his exploits in the 79-80 Anglo Scottish Cup – especially the final.

The tie against Bristol City at Ashton Gate in the two-leg final saw not only Alan in the Saints starting line up, but Tony Fitzpatrick in the Robins team. No doubt Tony had been highjacked into marking the card of the City manager as to the Buddies' strengths and weaknesses.

Two goals from Billy Stark down at Bristol set the Saints up for the return at Love Street. Fitzpatrick didn't play but Alan did and sealed the 3-1 second-leg win with a smartly taken third goal, generating a medal for the trophy cabinet.

While Bristol City won't register geographically as overseas opposition, Alan did manage to acquire a taste for the continental game, coming on as a sub against Elfsborg in the 1980 UEFA Cup.

He was also in the pool for the St Etienne games that same year. He was also in the national Under-21 squad against Sweden away but had to be content on each occasion with sideline views of these matches.

Towards the end of Alan's Love Street career, injury struck following a match with Clydebank. He was sidelined for seven months and while then boss Miller had faith in the Logan capabilities, he never managed to regain his early St Mirren form.

A new direction was required and a signpost diverted him to Firhill. It was former St Mirren full-back and good friend David Walker who fast-talked Alan into a three-season spell with Partick Thistle.

In effect, Alan's arrival in downtown Maryhill was fortuitous as he was a ready replacement for Kenny McDowall, who had moved to Love Street.

Life with the Jags was followed with the assertive Frank Connor kitting Alan out in a Raith Rovers jersey. However, his time at Stark's Park ended in controversy, Alan falling out with manager Jimmy Nicholl on a simple matter of principle.

Cammy Fraser, who had played with Alan at Kirkcaldy, persuaded him to move to Montrose. The travelling, while extensive, was eased with training facilities being arranged with Airdrie at Broomfield.

A return to the west and a step down to the Juniors found Alan operating for a single season with Kilbirnie Ladeside.

By now the Logan knees had taken a fair pounding and it was former boss McFarlane, in his professional capacity as a physiotherapist, who persuaded Alan to call it a day.

In his post-St Mirren days, Alan opted for part-time life as a postman. But such a calling demands Saturday deliveries with a 5am reveille required to satisfy the postal needs prior to heading for Firhill. Not the best of pre-match preparations

If Logan's lifestyle in the football industry was of sedentary proportions, it didn't change in his post-playing days. Following his dad's occupation, he eased behind the wheel of a Renfrewshire taxi.

His affinity to the game hadn't been totally lost as a close friend and former St Mirren colleague Gardner Speirs persuaded him to cast an eye around the local soccer talent in pursuit of the needs of Ross County, when Gardner was involved as manager Alex Smith's number two.

BRIAN MARTIN

"WHY did you sign me when you've a player like that on your books?"

These were Danny McGrain's words. They were directed at Hamilton boss John Lambie in praise of the performance of a young Brian Martin after a 3-2 win over Clyde in an August 1987 game at Douglas Park.

Brian reminisced: "Danny was my football hero. He was sitting in the Hamilton dugout after his career at Celtic had finished when he made these observations to Lambie.

"I'd had a pretty good game, laying on a couple of goals, but hearing these comments coming from your boyhood hero provided a tremendous boost to my confidence."

That confidence factor had been given a slight dent in Brian's early senior days. Airdrie Schools have always harboured a production line of players destined for the senior stage. Martin was a one such graduate from the St Margaret's High School, one time winners of the Under-16 Scottish Schools Cup.

Post scholastic football saw Brian settle for further advancement with the Plains Under-18 team.

The moustached Sam Goodwin was then first on the scene to spot the latent Martin potential and promptly signed him for Albion Rovers.

Brian said: "I had only played 10 games for Rovers when I snapped my Achilles tendon in a match down at Stranraer. I was out for about five months before Harry Hood came in as manager.

"He wanted me to play in one particular game but I said no as I was scheduled to be best man at my brother's wedding. I was told play or you'll be freed. Family comes first with me so I was out."

Fortunately an uncle of Brian's, Jim Black, engineered a couple of games for him with Stenhousemuir. As luck would have it, the first was against Albion Rovers.

On the day Brian was facing a professional sprinter in Ian Campbell. However, the Ochilview full-back was happy to endorse the fact that in addition to having an outstanding game, the flying winger failed to breach the Martin defensive prowess once. The 2-0 win over the Coatbridge side provided a taste of sweet revenge.

These early forays into the senior game served to prove a point for the teenage Mr Martin – he required subjection to a toughening up process.

That process was duly administered in the Junior game by Shotts Bon Accord, Brian remaining with the Hannah Park side until he was 21.

Billy Lamont was the Falkirk boss at the start of the 85-86 season. The Bairns had Premier League aspirations but their defence needed stiffening. Martin supplied the necessary needs, the Brockville club just managing to pip both Kilmarnock and Forfar Athletic by one point in moving up from the First Division.

Dave Clarke succeeded Lamont at Falkirk but he didn't fully appreciate the Martin talents. Lambie thought otherwise, having seen Brian play and score in a previous Premier League encounter against Hamilton.

The late 1980s were halcyon days for St Mirren. They had won the Scottish Cup, Ian Ferguson had been sold to Rangers and Martin arrived at Love Street as a possible replacement on the back of a £75,000 fee to Hamilton. Lambie was a happy chappie because a sell-on clause in the Martin contract yielded a £30,000 fee to Falkirk and Accies still earned a tidy little profit.

April 7, 1990, provided Brian with a momentous entry for his personal scrapbook. Saints at Parkhead and the Buddies registered a resounding 3-0 defeat. A memory relished and reminisced in jig time by the delighted St Mirren midfielder, who conceded much of the Parkhead damage had been orchestrated by the Paisley overseas contingent in Guni Torfason and Tomas Stickroth.

By now David Hay had succeeded Tony Fitzpatrick at the St Mirren helm. Financially, St Mirren's buoyancy was less than stable. The manager's budget had been overspent. He needed to recoup some cash and this resulted in Brian being transferred to Motherwell in November 1991, with a fee of £175,000 heading back to Paisley.

It was Brian's move to Fir Park that effectively brokered the deal that took Paul Lambert to downtown Lanarkshire.

Martin explained: "Tommy McLean was the Motherwell manager. He asked me if there were any other half decent players at Love Street. I told him to make tracks for Paul Lambert and Norrie McWhirter.

"Unfortunately Norrie's injury catalogue held him back but within a year Paul had donned a claret and amber strip. To this day, Paul has never believed I was responsible for initiating his move to Motherwell."

A player with a strong boned heavy built frame, we are indebted to the Motherwell publication The Men who made Motherwell Football Club for their pen pic assessment of Brian.

They said l: "Not by any means quick, his game was built around exceptional reading of events and a wonderful sense of commitment."

These characteristics were clearly developed during Brian's five-year spell at Love Street.

After his teenage Achilles misfortunes, Brian remained virtually injury free. The fact is mirrored by the stat that he was never listed as a substitute in league games with St Mirren and only once while at Motherwell. Indeed, he logged in a 100 per cent Fir Park attendance record in season 92-93.

The core of Brian's playing career was served with Motherwell. Some 236 league outings highlighted the potential that led to being selected for the Scotland tour of the Far East in 1995. The Caledonian participation in the Kirin Cup competition in Japan provided two international call-ups against the host country and Ecuador.

The strong going Fir Parker John Philliben – quaintly nicknamed "Softy" in the soccer environs – and a long-term pal of Brian's, had taken over the management strategies at Stirling Albion. Brian was recruited to bolster the Forthbank defence

Some justification of the move surfaced in a third round Scottish Cup replay against Hibernian in February 1999, the Binos winning 2-1. A certain Mixu Paatelainen, later to feature at Love Street, appeared in the vanquished Edinburgh side.

Alex Totten then wanted the Martin expertise back at Falkirk but the syndrome "Better the devil you know that the devil you don't" kicked in and former boss Lambie took Brian to Firhill for a 16-game fling with the Jags.

By now, a broken wrist and numerous slow healing cuts and bruises spelled the end of senior involvement.

A step down to Junior activity followed, with subsequent service being given to Lanark United, Wishaw, Shotts Bon Accord (again) and Cambuslang Rangers.

Finally, Stonehouse Violet took Brian on board as their player/manager.

Surprisingly, no one at the Stonehouse club could provide information on the origins of the Violet title. We've had a number of romantically named teams in the past, Dundonnell Bluebell and Glenbuck Cherrypickers spring to mind.

However, with local worthy Tom Forsyth – he with a 22 Scotland cap collection – sporting the nickname "Jaws" and featured as a local icon in a framed picture at the Stonehouse Social club, conceivably the team title might have been read as "Violent!"

A family man, Brian and his wife Ann still live in Airdrie. His non-football occupation now centres on being a team leader in the warehouse of a pharmaceutical company.

FRANK McAVENNIE

DON'T knock Milton. That suburban sprawl located in the North West environs of Glasgow has had many critics in examining the quality of its family life. In terms of football life, it veers from the lugubrious to being more salubrious - Kenny Dalglish was brought up in Milton, so was Frank McAvennie.

The local school playground was the mythical Hampden Park for the juvenile population, although in Frank's case, his Shangri-la was Celtic Park.

The playground format was simple - 20-a-side games were the vogue and the first team to score 21 were winners.

St Augustine's Primary was almost responsible for turning Frank away from football. He was told he was too small with a fragility factor likely to encompass severe injuries.

But in his teenage days Frank was made of sterner stuff. Despite being told after a trial with Kilsyth St Patrick's that he wasn't good enough, he embarked on a series of games with a group of his mates, performing for the quaintly named 200 Club.

The ability to nutmeg opponents at will and contribute a barrow load of goals saw Frank's games being closely monitored by a galaxy of scouts, one of which was a representative of Johnstone Burgh.

Having left school at 15 and embarked on a collection of wage earning activities - some 14 jobs in a four-year period - meant being given a signing on fee of £500 from Burgh opened the portals to a more acceptable lifestyle. It would satisfy the needs of his bank manager, to say nothing of the pleasures of those in the licensing trade.

Word was circulating in the Renfrewshire domains that here was a lad that could score goals. Bertie Auld, the Partick Thistle manager, had Frank on trial on three occasions but no offer of a permanent peg was forthcoming.

Cue St Mirren. A highly contentious trial for Saints against county rivals Morton seemed to put paid to any signing possibility at Love Street - Frank was ordered off after a bout of fisticuffs.

Jim Clunie was the Saints gaffer. He wanted someone with a bit of bottle.

He liked what he saw and Frank signed for St Mirren in November 1980, just before his 21st birthday.

Two weeks later, Clunie joined the ranks of the great football unemployed, Rikki McFarlane taking over as the Love Street manager.

Listed as a substitute against Partick in January 1981, Frank had to wait until September of that year to make his first full start - and what a start!

St Mirren were playing Airdrie at Broomfield Park. Frank had scored along with Billy Stark but the Buddies were 3-2 down and there were only minutes left for play. Many Saints fans had already left the ground when Stark scored the equaliser in the 87th minute. A minute later and enter McAvennie, who rode to the rescue with the the winner to generate utter bedlam on the terraces.

Hordes of St Mirren fans were caught in mid-stream on the stairways, some leaving for Paisley and others returning to the slopes to cheer the unlikely winners. Not too many score a double on their first senior start.

A 63-goal tally from 164 Saints outings - which led to five Scotland Under-21 caps - inevitably created interest from the English leagues, with Luton Town in the vanguard of potential purchasers.

Allan Marshall was the St Mirren director/secretary at the time of the negotiations.

He explained: "Luton had been after Frank for nearly 18 months but were always a bit light with their offer. They initially offered £100,000 and later upped the figure to £325,000.

"The St Mirren party comprising Frank, manager Alex Miller, myself and agent Bill McMurdo had flown down to Heathrow, the air fares being funded by Luton and their manager David Pleat.

"A deal had been agreed but the content of what Frank might expect to see in his pay packet was an aspect regularly side-stepped by the Kenilworth Road hierarchy. Deal or no deal? Definitely the latter!

"We were staying at a luxurious hotel in the sleepy township of Woburn - sleepy in that all the street lights went out at 11.00 pm.

"A couple of days before travelling to Luton, a chance phone call between Miller and Alex Ferguson revealed that West Ham were interested in Frank's future.

"When negotiations with Luton stalled, we made contact with West Ham manager John Lyall late that night. In fact, it was very late and we went on to meet John at a Watford services station in the early hours.

"These were pretty secret negotiations, remembering that it was Luton who had financed both the air fares and the hotel accommodation. John returned us to our Woburn hotel at around 5am and went on to fly up to Glasgow that afternoon and signed Frank for the Hammers at Glasgow Airport."

Not surprisingly, Frank made an immediate impact on the English scene. In a three-year spell at Upton Park, he netted 33 league goals from 85 appearances.

A scoring rate of a goal in almost every second outing created cult worship for the lad from Milton, even generating an invitation to appear on the BBC's Terry Wogan chat show, in company with Scotland icon Denis Law.

While in the Hammers employment, the international icing on Frank's soccer cake came with five full international appearances for Scotland. One of these caps was against Australia at Hampden Park in the 1986 World Cup qualifying campaign. The Tartan Army celebrated a 2-0 win with one of the goals being registered courtesy by Mr McAvennie.

While London life clearly appealed to Frank, there was a craving that he had yet to fulfil.

Playing for Celtic was very much a life-long ambition - one that was realised when Billy McNeill signed him for the Parkhead side in 1987.

The high spot from that particular sojourn came in the 1988 Scottish Cup final, Frank scoring both goals in the 2-1 win over Dundee United.

European competition then appeared on the McAvennie CV as he played against Honved in the 88-89 European Cup and scored in the 4-0 win at Parkhead.

He rejoined West Ham in March 1989 for a reported fee of £1.25 million, making a further 68 league appearances and scoring 16 goals, before moving on to Aston Villa for a mere three games as a substitute.

Subsequently, Frank travelled to Asia to play in the South China league.

He returned to Celtic and played two and a half seasons for the Hoops but by now the goal scoring sharpness had been marginally blunted.

St Mirren manager Jimmy Bone tried to resurrect the McAvennie scoring magic and brought him back to Love Street in season 1994-95, where he logged in only seven league appearances for Saints without scoring.

The McAvennie career was well peppered with numerous off the ball mischiefs. But if a PR accolade was ever required for Frank, he no doubt would be indebted to Jonathon Watson and his Only An Excuse cantrips in creating the McAvennie catchphrase - "Where's Ra Burdz?"

JOHN McCORMACK

STRONG willed, assertive, determined and with a mind of his own, John McCormack's personal motto could conceivably have been bracketed with the "Whae dare meddle wi' me" syndicate.

That positive attitude was sufficient to persuade his parents to allow him to stay on at St Mungo's Academy – a scholastic establishment rich in developing football talent and regular participants in teenage cup finals. However, John would freely admit to being less than sure footed on the lower rungs of the academic ladder.

He explained: "My prime reason for staying on was simply to play in the first 11. I didn't enjoy the academic side, although I was up for certain subjects. One of them was accountancy and that was my only Higher."

Of the three McCormack brothers – Billy and Steve were the other siblings – John was happy to follow the well-trodden path to join Drumchapel Amateurs under the legendary guidance of Douglas Smith.

A move to Duntocher Hibs followed by securing a peg at Provanmill Park, home of St Roch's, and it was a highly desirable club switch for John.

John said: "I'd always wanted to play for St Roch's as my dad used to take me along as a nipper to see them play. I always had a firm belief in my ability that I would eventually step up to the seniors and fortunately Bill Munro and Sam Henderson gave me that opening with Clydebank.

"The good news was that I went full-time with the Bankies, the bad news was that my wage packet was immediately halved. Fortunately Ricky Agnew, a Clydebank director, helped out by employing me on a part-time basis in one of his garages repairing punctures."

St Mirren manager Jim Clunie was anxious to bolster the Love Street central defence and the no-nonsense approach of McCormack was the answer in plugging any defensive leaks.

Jack Copland and Jimmy Bone were the top men when John initially set foot in the Saints dressing room, with Bone, being mischief maker in chief, dubbing John as "Cowboy" McCormack.

John explained: "There was another sporting type around at that time.

John McCormack the boxer apparently had a born in the saddle bow legged approach to the fisticuff game, which prompted the nickname "Cowboy". The moniker stuck but I'd like to think I had other physical attributes that the fans could wax lyrical about."

Getting paid for doing something he would gladly have done for nothing was a more than satisfying St Mirren experience. And perhaps playing against St Etienne in the 1980 UEFA Cup, Michel Platini et all, takes centre stage as John's Paisley highlight – especially with mum and dad looking on.

Having served under Clunie and Rikki McFarlane, Alex Miller was the man in charge when John's Love Street stay ended.

Cowboy recalled: "I'd spent four years with St Mirren and I didn't want to leave but Alex Miller apparently felt I was too strong a character for him to handle. I was persuaded to move eastwards to join Archie Knox at Dundee after a couple of verbal run-ins with the Paisley gaffer".

John's post Dens Park career saw him join Airdrie, followed by a final playing fling with Partick Thistle under Billy Lamont.

Never selected for any representative honours, John was "picked" only once by the national team manager.

He explained: "It was at a dinner for Jackie Copland when Jock Stein picked my name out of a hat in a raffle for a trip to Paris. I said to Jock, 'I hope that's not the last time you pick me'. The Big Man's response was typical – 'Take me with you and it might not be the last!'

"At the time I left Firhill my marriage had just broken up and I worked as an assistant manager in a sports centre, which meant a lot of shift work.

"I received a phone call from Simon Stainrod at Dundee after I'd lettered every club in Scotland. He wanted me to take over Dundee's Reserve team and when Simon left I fell heir to the manager's job."

The subsequent termination of John's contract at Dundee is one of the unfathomed mysteries of the football industry.

He said: "I still don't know the answer to my leaving. I can handle the media, I can handle the players but I couldn't explain to my family why I was sacked.

"It was Peter Marr that showed me the door. There we were, top of the First Division, five points clear and on track for promotion. We had just beaten Stirling Albion and I was told 'OUT'. Apparently they wanted to go in a different direction."

With such a managerial record, clearly the McCormack administrative talents wouldn't be confined to cold storage for long. Queen's Park saw to that.

He said: "My new wife Gail was a civil servant in a Jobcentre. She wanted a career break with our twin boys Josh and Jack until the youngsters went to school. I told Queen's Park no to part-time and they eventually gave me a salary that was acceptable, making me the first full-time manager in the club's history."

It was now Queen's that wanted to go in a different direction, having lost 13 players in one season to the paid ranks. It proved to be the right direction as the Hampden club won promotion to the Second Division in the millennium season. The fact that they dropped back down the following year is typical of the challenge facing any Queen's Park chief.

John explained: "You can't get players on loan. You can't offer players financial incentives and if a player does well you're going to lose him at the end of the season. Every year you have to rebuild a new team."

While the Hampden challenge was successfully accomplished, a yearning for a more professional approach was satisfied when John joined Renfrewshire rivals Morton.

Again promotion success came the McCormack way, before the disastrous 2003-04 season. St Mirren, despite the traditional terracing acrimony, will always welcome the Cappielow club operating in the same league – for obvious financial considerations.

Around the mid season mark that desire seemed on track. Top of the Second Division, eight points clear of Berwick Rangers, Morton went on to lose the plot, with 15 points being surrendered in their last six games.

Clearly team motivation had been substantially diluted. Morton had lost their way and McCormack was forced to relinquish his Greenock hotseat early the following season.

John has readily made his mark on the Scottish game, both as a player and a manager. And the general expectation is that his career in the industry has not yet hit the buffers.

FRANK McDOUGALL

RUMBUSTIOUS is an adjective of onomatopoetic proportions that springs readily to mind. Not a term used in any derogatory sense, but an apt description of those goalscoring frontmen who opt for the shortest distance between ball and the opposition nets.

Jock Dodds of Blackpool and wartime Scotland fame was one, although his middle name of Ephraim seemed to generate, on paper at least, a more placid approach to the game.

Billy Houliston, Queen of the South's prolific post-war marksman, was another, and the epitome of the bustling striker, always a menacing prospect for the opposition.

Perhaps not over physical but none the less assertive in the goal-grabbing business was one Frank McDougall - a particular favourite of the Paisley faithful in the early 1980s.

The McDougall potential was first spotted and taken on board by Hearts, who signed the 16-year-old schoolboy in 1974. Always a centre-forward, Glasgow-born Frank's affinity to the Gorgie Road environs was short-lived and he returned to the west for, in his words, "a wee stint" with Partick Thistle.

Still able to find the net but not with an acceptable frequency to satisfy the Maryhill Magyars, Frank, perhaps a little disillusioned, opted for life with the Juniors and with Perthshire in particular. Daytime activities allied to part-time football saw Frank employed in erecting pyramids of scaffolding in the West of Scotland.

Around the late 1970s, the astute husbandry of Clan Steedman at Kilbowie Park was instrumental in transforming Clydebank into a prominent force in Scottish football. Indeed, they were Premier League material in 1977-78, with Jack Steedman falling heir to the presidency of the Scottish League from 1988-91.

It was Jack and his scouting team who endorsed the McDougall skill factors by bringing the then 20-year-old to the ship-building community of Clydebank.

And Billy Stark, Tony Fitzpatrick, Doug Somner and Lex Richardson were the top men at Love Street when manager Jim Clunie signed Frank for a club record fee of £180,000 at the start of the 1979-80 season.

The first recorded McDougall competitive outing in black and white was on August 11, 1979, with Saints registering a 2-2 draw with Kilmarnock on the first league outing of the season, Stark and Robert Torrance netting the goals.

Saints legend Fitzpatrick was a playing colleague of Frank's and Tony remembers him well.

He said: "Frank actually came to St Mirren on trial before he went to Clydebank. He was strong, very determined and particularly good in the air. He scored some unbelievable goals but didn't receive the full acclaim for his efforts until he joined Aberdeen."

Ask Frank for his St Mirren highlights and his reply is masked in poignant ruefulness.

He said: "I played in four major cup semi-finals for St Mirren and didn't win one! In 1981-82 Saints lost to Rangers in the League Cup and Aberdeen in the Scottish Cup. In the next two years, we went down to Rangers and Celtic. Frustrating? Absolutely!"

A prolific scorer at Love Street, Frank amassed some 62 goals on his St Mirren CV. Playing at the same time as Frank in the early 80s and a marksman of considerable note down south was one Luther Blissett of Watford, the West Indian winning 14 England caps.

It was the pawky humour of Clunie who nicknamed Frank as "Luther Blizzard" in recognition of his scoring ability. The name Luther stuck!

Two goals in particular endeared Frank to the Paisley faithful. A fourth round Scottish Cup tie against Morton at Cappielow in February 1983 saw the Saints centre knock in both goals in the 2-0 turnover.

The football path linking St Mirren and Aberdeen has been a well trodden route over the years. Alex Ferguson was one who made the journey and he was in the market for some additional punch for the Dons' forward line. Fergie secured the McDougall transfer for the start of the 1984-85 programme and a cheque for £100,000 enriched the St Mirren coffers.

Ironically, Frank's debut for Aberdeen saw him return to Love Street for the second game of the 1984-85 season. Not surprisingly, the Buddies in the North Bank were a mite apprehensive about his return.

Proof of his progress in the north east saw him not only top the Granite City team's scoring charts, he also topped the Premier League ratings.

Further Paisley irony surfaced with former Saint Stark being the Pittodrie side's runner up with 15 goals that same season.

Frank tasted and enjoyed European football playing against St Etienne in the 80-81 UEFA Cup. However, a slight European playing indiscretion saw Frank receive a four-match ban which barred him from a number of Aberdeen's continental counters.

He recalled: "Alex Ferguson didn't know about the ban and being Fergie, he promptly cracked up. It meant I missed out on the 84-85 European Cup competition plus the first two ties the following year.

"I'd like to think I was partially forgiven when Aberdeen played the Swiss side Servette in the second round of the European Cup in 1985. We had held them to a 0-0 draw in Switzerland and I scored the only goal of the tie in the return at Pittodrie."

Frank's time with the Dons ensured a well stocked trophy cabinet and he enjoyed Premier League plus Scottish and League Cup successes. Also on show is the European Golden Boot for his 22-goal haul in the domestic 84-85 campaign.

Pose the question as to which goal Frank relishes in the most memorable category, the pride factor is self evident.

He smiled: "It's always nice to score against Rangers and Celtic. I managed two hat-tricks for Aberdeen against the Ibrox side and bettered these strikes with four against Celtic at Pittodrie on November 2, 1985. I'm the only player ever to score four in one game against the Parkhead team."

There were many highs in Frank's playing career but there were major lows, too, with injuries never far away.

A cartilage injury with St Mirren was followed by two broken legs during his time at Love Street, but worse was to follow.

Frank's last game for Aberdeen saw the Dons play Hibernian at Pittodrie.

He was on the bench but a niggling spinal column injury was later confirmed as a severely damaged back and he was never to play again.

With football now behind him, Frank moved into the licensed trade, with home being established in Bury in the Manchester suburbs.

KENNY McDOWALL

KENNY MCDOWALL owes a tremendous debt of gratitude to his father for giving him a perspective on the values of life.

He left Kingsridge Secondary in Drumchapel as a 16-year old, determined to fashion a career in football. Kenny's Dad thought otherwise.

"You get a trade behind you," was the parental advice. In fact, it was an order that was satisfied with a five-year bricklaying apprenticeship with the John Lawrence construction company.

Any youngster with latent footballing potential and living in the north western environs of the Glasgow conurbation invariably found the soccer traffic signals directing him to the famed Drumchapel Amateurs side.

The venerable Douglas Smith, architect of the youth side's meticulous organisation, has fond memories of Kenny.

Douglas said: "As a 14-year-old he used to come down to my home at Cardross, where we used to enjoy some fairly hectic five-a-side games on our tennis court. He spent many years as a youngster driving my car illegally up and down the driveway!

"On one occasion Drumchapel were playing on the continent. Kenny had gone into an over robust challenge with the opposition keeper. Kenny was pole-axed and appeared badly injured. When we got to him, he whispered out of the corner of his mouth – 'I'm OK, but if I get up right away the ref will book me!' His enthusiasm was never in doubt."

Still at school and playing for The Drum, Kenny signed an "S" Form for Partick Thistle in 1978, with Bertie Auld, the then Jags manager, reminiscing on his new addition to the Firhill ranks.

Bertie said: "I was fortunate enough to have Kenny playing in the Thistle youth team alongside the likes of Mo Johnston. He was the type of player every manager would like to have. A natural goalscorer, he had enthusiasm and commitment in abundance. What set him apart from the other lads was the fact that he was prepared to listen. That's a major feature in the football learning process and Kenny was quick to learn."

Saints manager Alex Miller was seeking that degree of commitment to augment his strike force and Kenny moved to Love Street when he was 21.

The nine years spent with the Paisley Saints provided a rollercoaster ride of emotions with numerous highs and lows.

A member of St Mirren's 1987 Scottish Cup-winning side, Saints manager Alex Smith spoke highly of Kenny's contribution.

He said: "As a player he was fearlessly competitive, gave everything he had, helped everyone round about him, scored some great goals – particularly with his head - and played a major part in the winning of that Cup."

The tempestuous nature of the McDowall attacking play was never more on show than on the opening day of the 1989-90 league campaign. Rangers had won the previous season's Premier League title.

The date was August 12. A few grouse no doubt plummeted to terra firma that day but it was the hopes of the Ibrox faithful banking on a winning start to their league programme that were shot down by the tenacity of McDowall.

Ibrox was bathed in sunshine, the title pennant had been unfurled and, let's face it, visiting teams aren't generally programmed to win at the Ibrox citadel. A cross came in, both Kenny and keeper Chris Woods went for it.

Kenny's cranium was a microsecond ahead of the Rangers custodian, who was unceremoniously decked in the process. The ball finished in the net with the Light Blue denizens baying for a free-kick. But as subsequent pictorial evidence proved, Woods had a foot on the ground, providing complete validity to the challenge, and the goal was the only counter in a torrid game.

Veteran soccer scribe Willie Hunter remembers the Saints man well and being on the wrong end of a bone-crunching McDowall handshake.

Hunter recalled: "Kenny got his nickname Koj from Kojak the TV cop. Paisley people found the three letter word easier to say than the five letter one. Besides, Koj sounds like a coach. Especially when Jimmy Bone bellowed the name from his soft seat in the directors' box in the stand during reserve games.

"He was good at handling wild men. He was afraid of nobody. And he wore gaudy waistcoats and sucked lollipops. Kojak did, that is. Our Koj isn't like that. Except for the bit about being fearless.

"Then some wag noticed another resemblance. Both Koj and Kojak are clear headed, the centre parting is measured in yards!

"Koj belongs to a line of football notables that includes Vialli but goes back to Bobby Charlton and the immortal Jimmy Delaney. They are all much the same from the ears up!

"Don't let me sound as if I know Koj. We've met once to say hello and shake hands. He is firm about that as about most things. But he gave me my hand back and it soon returned to its normal shape, thank you."

Financial restrictions had manager Bone labouring on a single ticket. Some coaching back up was required and both Kenny and Campbell Money were elevated to joint first-team coaches. With Kenny's playing career in some decline due to a niggling cartilage problem, the appointment gave him a leg up onto the coaching ladder.

For someone who had joined Saints on September 22, 1984, and made his debut as a substitute against Celtic on that same day, to have contributed 209 black and white appearances and raked in 24 goals – one of them against Tromso in Sweden in the European Cup Winners' Cup – some form of earned gratitude had to be found.

It came on May 7, 1996, Kenny being awarded a testimonial match against Morton, with a curtain raiser being a match between a St Mirren Legends side and the Paisley Business Brigade.

The joint coaching structure was regrettably fractured when Money opted to try his hand at management in taking over at Stranraer. With bonhomie on a high after the testimonial celebrations, it seemed that Kenny had been dealt a more than stronger hand.

That was until the start of the following season. Saints were feeling a financial pinch. Cost-cutting reared its ugly head and Kenny's coaching position was one of the unwilling sacrifices.

Bone wasn't in any way impressed at the financial downsizing and immediately offered his resignation in protest.

Kenny on the scrap heap? Not a bit of it.

Happily ensconced in the Milngavie suburbs to the north of Glasgow with the support of his wife Liz and young daughter Alana, it was a safe bet Kenny would bounce back.

With a full house in coaching certification and his in-depth knowledge of the game and his man-management strengths, Partick Thistle initially enlisted his coaching services, before the powerhouse who are Celtic appeared on the scene.

Now fully embroiled as coach of the reserves at Celtic Park, it's a million light years away from his bricklaying days. However, Kenny is still in the building trade – fashioning promising football careers.

DONNIE McDOWELL

LIFE at St Mirren was never one of docile proportions in Donnie McDowell's time. His arrival at Love Street in the mid 1970s came on the back of an acrimonious send off from manager Bertie Auld at Partick Thistle.

Donnie explained: "Thistle were due to play a pre-season friendly against a Danish side at Firhill. I'd injured my ankle and Bertie wanted me to take a pain-killing injection. For an important league or cup game I might have said yes but for just a pre-season friendly I flatly refused.

"From that moment on I was finished at Firhill and banished to the Reserves – but I was still able to score a load of goals.

"For a Partick Thistle Reserve game, the players' boots were always set out in the dressing room in readiness for the game. On one particular occasion my boots were missing and I was given the message that Auld wanted to see me.

"He was fed up with my moaning at the lack of first-team football. I was fed up being a full-time player in the Reserves. I was told that Rangers had taken a shine to me but if I was in any way interested, Alex Ferguson of St Mirren wanted to talk to me.

"I talked with Fergie, was impressed and signed for St Mirren. But when I went to collect my boots at Firhill they had vanished. This was Bertie at his mischievous best and Fergie wasn't over impressed at the disappearance of my footwear. He was on the phone in jigtime to Firhill lambasting Bertie for his childishness."

Donnie arrived at Love Street early in season 1974-75, at a time when league reconstruction was the current topic of informed conversation, pending the arrival of the new Premier League.

St Mirren were languishing in 13th place in the old Second Division and needed to make sixth to gain a place in the proposed new First Division.

That St Mirren achieved that goal was in no small way due to Donnie's predatory scoring instincts. Some 39 goals from 93 outings in total is a scoring rate of the highest order, with perhaps a certain goal against Hamilton at Douglas Park being the pick of the bunch.

Donnie recalled: "Hamilton were above us in the league and I managed to hit a 30-yard screamer for the only goal of the game. While it was nice to score, what was more important was the result kept us in that coveted sixth spot."

And all this from a lad who had received his secondary education at Allan Glen's School – a rugby playing establishment!

McDowell went on: "I never played secondary schools football. All my football energies were channelled into playing for the 150th Glasgow Boys' Brigade Company, before I joined the Partick Thistle youth side when I was 15.

"I moved up through the age groups to eventually graduate to their Under-18 side, well known as Sighthill Amateurs. They had in their ranks such future Partick Thistle icons as Alan Rough and Andy Anderson. They earned the reputation of being the top amateur youth side in Scotland – even better than Drumchapel Amateurs."

The legendary Willie Thornton was the man who introduced Donnie to Firhill. The former Rangers man was followed by youth coach Davie McParland, who alerted Ferguson that the Jags had a striker who was surplus to Maryhill requirements.

With such notables as Robert Reid, Walter Borthwick, Davie Provan and Alex Beckett in the St Mirren line up, more might have been expected from Donnie's Saints debut in a trip to Cowdenbeath. The Blue Brazilians were destined to finish second bottom of Division Two with a meagre points harvest of only 21.

That grey day in November 1974 saw St Mirren at their charitable best, registering a 1-1 draw and donating a point to the Central Park team's slim points tally.

Not surprisingly, high on Donnie's most memorable list was the winning of the 76-77 Division One championship and promotion to the Premier League.

Not quite so high on that listing was the Ne'erday match with Morton at Cappielow.

Donnie recalled: "We won 6-3 but I didn't even manage to score – and I was ordered off for the first time ever in my career. The pitch was pretty frosty and I was chasing a long through ball. Jim Liddell, the Morton keeper, tried to clutch the ball to his chest as I came running in. It bounced off his torso and I tried to head it.

"The keeper recovered to make a positive clutch and I moved back but Liddell took offence and swung a fist at me. A bit of a melee developed but I was no where near the epicentre.

"The referee Alan Ferguson then took centre stage, sending me off for apparent head-butting and Liddell for retaliation."

Donnie's day of embarrassment was further compounded that evening as he met his girlfriend Margaret's parents for the first time – Donnie later marrying the young lady.

He explained: "We were sitting in their house when Sportscene appeared on TV and flashed up pictures of the Morton-St Mirren derby and the double sending off. What was embarrassing was the fact that Margaret and her parents didn't even know I played football!"

Fortunately, that red card was later rescinded after an appeal to the SFA.

Donnie's time at Love Street – he was there for just over three seasons – preceded St Mirren's European adventures of the 1980s. Yet his footballing passport was well utilised on overseas missions.

The spectre of Cowdenbeath came back to haunt Donnie and his St Mirren colleagues, the Fifers seeing off the Saints 3-0 in a third round Scottish Cup tie at Central Park in January 1976.

To say that Ferguson doesn't take too kindly to losing is a slight understatement, especially losing to a side the St Mirren Reserves could have beaten. As a result, he dropped five regulars for the next league game, then reinstated them for a friendly with Legia Warsaw at Love Street.

The Polish side were one of the top European sides at the time but Saints sent them home to think again on the back of a 1-0 win. Donnie well remembers the game as he came off the bench to replace Jackie McGilvray and score the winner.

Also incorporated into Donnie's meanderings were a couple of games against Notts County in Malta, to celebrate the Queen's silver jubilee. Saints drew the first but lost the second, with conceivably the County-St Mirren affinity from their 1922 Barcelona get together having an input to that tournament invitation.

Donnie explained: "We also toured the West Indies and helped a number of countries with warm up games prior to the1978 World Cup. We played Barbados, British Guyana, Surinam and Trinidad & Tobago and beat all four. I was substituted in one game to make way, would you believe, for Fergie, before Davie Provan substituted Fergie after just 20 minutes!

"After beating British Guyana, we were invited to a reception at the British Embassy. Jackie McGilvray and I were deep in conversation with an official who assured us that after our 4-1 win, we most assuredly would not win the second game the following day. He was right – he was the referee! We lost 2-1 and he sent off two St Mirren players, including Alex Ferguson."

What was interesting in the current climate of suggested refereeing incompetence was the public apology after the game from the British Guyana FA for the performance of the match official. Nice touch!

Season 1977-78 saw Donnie setting up camp with Kilmarnock for a couple of years, before moving to Falkirk and winning a Division Two championship medal with the them. Post Falkirk and Donnie opted for a season with Petershill. But in Donnie's own words: "By now the legs had gone."

If you are ever accorded the privilege of visiting the McDowell homestead, you will be immediately confronted with a couple of huge bearded collies. They contribute substantially to Donnie's leisure time activities.

The McDowell legs might have gone football wise, but dog walking ensures the lower extremities are kept in prime condition for his nine to five job as a computer expert in the IT industry.

ANDY McFADDEN

COLLINS New English Dictionary comes up with a clutch of suggestions in support of the word "devotion". "The giving of oneself to a cause", "Unselfish obedience to duty" and "A committed zealous support" are but three interpretations. And who would argue that they all fit comfortably on the broad shoulders of Andy McFadden – especially during his time with St Mirren?

Another whose early days saw scholastic endeavour at the now defunct Stanely Green School – Archie Gemmill was a playing colleague – both must have energised the saliva glands of any watching Senior scouts at the latent potential on view.

Andy said: "When I was at school I was a right-half, or an attacking wing back in today's parlance. Once I had turned 14, I signed provisional forms for St Mirren. The deal was that I played for the school in the morning and for Port Glasgow Rangers – a Juvenile team – in the afternoon.

"By the time I had reached 17, Doug Millward, who was an exceptionally nice guy, had taken over. I was called up and converted into taking root in the centre-half berth. If the St Mirren Reserve side were short of players, I filled in for them. That was the time when both the first team and the Reserves played on the same day."

Mid-term in the 66-67 season and Saints were vulnerable in fielding a somewhat less than stable defence. Jim Clunie's playing day were over, Cammy Murray alternated between right-back and centre-half while Jim Kiernan was Mr Versatile with his array of half-back duties.

Manager Alex Wright sought to remedy the situation by giving McFadden his debut at right-half against Airdrie at Love Street. Willie Renton was secured from St Johnstone and also made his first appearance in black and white. But the infusion of fresh blood failed to do the business, Airdrie winning 3-0.

Andy remembered: "I was only 17 at the time and to be honest I was only a big raw boy hitting everything that moved. Alex Wright was over critical of his senior players in failing to give me any help or support. He sent me back to the Reserves but I did play in the last game of that season against St Johnstone at Love Street. We drew 0-0 but I was much happier – I was back

169

on the centre-half beat."

Ask Andy for a career highlight and his response is delivered in jig time – the 67-68 championship-winning season!

He said: "You know I never played in a losing game in that campaign. Sure, St Mirren did lose one game against East Fife, but I didn't play – I missed out with a pulled muscle!

"What was a total anti-climax was the medal presentation. Some grandiose occasion perhaps? No sir. We came in from training one night and were told to report to the boardroom. It was like standing outside the headmaster's room.

"We thought we were in big trouble but it was the St Mirren chairman presenting us with our winners medals. I was happy enough but some others weren't so pleased as there were only a limited number of medals on offer."

A promising career looked assured but there was injury trouble on the McFadden horizon. A recurring problem arose with a number of shoulder dislocations.

Andy explained: "I went to see a consultant about the problem but never had an operation. I think on reflection the difficulty was inoperable. It was a wee hole in my shoulder joint and I had three such dislocations in my time with St Mirren."

Never one to grab the goal scoring highlights, Andy only ever netted four goals in his 135 St Mirren outings. But two of them came in one game with Dundee at Love Street.

He added: "Iain Munro and big Gordon McQueen were in the side. We were losing 3-0 at half-time and in the second period I swapped my beat with Iain and went upfield. Talk about being in the right place at the right time – although we still lost 4-2!"

Andy had experienced the managerial foibles of Millward, Wright and Wilson Humphries before Tommy Bryceland took centre stage. Tommy didn't fancy this recurring injury situation and immediately posted a P45 to the McFadden Paisley homestead.

Wright, by this time, had moved on to Dumbarton. He remembered the strong central defender's capabilities at Love Street and took Andy over to Boghead. He was only 23 when he left Love Street. Did a revitalised career beckon?

Andy revealed: "The move didn't help. In fact, it only exacerbated the problem. The dislocations occurred on a more regular basis and I had the task of yanking my shoulder back into place. Painful? You bet it was!"

The pain barrier effectively ended a more than promising career, one that never once saw any representative selection.

McFadden recalled: "At school I was in line for a schoolboy cap but

Stanely Green wasn't a favoured site of learning by those with team selection responsibilities. The nearest I ever got to a representative game was to play for St Mirren's Under-17 side against their national counterparts – I think we beat them 5-0!"

So who did Andy lay out the red carpet for in terms of exerting the biggest influence on his football life?

He said: "Definitely my dad. He was a Junior internationalist and used to regale me with tales of his uncle Peter Doherty, the Irish internationalist, who won his 16 caps over the period 1935 to 1951. He would have won a barrowload more if it hadn't been for the war.

"And then there was Willie Fulton. I learned a lot from him. He used to sit me down and give me advice. The fastest man around at that time was Jim Forrest, who went from Rangers to Aberdeen. He was quick. The guy could travel and even if I say it myself – I was no slouch. Willie would reassure me saying, Don't worry Andy, if he beats you I'll be at your back.' Willie provided the complete calming influence."

A soccer career in tatters in his mid 20s, the Andy McFadden legacy was not lost on the far flung horizons of the Scottish game. Thoughts on management must have loomed large in his mind. Brora Rangers from the Highland League were in need of a player/manager. Would Andy consider the position ?

He explained: "I was really taken aback and deeply honoured that they thought I could do the job. But, on refection, I turned it down. I was too young and hadn't a grounding on the administrative side of things, plus the fact that the injury situation made playing a no-go option."

Never a full-time player, Andy is a joiner to trade and a glance at any newly fashioned staircases, doors or screens in the Paisley area might well have been carpentered by the resolute McFadden.

STEVEN McGARRY

THIS substitute business… It was wee Archie Gemmill who started it all as the first ever substitute in the Scottish game when he came on to replace Jim Clunie against Clyde in a League Cup match at Shawfield in August 1966.

Alan Logan in the 1980s took the replacement business to a new level when he logged in 73 substitute appearances. But it was Steven McGarry who created a new art form in this style of a soccer occupation – his listing of 92 substitute placements as against 104 starting appearances creating a new St Mirren record.

But it was a frustrating experience and Steven made the plaintive plea: "I hope I'll be remembered at St Mirren for something more than just a clutch of sub appearances!"

In truth, he will be. Born on September 28, 1979, he shares his birthday with such notables as singer Helen Shapiro, actress Bridgette Bardot and actor Peter Finch. Even as a nine-year-old his football endeavours were attracting attention of the then St Mirren Director for Youth Development, Charlie Palmer.

Charlie, a former Saints full-back from the early 1970s, perceived a latent talent in young striker Steven as he performed on the Racecourse pitches with the St Margaret's Boys' Club.

Captain of his school team at St Brendan's High in Linwood, the team selection process was generally achieved on an ad hoc basis, with Steven being hauled out of class to select the starting line up in tandem with a soccer-minded teacher.

St Mirren Youth Development Officer Joe Hughes, aided and abetted by Palmer, having already secured the McGarry autograph on an "S" Form, was keen to have young Steven sign for Saints on a full-time basis.

But Steven's mum insisted on a college course, the national certificate covering Sport, Leisure, Recreation and Health at the Reid Kerr College. This offered Steven a basis for possible future career prospects on his après playing days.

The boys' clubs of St Convals, St Margaret's, Celtic and St Johnstone all had playing associations with Steven before he eventually went full-time at

Love Street.

And so well did he perform that an early run with the Reserves was promised. Stranraer at Love Street provided the opposition for the hitman's first game.

Steven recalled: "I nearly didn't make it. I'd lost my boots and had to borrow a pair from Matt Kerr. I came on a sub with Paul McIntyre going on to gallop up the right wing and sending over a peach of a cross which I managed to net with my first touch. A 2-1 win – it was some start!"

That debut provided great satisfaction for Clan McGarry, who were somewhat less than enthusiastic with Steven's senior debut against Partick Thistle at Firhill on the last day of August 1996.

Steven explained: "All my pals were at Firhill but none of my relations. My aunt was getting married that day and I was over the moon to see my name on the squad list. Charlie Palmer told me if I wasn't in the starting line up or on the bench he would escort me to the wedding. I think he knew I'd be playing so I didn't need his taxi service."

There's no doubt the winning of the 2000 First Division title takes centre stage in the St Mirren most memorable category. Scoring the second goal with a glancing header in the 1999-00 title-clinching game against Raith Rovers was simply the icing on the promotion cake. McGarry's Saints Young Player of the Year in that millennium season provided added cause for celebration.

The 27 competitive goals in the McGarry St Mirren locker generated a number of gems. His first ever was against Renfrewshire rivals Morton, creating, as always in derby games, a euphoric mayhem among the Love Street faithful.

A double dumping Rangers at Love Street in a 1999 pre-season game was equally rewarding but the favourite McGarry strike was against Livingston at Almondvale in the 2000 promotion-winning year.

Steven explained: "A break was on and I charged up field only to be confronted by Ian McCaldon, the Livvy keeper. He is a big lad and an imposing figure but I saw him off his line and managed to chip him from all of 30 yards. That was a very satisfying goal."

Capped by Scotland at Under-17 and Under-18 levels, Steven worked under national coach Alex Smith with the Under-21 group and picked up three caps against the USA, the Czech Republic and Portugal in 1997.

Finance, or more properly, the lack of it, can be an ongoing cancer at many clubs. St Mirren's solvency was questionable around the summer of 2002.

McGarry said: "Stewart Gilmour told a few of us that we were free to leave if we found another club. My agent phoned around and Boston United came to the surface. I went down to have a look. They are a well run club but I didn't enjoy Boston, it wasn't the best of places and I would have found it difficult to live there.

"Boston wanted to give me a two-year contract but I felt a loan period would have been a better deal. Inverness Caley Thistle were interested and I spoke to them but it was Ross County who came in with the promise of regular football. It was a done deal for me."

Tom McGarry, Steven's dad, is a devoted Buddie. Resplendently garbed in his St Mirren jersey at every game, what were his reactions on the first occasion Ross County met St Mirren at Love Street?

Steven revealed: "I think in his mind he had worked out a compromise. He wanted St Mirren to win 3-2 with me scoring twice for County!"

Steven's claim to fame on the Dingwall club's books saw him in the County line up when they appeared in the 2004 final of the Bell's Challenge Cup. The cup wasn't full to overflowing, however, County losing out 2-1 to Falkirk at McDiarmid Park.

Of more pleasurable Dingwall associations for the McGarry memory bank was the last league game of the 2002-03 season against Ayr United up at Victoria Park. Arbroath were already fated to enjoy Second Division fayre. The second from bottom spot was being contested by Ross County and Alloa Athletic.

The Wasps from Recreation Park thought they'd saved their First Division bacon by thumping St Mirren 4-0 at Alloa. But it was McGarry who demonstrated some Highland enterprise by scoring twice in a 4-1 win over Ayr to keep County's First Division credentials afloat on goal difference.

The old adage of "Nothing is forever" was most certainly applicable to Steven's future with Ross County.

County director and former chairman Roy McGregor confided that the lack of goals might be a contributory factor in releasing Steven to further his career elsewhere.

A new window of opportunity was required and Raith Rovers were the initial favourites to secure the McGarry future.

However, it was with some surprise and no little satisfaction for Steven that Terry Butcher offered a post at Motherwell, Steven going on to resample SPL football with the Fir Parkers against Dunfermline at the end of January 2006.

Another crack at the topflight is no more than he deserved.

FRANK McGARVEY

THE football encouragement Francis Peter McGarvey received in his teenage days was remote and scant in the extreme. One of a family of five, his three older brothers didn't play and weren't interested while his father only came to see him once - and left at half-time!

A much more productive back up came from Ian French, the manager of the Colston Youth Club, who kept arranging trials for the teenager.

Frank mused: "I had a succession of trials for Junior teams and also had one for Clyde. The standard good bye was, 'We'll call you, don't you call us!'

"I was a bit naïve at the time and didn't really know what that meant. I kept waiting for the phone to ring.

"I was asked eventually to play a trial for Kilsyth Rangers. To be honest, I was becoming fed up and made up my mind this was going to be my last trial. I was all set to wave football goodbye when the Kilsyth officials signed me and presented me with a £25 signing on fee. At that time I was earning only £8 a week, so I was immediately in dreamland."

A couple of months later Rangers expressed an interest in Frank's playing future - an interest that went into terminal decline when they heard which scholastic establishment had contributed to Frank's academic wellbeing.

Rangers did add some fertiliser to the soccer grapevine and told Alex Ferguson about the McGarvey potential, with Frank autographing a St Mirren recruitment form in time for the 1975-76 season.

In the St Mirren party for the pre-season Isle of Man tournament, Frank also played in a warm up match against KR Reykjavik and scored four.

Obviously now in contention for a starting role, disappointment clouded over Frank in the opening fixture, a League Cup tie against East Fife at Love Street. He was only on the bench but the cloud soon lifted when he arrived on cue, the wearer of the No.12 shirt netting the winning goal in the 2-1 result.

A member of the 76-77 promotion-winning side, it was a hat-trick from Frank against Dundee at Dens Park that secured the title and promotion to the embryonic Premier League.

After four seasons in St Mirren colours and a haul of 61 goals, Frank felt compelled to try his luck at a higher level. Liverpool satisfied that need in 1979 and provided a cheque of £300,000 for the St Mirren exchequer.

It was a sweet and sour move. Frank spent 10 months languishing in the Anfield reserves and was eventually given a first-team start as he was about to ask for a transfer.

The less bitter moments of his time on Merseyside came with the acquisition of seven full Scotland caps - the first against Nigeria in 1979, his last in facing Wales in 1984.

While Frank voiced his leaving of Liverpool as the greatest mistake of his football life, he was seemingly partially pacified with his move to Celtic, a reported fee of £325,000 taking him to Parkhead.

What was ironic about the move was his debut for Celtic, as the Hoops took on St Mirren at Parkhead. Saints' contribution to a 2-2 draw was a brace from Dougie Somner.

If the McGarvey trophy collection was at this time of Old Mother Hubbard proportions, it took a turn for the better in his time in green and white.

Two league championship gongs plus a winner's medal in the League Cup was only bettered with the memory of that late diving header to dispose of Dundee United in the 1984 Scottish Cup final.

One other McGarvey claim to fame saw him establish a record of being the first player to score 100 Premier League goals.

Despite Frank's ton up in the striking department for Celtic, manager David Hay had high hopes of landing Mo Johnston as his first choice striker.

Frank was out of favour and was surprisingly allowed to return to St Mirren in June 1985. And the move culminated in another Scottish Cup winner's badge in 1987, gleaned once again at the expense of Dundee United.

Frank said: "I had looked forward to playing alongside Frank McAvennie but that dream went up in smoke when he was transferred to West Ham."

Outwardly, the McGarvey physique was seriously slim, perhaps even frail and lightweight, yet he managed to dodge the crunching tackles and escape serious injury. In truth, he only missed one game from each of the 75-76 and 85-86 league seasons.

After a total of nine St Mirren campaigns, Frank is accredited with a 91 goal tally - a figure that rates him second on the post-war scoring ladder, with only wee Tommy Gemmell three ahead of him.

He was appointed St Mirren player-assistant manager in April 1988, and while the position was an acceptable starter on the coaching front, Frank wanted to be his own man and moved to Palmerston Park for a season as player-manager of Queen of the South. However, a degree of acrimony ensued and the Doonhamers terminated his contract in March 1991.

A move to Clyde in a simple playing capacity followed, as did another 22 league strikes.

Frank always maintained a more than passing interest in the Junior game and gave vent to his grass root feelings by ending his playing career as player-assistant manager of Shotts Bon Accord.

Meticulous regarding his appearance, it was a McGarvey custom always to appear clean shaven on the playing pitch. And the application of razor and shaving soap was undertaken on occasion pre-match in the dressing room.

He explained: "I like to be smart. I don't much care for a bearded growth. Being clean shaven makes me feel better and if that's the case, I always played better."

Working in the building trade after the cessation of football hostilities, a need for peace of mind on Frank's behalf could always be found at the Millport Golf Club - arguably the course with the most scenic views in Scotland.

Nominated as a striker in a Saints Club Magazine poll to select St Mirren's finest post-war line up, few would argue with the result when Frank's name topped the readership listings in the goal getting department. His scoring returns were prodigious.

KEVIN McGOWNE

IF there is a common denominator in Kevin McGowne's football career then it's quite probably Alex Totten.

It was Alex whose post-match TV interviews always created doubt as to why any of his managed teams had lost. It was Alex who recruited Kevin for St Johnstone after the defender had served the Paisley Saints for three seasons.

It was Alex who brought Kevin back to Ayrshire to join his home town team Kilmarnock. And, somewhat perversely, it was Alex's team Falkirk that Kevin's Kilmarnock side faced on the day of the McGowne career highlight – the winning of the 1997 Tennent's Scottish Cup.

Never catching the eye of any national or local squad selection panels, that bypass in his teenage days Kevin attributes to being a late starter.

He did start at St Joseph's Academy in Kilmarnock, linking his scholastic playing activities with Saturday afternoon or Sunday morning outings with a galaxy of boys' clubs, Ayr United, Kilmarnock and Bellfield, to name but three.

At 6'-1" and around the 13 stone mark, here was a striker who could play a bit. As Kevin reminisced: "I was never lightning fast but was able to harvest a considerable collection of goals."

It was that collection that negotiated the passage from the Bellfield Under-18 side to Hurlford Juniors.

The goal getting continued at the Blair Park junior club, a facet that greatly interested St Mirren scout Peter Donald. It was Peter, the father of the Scottish Football League secretary, that brokered Kevin's move to St Mirren Park in December 1988.

Kevin explained: "I only signed on with St Mirren in a part-time capacity. I played the remainder of the 87-88 season with Hurlford and turned out in a number of reserve games for Saints. Obviously the part-time deal necessitated another job and I worked as a storeman for three years in a curtain factory in Darvel."

Kevin's first outing as a St Mirren player came in a reserve match against

Motherwell at Fir Park.

He went on: "We had out a strong side that night and had a pretty convincing 6-2 win. I was playing up front alongside Frank McGarvey and wee Billy Davies was also in the team. It's great to launch your career with a win but I was somewhat disappointed that I didn't manage at least one of the six goals."

Kevin's first start for the senior side came in the first round of the 1990 Scottish Cup against Ayr United. He didn't feature in the 0-0 draw at Somerset Park but was called into action for the replay, St Mirren winning 2-1 thanks to goals from Davies and Kenny McDowall.

Former Saint Gordon McQueen was involved with the Love Street coaching staff at this time. Gordon was el supremo with the reserve side and with his defensive background with St Mirren, Leeds United and Manchester United, it wasn't surprising that he was responsible for rewriting Kevin's soccer CV in converting him from a frontman to a strong going right or centre-back.

Financial viability can on occasion be the catalyst that determines a player's career path. It certainly pointed Kevin in a new direction.

He recalled: "Davie Hay had left when St Mirren were relegated in 1992. Jimmy Bone took over but the club were apparently on a financial sticky wicket. Quite a few players left and that's when I first met up with Alex Totten when I joined St Johnstone.

"The move allowed me to stay in the Premier League but when the leagues were rearranged at the end of the 93-94 campaign, three teams were relegated to the newly formed First Division. Partick Thistle stayed up but St Johnstone were banished to the 10 team First Division on the back of goal difference – that difference being a mere one goal."

Life at McDiarmid Park went into marginal free fall under John McCelland's direction, before Paul Sturrock arrived to steady the Perth Saints.

After four seasons in Perth, Kevin renewed his Premier League association, with Totten taking him down to Kilmarnock's Rugby Park. Ironically, a year after Kevin left St Johnstone, the Perth side clinched promotion back to the Premier Division on the back of a massive 20 points difference from Airdrie.

But such promotion disappointment was consigned to the back burner as McGowne enjoyed Scottish Cup success with a 1-0 win over Falkirk. And in the Bairns dugout? None other than a resplendently kilted Alex Totten.

Kevin said: "Winning the Scottish Cup with a provincial side was massive. Looking back, the game is a bit of a blur but what will always be a treasured memory was the trip through Kilmarnock in an open top bus."

Season 2002-03 was a stalled one for Kevin. Some 12 league games for Dundee United plus seven for Partick Thistle followed before the John

Coughlin-Gus MacPherson double act brought Kevin full cycle back to St Mirren Park to provide some solidity to the Buddies defence. Kevin signed on in July 2003.

While that Scottish Cup triumph with Killie remains a proud memory, Kevin rates the winning of the 2005 Bell's Challenge Cup with almost equal fondness.

He said: "It was a magical experience to lift the cup as the club captain. I never had that opportunity before. What was particularly satisfying was the buzz it gave the younger players just to feel the euphoria and enjoy the winning experience."

At least that Scottish Cup medal now has a companion in the McGowne trophy cabinet. But there's more!

Obviously Kevin's defensive beat has restricted his scoring opportunities, but occasionally a gem or two turns up. Just like the big red bus syndrome, you wait for ages and two come along at once.

Such was the scenario back in Perth at the beginning of the 2005-06 season. The first league match at McDiarmid Park saw Kevin net the winner in a 2-1 return. Three days later the Buddies were back up the A9 to face St Johnstone in the second round of the League Cup. One nil this time to the Paisley Saints, the winning goal coming courtesy of another McGowne strike.

Such scoring prowess was conceivably instrumental in Kevin receiving the Bell's Player of the Month for August 2005.

In all his football wanderings it is remarkable the number of past and future St Mirren playing associations that Kevin has experienced.

Sergei Baltacha, Guni Torfason and Tommy Turner at Perth is more than matched with MacPherson, Martin Baker, Ally Mitchell, Tom Brown and Mark Reilly at Rugby Park. Clearly the big happy football family as opposed to colleagues in crime is a positive aspect at St Mirren Park.

So who would Kevin rate as his most difficult opponent?

He said: "It would be easy to say Henrik Larsson at Celtic. He did me in many a game but I found Mark Hateley really difficult to handle. He was a big physical player and I'm convinced he had the sharpest elbows in the business!"

From his home in Perth you'll find Kevin on a daily basis walking his Dalmatian dog. Deep in contemplation, he'll be pondering over life after football. Given the chance he would opt for full-time golf but that option might not even provide sufficient recompense to feed the family dog!

While the 1997 Scottish Cup final still tops the ratings in the McGowne memory banks, season 2005-06 isn't far behind. As the well respected Saints skipper, he had the honour of lifting aloft two national trophies in that campaign – the First Division championship and the Bell's Challenge Cup. Not many can include the lifting of such silverware in their soccer biographies.

JACK McGUGAN

IF Jack McGugan was the youngest player in St Mirren's 1959 Scottish Cup winning side - he was 19 at the time - his teenage health caused considerable pre-match anxiety to his older compatriots in the Love Street camp.

Prone to suffer severe attacks of tonsillitis, he was the one player to miss out on the Wednesday evening training session prior to Hampden. In fact, he was ill in bed semi-speechless with his tonsillitic troubles.

Local concern in Paisley was high. Would the strapping Saints centre-half be fit to face Aberdeen? Even the local media forsook the current front page headlines of the day and waxed lyrical about his chances:

We do not care for Miss Fonteyn

Or Panamanian Consuls,

But let our hopes be not in vain

For Jack McGugan's tonsils.

Fortunately, his prescribed medication cleared the problem and Jack went on to exert a stranglehold on the Dons inside trio of Davidson, Baird and Wishart.

Some considerable stretch of water had passed under the McGugan bridge since arriving on planet earth in Airdrie in 1939 and that momentous cup final day. The local academy had become something of a Mecca for the nuts and bolts operation in assembling the way forward for aspiring footballers.

Joining the Saturday morning touchline troops of loud voiced fathers and menacing mothers with lethal umbrellas, there were scouts a plenty. One such onlooker represented Stoke City, and this scout was instrumental in taking the young McGugan down to Victoria Ground hoping he would make the grade in the English game.

However, life in the Potteries and many miles from mum's home cooking soon sent Jack scuttling back over the border, where, playing as an inside forward, Hearts developed an interest in his future.

The Tynecastle hierarchy found him a peg with Slateford Athletic Juveniles but he soon returned to his West of Scotland roots, stepped up to the Junior ranks and joined Pollok over at Newlandsfield Park.

Jack takes up the story: "I'd heard that St Mirren were interested in me and that their scout, Jack Gilmour, was coming to run the rule over me in a match against Rutherglen Glencairn. I don't think he could have been too impressed with me - I was sent off!"

If the intention of building a team from the back is to provide a muscular structure to dim the lights of the fleet footed frontmen, then McGugan was a prime candidate. The man who eventually succeeded Willie Telfer had served a five-year apprenticeship as a blacksmith and despite the red card nonsense in that Junior game, manager Willie Reid went on to harness the bulging biceps to the St Mirren cause in 1956.

If that game for Pollok caused Jack some embarrassment, his debut for St Mirren was also well cemented onto the howler category. Clyde were the visitors to Love Street and Jack scored a cracker - only it finished up in the back of his own net!

Clearly the '59 cup final was the McGugan career highlight. But for the Saints teenage centre-half the excitement of the occasion blotted out any poignant memories of the day. In truth, it was a severe case of acute oblivion - he remembered little of the game.

He nearly made a niche for himself and almost eased into the national side. Together with Tommy Leishman and Tommy Bryceland, the trio were invited to train with the Scotland squad prior to the May 1959 game with West Germany at Hampden, a match the Scots won 3-2.

A further step up came when, in tandem with Leishman, Jack was selected for the summer continental touring party. He eventually made the national side, playing a Jutland X1 in Aarhus, but failed to get the nod against Holland in Amsterdam and Portugal in Lisbon.

Jack's five-year spell at Love Street ended with a move down south to join Leeds United, where he stayed for 18 months.

The Wirral peninsula in England provides a high standard of domestic living and Jack emigrated from Yorkshire to sample the lifestyle with Tranmere Rovers. The quality of life at Prenton Park was pretty pleasing until the arithmetic ramifications of goal difference cooled the Tranmere ardour in 1966. The English Fourth Division had seen Tranmere score 23 goals more than Colchester United, but the Essex club had conceded considerably fewer, thus trumping the Tranmere promotion bid.

He was a canny player in his time with Kilmarnock and when Gerry Mayes took over the reins at Somerset Park, McGugan was among the first on his mostwanted list to bolster the Ayr United rearguard. A similar scenario subsequently developed at Cappielow Park, with the impresario that was Hal Stewart enlisting Jack's services for duty at Morton.

Still the final entries of McGugan's playing CV hadn't been logged before the rural niceties of Cambridge United enticed him back south for a spell.

Prior to hanging up his boots, Jack also had a final fling with the steel workers of Corby Town, before opting to down his domestic anchor in Cambridge where, with his wife Janette, they made a credible contribution to the UK population figures with two daughters, a son and six grandchildren.

The days of sweating over the blacksmith's furnace have long since gone. And on his retirement from the game, the charisma that is Jack McGugan's was well suited to satisfying the needs of being Mine Host in a number of English hostelries.

The current technical revolution has also caught up with the former Saints man - he is now on hand to tame the gremlins of any company computer systems that malfunction.

BOBBY McKEAN

A NUMBER of former St Mirren players have regretfully passed on before their time, some in unforeseen circumstances. Donnie Kerrigan and "Cockles" Wilson are two that spring to mind – but the demise of Bobby McKean was tragic.

Bobby's post playing days at school saw him provide a variety of touchline trickery on the Junior stage with Blantyre Victoria.

Alex Wright was the Saints manager at the time and his persuasive ways brought the speedy winger to Love Street in 1969.

Bobby had to wait until August 12, 1970, to make his first-team debut, Wright providing a seat on the bench for him in the League Cup tie with Kilmarnock at Love Street. Killie enjoyed a 3-1 win at the time when only one substitute was allowed in the team pool.

That term, the McKean wing play earned him 25 starts in all games, plus a further eight substitute appearances. His goal tally was a mere three.

However, while his goal-getting ability grew to double figure proportions the following season, it was the 73-74 campaign that Bobby's credibility really took off.

One outstanding McKean contribution occurred in a league match with Brechin City at Love Street. The game finished 3-1 in St Mirren's favour. All three goals were spot-kicks and all were expertly converted by Bobby.

That same season his goal count reached a remarkable 22, covering the three major competitions. It was an outstanding return from a winger.

His efforts were rewarded with the St Mirren Junior Supporters' Player of the Year trophy plus the St Mirren Supporters' Player of the Year accolade.

There was never any question that McKean was an ambitious young man keen to make a lasting impression in his chosen vocation. As such, a transfer request was posted and turned down by the board and then manager Willie Cunningham.

Clearly an unhappy or discontented player can become a cancer in dressing rooms and, consequently, a move away from Paisley for Bobby became highly desirable.

Willie Todd was the St Mirren vice chairman at the time and well remembers the situation.

He explained: "Bobby was one of the most skilful right wingers I have ever seen. He played in the same team as big Gordon McQueen. He was a pacy player and his ball control was adept enough to beat a player and deliver a quality cross.

"Rangers watched him a number of times and initially offered £25,000 for him. St Mirren turned down the offer – we thought it a bit derisory. The Ibrox hierarchy reconsidered and upped the fee to £35,000, which we accepted. It was one of the biggest ever transfer fees at that time."

The move was finalised in September 1974

Estimates in the evaluation of transfer fees are notoriously inaccurate. The McKean fee was reported in the Paisley Daily Express as £50,000, while the Rangers Press Office quantified the figure at £60,000. Clearly such financial transactions generate a raft of inflated figures.

McKean's reaction to the move was more philosophical. He said at the time: "I have got to better myself. I've seen many other players leave St Mirren to better themselves and I thought the time was ripe for me to depart."

The St Mirren full-backs during this period, Cammy Murray and Tony Connell, knew a thing or two about trimming the aspirations of exuberant wingers.

Tony said: "He was a complete breath of fresh air. A young guy, he was so confident and just a natural winger, something you don't see much of nowadays.

"You can generally make an assessment of a boy's character when you first see him. Bobby was very level headed, wasn't one for the drink and as I said, really was a breath of fresh air."

Murray was equally forthcoming in his appreciation. He said: "Bobby was quick and direct and had the ability to drive past players. Light on his feet, he was always able to find space to receive a ball. As a full-back that was always my first thought when I had the ball – where was my winger?

"I used to travel with him. He stayed in East Kilbride and I used to bring him into Love Street for training. He was always a perky character and I was shattered when I heard what had happened to him."

Bobby went on to play 119 matches for the Ibrox club, scoring 17 goals and winning two League titles in 74-75 and 75-76. He was also in the winning Rangers Scottish Cup team when they defeated Hearts 3-1 in 1976.

A taste of European activity was also logged on to the McKean CV, Bobby participating in the 76-77 European Cup against FC Zurich. The following season he was also active in the European Cup Winners' Cup against Young Boys of Berne and Twente Enschede from Holland.

One further honour was a full Scottish cap against Sweden, also in 1976, coming off the bench in a 1-0 win.

Then came the fateful day of March 16, 1978. Bobby was in the Rangers pool for their League Cup final clash with Celtic two days later. Clearly he had something to look forward to.

He had been visiting friends and had initially phoned home to tell his wife Fiona he would be staying over. He apparently changed his mind, returning home in the early hours only to find Fiona, a heavy sleeper, had securely locked all the house doors.

Bobby's efforts to rouse Fiona only succeeded in waking some neighbours, who offered him a bed for the night. However, he opted to sleep in his car in his garage, leaving his engine running to keep warm.

At only 25, he was discovered the following day having succumbed to the carbon monoxide fumes.

His funeral service was conducted by the Rangers Chaplain, the Rev. James Currie, at the Martyr's Parish Church. Rangers, Celtic and St Mirren players attended the service.

The general consensus of football opinion was that here was a sad and tragic loss, particularly for his wife Fiona and daughter Ashleigh, but also for the wider spheres of the Scottish game.

BARRY McLAUGHLIN

HAVING his birth certificate date stamped as April 19, 1973 – a birthday shared with TV presenter Sue Barker and comedian Dudley Moore – the Christian names of Barry John might have suggested that the young Mr McLaughlin's future sporting interests might well revolve around the oval ball game. Not so – his Paisley-born sporting genes were destined for success on the round ball arenas.

Having caught the eye of the St Mirren scouting staff, Barry was a mere 13 when Alex Miller's regime were instrumental in having the McLaughlin signature appended to the all embracing "S" Form.

But there was a problem on the immediate horizon. A bright lad at school, Barry saw a clutch of Highers safely accumulated, providing thought that a career outside football might be a more positive way of earning a living.

His folks also agreed and Barry joined the Royal Bank of Scotland on leaving school.

But it was Jimmy Bone that brought Barry into the first-team fold after David Hay had persuaded Barry to sign pro forms in August 1991.

A summer evening just a year later at Douglas Park, in a league match with Hamilton Accies, the 6'-1" 19-year-old made his senior debut – wearing the No.9 shirt. A long loping stride pattern saw the debutant cover every blade of grass but to no avail, the game petering out in a scoreless draw.

There were just three outings in his first season but 27 and 34 in the next two league programmes meant a St Mirren future seemed assured – and the banking exams were seconded to the back burner to be replaced with a full-time contract at Love Street.

The first goal to be incorporated into the McLaughlin scrapbook came in his second full season, Barry coming off the bench to score against Dunfermline in a league match at East End Park.

With Barry's physical attributes more suitable for repelling cross balls and delivering the telling tackle, it wasn't surprising his modus operandi quickly changed from a front running role to one of defensive solidarity.

Not surprisingly as a defender, goals weren't a regular commodity but one memorable McLaughlin strike against Aberdeen at Pittodrie in the 1995 League Cup sent the Paisley pulses racing. With no score at the time, Barry found himself in the Dons penalty box. A quick pivot and a blast over his shoulder saw the proverbial rocket fly past Theo Snelders.

One up, could Saints do it? Alas, they couldn't, as a couple of goals from Scott Booth and one from Billy Dodds blunted Saints' progression.

While that goal energised the saliva glands, there was one further Barry Mac strike well entrenched in his memory banks.

He recalled: "Our last home game against Raith Rovers in our millennium title-winning season was pretty special.

"We had won promotion the previous week down at Somerset Park, now we wanted the title.

"Nearly 8,500 turned up at Love Street and after big Mark Yardley and Steven McGarry had given us a two-goal lead, I managed to knock in the clinching third goal – clearly a magic moment for me".

What wasn't such a magic moment for Barry occurred in a pre-season visit to Blackpool in July 1999. A two-night break at the Hilton Hotel incorporated a warm-up game against Blackpool at their Bloomfield Road ground.

Manager Tom Hendrie implemented a strict code of pre-match discipline and there was an early Friday night curfew, with the players being given reign to strut the promenade the following evening.

However, early on the Saturday morning the news broke that Barry's mother had unexpectedly passed away at her home on Paisley.

The Saints centre-back was obviously excused duty and returned home by car with his girlfriend Louise, later to become his wife. There was some thought of calling off the Blackpool game but the mood of the team was positive – they had to win it for Barry's sake – and they did, 1-0, thanks to a Junior Mendes goal.

The McLaughlin mantelpiece was by now in need of an extension due to the arrival of numerous playing baubles, the Paisley Daily Express Star Saint for the 1999-00 campaign and the St Mirren Player of the Year for 98-99 being two of the most notable.

With his banking background and the ability to communicate, it wasn't too surprising when Barry was invited to provide a helping hand to Campbell Kennedy's commercial operation.

However, despite being well known on the park wearing black and white, there were occasions when Barry seemed to wear a cloak of anonymity.

He said: "I went along to the Station Bar in Paisley with Campbell. Make no mistake about it, this is a St Mirren theme bar. I was introduced to the manager and he asked me who I played for prior to working in the commercial department. I was mortified – a St Mirren theme bar and he didn't even know I played for the club!"

Barry did, in fact play, making 283 starts with a further 13 as a substitute. His overall goal tally was 14.

With a firm central defensive partnership with Scott Walker behind him, it was time to move on and St Mirren chairman Stewart Gilmour brokered the only First Division funded transfers of the 2002-03 close season. Walker moved to Dunfermline and Barry headed for Rugby Park, Kilmarnock, on the back of a reported £30,000 transfer fee.

Prior to leaving Love Street, Barry's 11 years' service at St Mirren culminated in his receiving a Testimonial Year. The usual dinner and golf outing events were securely packed away but the anticipated testimonial match never materialized, primarily due to Barry's move to downtown Ayrshire.

Barry's time in Killie's blue and white wasn't over gilded in playing success, with thoughts surfacing after two Kilmarnock seasons of pulling the plug on full-time football.

At the start of the 2004-05 season, Barry reverted to the world of cheques, investments and current accounts, operating under the Royal Bank of Scotland umbrella. Still keen to play the game, it was Campbell Money who secured the McLaughlin part-time signature to bolster the defensive frailties of Ayr United.

A particularly poignant match for the new Somerset Park defender was Ayr's third round Scottish Cup clash with St Mirren in February 2005.

Barry said: "It was good to meet up again with a number of former colleagues and when I was injured in the game, the acknowledgement I received from the St Mirren fans was pretty pleasing."

Paul Lambert has a lot to answer for in the generation of players' nicknames. It was Paul who created "Trigger" for Barry but any similarity between Barry and Roger Lloyd Pack's performance in Only Fools and Horses is definitely a figment of Mr Lambert's fertile imagination!

HUGH McLAUGHLIN

INTERESTED in an example of football self motivation, then have a peek at Hugh McLaughlin's teenage way of life. A youngster with aspirations of pro football, he was serving an apprenticeship as an electrician in Strathaven. But a three nights a week training schedule with Third Lanark from his home in Larkhall had to be fitted into his weekly programme.

No quick trip on the suburban railroad, no car, so it was bus transport all the way. A bus from Strathaven to Hamilton was followed by bus from the Ducal Township to Glasgow's Duke Street and then a 'Fitzpayne Taxi' – or corporation bus for the non Glasgwegians – en route to Third Lanark's Cathkin Park. The return journey was equally tenuous and Hugh's parents were glad to see him home each evening.

Hugh said: "Sure it was a busy time. In my early teens I was playing for my school Holy Cross in the morning and for Glasgow United in the afternoon. The United team were the nursery club for Third Lanark, hence my evening training sessions at Cathkin. I was considered a striker in those days and managed to bang in a few goals."

A number of signing overtures had been cast Hugh's way. Firstly by his head teacher at Holy Cross and secondly by Tommy Gemmell of subsequent Lisbon Lions fame and a playing colleague at the time. Both were rejected as a promise to sign for the Cathkin club on his 17th birthday had been given. That signing never materialised.

Hugh explained: "I had committed a wee indiscretion while I was training with the "Hi-Hi's". I was only 16 and a local scout had goaded me into going down to Newcastle for a trial. It was the middle of winter and Glasgow United weren't doing much at that time.

"I went down and played in a youth match at Bradford. We won 2-0 and I scored both goals. That night I was a bit of a local hero on Tyneside.

"I came back to Glasgow and still there was little football with Glasgow United, so I went back down to Newcastle, played in another youth match against Wolves. We won 7-2 and I managed a hat-trick.

"The following Tuesday evening I went into Cathkin to do some training and was asked by the manager George Young to go to his office. His questions were searching and I was pretty naïve at the time and was completely floored when he flung a newspaper down in front of me. The headline said it all – Newcastle interested in Third Lanark star!

"Although I was an amateur, I had broken a code of ethics with Thirds and was told to pick up my boots and not to come back!"

End of the world? No, not really. Hugh went on to sign for Ayr United when Gerry Mays, the former Kilmarnock player, was in charge. Just over 18 months at Somerset Park and Neil McBain succeeded Mays as manager. McBain spent little time in demonstrating he wasn't a fan of the McLaughlin style of play and promptly released the youngster. Indeed, he released 14 players in one go. As Ayr United historian Duncan Carmichael pointed out, it was a disastrous cull.

In those days it was difficult to achieve a fast-track mid season reinstatement to the Junior game. But a direct passage to the amateurs was on and Hugh signed for the local Larkhall team Raploch Victoria.

Still only 18, he went on to join Larkhall Thistle with a ready collection of goals to his credit.

By this time Third Lanark were on a slippery slope thanks to financial mismanagement. Boss Young had been succeeded by Frank Joyner and the former Dundee man was oblivious to any previous McLaughlin indiscretions, harnessing his goal getting ability in time for the 65-66 season.

Hugh recalled: "I spent two seasons with Thirds before they went into liquidation. It was sad to see a club go under after such a 95-year history."

When a club hits the financial buffers, all the players' contracts are then held by the SFA. It virtually became an open market or car boot sale and Alex Wright, having had the misfortune to see St Mirren relegated, captured both Hugh McLaughlin and Tony Connell in a quest to reverse Saints' fortunes.

The new brooms swept pretty clean. Hugh was in for his first Saints game against Berwick Rangers at Love Street in the first game of the 67-68 season, the League Cup tie ending in a 2-2 draw.

While Hugh turned in 16 league appearances that season and St Mirren claimed pole position in the league, his pleasure in winning promotion was marginalised in abject disappointment.

He explained: "I didn't get a medal. The Scottish League officials were pretty stingy in handing out the winners medals. There were only a limited number on offer and I somehow or other didn't qualify. To put it bluntly, I was mad."

A five-year spell with St Mirren and over 100 appearances logged in, Hugh began to move further back in the team, occasionally even wearing the No.3 shirt. His final season at Love Street brought further disappointment.

He said: "I was captain of the team when Tommy Bryceland released me.

Added to that, there had been a wee whisper I was in line for the Player of the Year award. However, when it got out that I was being freed, the award bypassed me and went to Gordon McQueen."

From St Mirren, the McLaughlin skill factors then found favour with Queen of the South. But here again, Hugh's committed dedication wasn't to the liking of Queen's chairman Willie Harkness.

Hugh explained: "It was in essence a trivial mater, but Willie made the point I wouldn't play for another senior team ever again. I managed to arrange training facilities with Motherwell before the Dumfries club's top man contacted me again.

"Would I play for them on Saturday? Believe it or not, it was against St Mirren at Palmerston Park. They seemed to think I'd have some sort of psychological edge over my former team. It must have worked – we won 4-2."

After the Dumfries saga it was reinstatement to the Junior scene and Hugh at last received a coveted medal, Cambuslang Rangers beating Linlithgow Rose 3-1 in the 1974 Scottish Junior Cup final.

Born in Larkhall, Hugh and his wife Eileen still live in the town with their leisure pursuits dedicated to the local bowling green – both playing at different clubs and developing a degree of matrimonial rivalry.

While the time-served electrician blew the occasional soccer fuse with a number of clubs, his self-motivation factor will be well remembered for being the bright spark, turning in many gutsy performances for the Honest Men and Thirds, but particularly for the Paisley Saints and for Queens.

ALLY McLEOD

FEATURING Ally McLeod in St Mirren's top post war 100 generates one vital question – which one? Ally the ex-Scotland manager or "four-goal" Ally of Ibrox fame. In this particular chapter, it's the Scotland man, born in Glasgow's Govanhill district on February 26, 1931.

Sporting a hair style generously prescribed as "tow headed", Ally played for the Queen's Park secondary side in the morning, signing for Third Lanark as a 17-year-old and playing for the Cathkin club in the afternoon.

It was former Scotland right-back Jimmy Carabine who introduced Ally to life with the "Hi-Hi's", the winger taking over from the elegant Bobby Mitchell later to star with Newcastle United, and the little Pole Felix Staroscik.

One Third Lanark game provided a particular memory that nearly landed Ally in big trouble.

He explained: "Jimmy Carabine called me into the office and told me he was giving me a rest. I was 17 at the time and probably hadn't been playing too well. He told me to stay away from Cathkin.

"I took my boots and went down to the Queen's Park Recreation Ground. I met wee Bobby Collins there and he'd been told the same thing by Celtic. So we got into this bounce game on a 'Cock or a Hen' basis. The game had been going for 20 minutes when my mother arrived and said, 'Ally, there's been a call off, you've to get back to Cathkin'.

"It was a Scottish Cup tie against Aberdeen and I played. I'd have been on the Cathkin carpet had they known I'd just been playing in a bounce game."

A National Serviceman with the Royal Scots, Ally's call to the Colours coincided with the start of Third Lanark's financial freefall – and it was St Mirren's Willie Reid who latched on to the unpredictable McLeod wing artistry on the back of a £4,000 transfer fee.

His debut game in black and white featured a 2-0 defeat by Partick Thistle at Firhill on Guy Fawkes night in 1955. But the fireworks really took off eight games later with a 7-2 thumping of Airdrie at Love Street which incorporated a hat-trick from Bobby Holmes. Bobby well remembers the occasion and Ally's first goal for the club.

Holmes said: "Ally was an eccentric. You never knew which direction he was going to take, mind you he was simply brilliant in laying on a scoring chance for you."

Clearly the McLeod talents were not lost on the big-spending English sides, with Blackburn Rovers' Johnny Carey taking Ally to Ewood Park. That meant Ally left behind a minimal legacy at St Mirren Park of only 19 outings and a somewhat meagre two goals.

A seven-year spell with Blackburn saw the mercurial Ally play a big part in Rovers winning promotion to the top flight in 1958. Rovers had to beat second placed Charlton Athletic to go up and they won 3-0 with Ally scoring twice.

Another big occasion down south saw Blackburn up against Wolves in the 1960 Wembley FA Cup final. Ally didn't pick up a winner's medal – Rovers lost 3-0 – but he did catch the eye of those that mattered, winning the Man-of-the-Match Award.

If Ally's time at Blackburn was the zenith of his playing career, he most certainly enjoyed an Indian summer during a spell with Hibernian. Then came a return to the misfortunes of Third Lanark before Ally finally moved on to Ayr as their player-coach.

With a foot on the administration ladder, Ally experienced mixed fortunes with the Somerset Park side, The Honest Men having an elasticating time between the First and Second Divisions.

Dick Donald's Aberdeen side had been undergoing some managerial surgery, with a replacement required for Alex Stuart. Ally answered the call in 1974, with the terms of his contract being financially fluent.

Ally said: "Aberdeen were an honest club. When I went to Pittodrie they offered me a salary of £12,000 and I said no. They thought I wanted more. I told them I'd take £9,000 and the minute I win something they could treble my salary. I won the League Cup in 1976 and my first salary cheque thereafter was duly trebled."

After two and a half years with the Dons, sweet-talking SFA Secretary Willie Allan persuaded Ally to take on the Scotland job in 1976.

Scotland had been unbeaten in the 1974 World Cup finals in Germany, and with confirmed qualification for the finals in Argentina four years later, Caledonian excitement reached an over the top fever pitch in anticipation of success in South America.

Charismatic, irrepressive, eccentric and enthusiastic can be used to describe the McLeod character. However, a touch of embarrassed deflation almost floored the Scotland manager with the over exuberance of the going away party orchestrated by the SFA at Hampden Park prior to departing for Buenos Aires.

In truth, Andy Cameron's rendering of "We're On The March With Ally's Army" didn't lighten the embarrassment. Given that hindsight is a precise science, would Ally have made changes in relation to the Argentinean campaign?

He said: "Possibly I was too loyal to certain players, even when they had been having a sticky spell. I've proved the point that if a manager only uses 16-19 players in a season, he wins championships. If he uses 22-26, he faces relegation!"

"I've always stuck by a core of players for my teams. On the national front, perhaps their sell by date had over run. I made a few changes from Willie Ormond's 1974 team, but there were signs of some players getting over that age hill. That was a big mistake – I was too loyal to them."

Post Argentina saw Ally return to Somerset for just five weeks before Motherwell chairman Bill Samuel prised Ally to Fir Park as a replacement for Roger Hynd.

That spell with the Steelmen ended, as the majority of managerial posts do, in a sacking. But Ally was quite philosophical about the termination.

He said: "All credit to Motherwell. At a later function, Bill Samuel made a public admission that his one major error as chairman had been to ask me to leave. Jock Wallace took over the squad I'd built."

Fluent in dugout histrionics, Ally's verbal outpourings made him a marked man with referees.

Ally recalled one Ayr United visit to Tynecastle: "I had been ordered to the stand for my misdemeanours. I was at my usual shouting best when I received a tap on the shoulder from a Hearts director who was on the SFA Executive Committee. He told me, 'One of the greatest mistakes we've ever made was banning you to the stand from the dugout.'"

From Fir Park, it was onto Airdrie for a year but combining football management in Lanarkshire with a co-career as a publican in Ayrshire wasn't too compatible. Ally left Broomfield to go to Ayr for a third time.

The curtain finally came down on an illustrious career in soccer administration with Queen of the South, which established a record possibly never to be equalled.

In a Reserve League match at Love Street, the Doonhamers were short of players and Ally listed himself as one of three Trialists. Although Queen's were thrashed 8-1, the Dumfries boss had the temerity to net their sole goal from the penalty spot.

The iconic Stanley Matthews of Stoke, Blackpool and England fame was 50 years and five days when he played his last game. Ally was 61 years and 47 days in his final game.

After a long battle with the debilitating Alzheimer's disease, Ally died on February1, 2004. Ally's input to the St Mirren archives was fairly minimal, but his contribution to Scottish football folklore is vast.

ALLY McLEOD

IT'S against all the standards of acceptable protocol. The legions clad in light blue within the Rangers citadel that is Ibrox don't take too kindly to visiting players scoring four of the best against them. It's a behavioural no-no, but Ally McLeod, clad in the black and white of St Mirren, did just that.

The date was August 23, the year 1973, the competition being the sectionalised version of the League Cup. To be honest, by the time the six ties had been completed Rangers had virtually won the section. Indeed, the previous Saturday, Saints had suffered a 4-0 turnover at Love Street at the hands of the Govan brigade.

The mists of time have slightly clouded Ally's recollections of the game.

He said: "My memories are fairly vague. I think it was Alfie Conn who scored for Rangers in the first couple of minutes. We were up against it, but we had quite a young team at the time and that's when you have no inhibitions about playing at Ibrox.

"The home crowd generate an intimidating atmosphere and that can easily equate to a goal of a start."

Modest about his foursome at Ibrox, Ally had a series of other Man-of-the-Match type occasions, scoring four against Arbroath at Love Street, with Forfar Athletic and Cowdenbeath both on the receiving end of McLeod hat-tricks.

Bellahouston Academy was the McLeod Alma Mater, where both football and rugby were on offer. The energetic Ally was a devotee in playing both codes.

However, it was soccer that emerged as the greater attraction. And it was a pastime he successfully integrated in going straight from school to work with the Bank of Scotland.

Away from his teller duties, he found favour with Renfrew Juniors and while on duty at Western Park, Saints boss Alex Wright spotted the latent potential bringing him to Love Street for the start of the 70-71 season.

In the St Mirren line up for the first game that season, the end product wasn't destined to be a memorable jewel in the McLeod career crown,

Dundee taking the honours with a 1-0 win in the League Cup at Dens Park.

The launching of the McLeod senior scoring account saw the United half of the City of Discovery's two sides visiting St Mirren Park on April 24 1971, Saints winning 2-1 with Ally and Dave Millar on the scoresheet.

Most of Ally's playing comfort zone was spent in midfield, particularly with Southampton and Hibernian. But in his time at Love Street, he was an undoubted frontman with a more than acceptable scoring return of 60 from exactly 100 St Mirren outings.

Marking time at Love Street while awaiting permanent first-team selection, Ally also turned out for the Reserve side under the jurisdiction of Willie McLean, brother of Jim and Tommy.

Ally recalled: "Willie was an outstanding coach. I learned a lot from him and then Wilson Humphries took over. I was a part-time player until that time. Wilson then arranged for the club to go full-time and around a dozen of us were offered full-time contracts, with Gordon McQueen, Bobby McKean and Iain Munro the backbone of the team."

One further McLeod scoring gem is neatly pigeon holed in the sweet and sour category. Last game of the 70-71 season saw Celtic arrive at Love Street – the match being Ally's 10th game for Saints. Celtic needed a win to clinch the championship, while St Mirren required the points to escape relegation.

Ally scored both goals in the 2-2 draw but the Hoops retained the title and St Mirren went to source the geographical locations of the residents in Division Two. What was all the more galling was the fact that McQueen hit the bar with a late header. Had that chance gone in, St Mirren would have stayed up.

After three seasons with St Mirren it was time for Ally to move on, with Southampton at The Dell being his next port of call. Two campaigns on the south coast culminated in Eddie Turnbull bringing the sharp shooter back up north for duty with Hibernian.

Ally explained: "Alex Wright was my soccer guru during my time at Love Street. He was also the one who looked after your interests both on and off the park.

"Most of my later knowledge about the game came from Eddie Turnbull. Eddie was the complete enigma. I would rate his man management ability as 0/10 whereas his football knowledge was a clear 10/10! As a manager, he was miles ahead of his time."

The Easter Road experience saw Ally spend nine seasons in Edinburgh with a goal tally of 72 from 208 league starts. Latterly, he negotiated and signed a four-year deal on the understanding that at the end of that period he would be a free agent at the still viable playing age of 32.

The McLeod thinking saw him anticipate still being able to contribute for another two or three seasons in the Premier League, and Dundee United's Jim McLean homed in on that mature viability by offering Ally a peg at

Tannadice.

Ally said: "I drove up to Dundee on a beautiful Saturday morning full of the joys to complete all the necessary signing documentation. I then went down to Largs the next day to take my final coaching badge. Dundee United had kitted me out with all the gear, tracksuits, boots, strips, etc. I was feeling good.

"Four days later at the Inverclyde Centre, I did my knee in and, as a result, missed all pre-season training at United. I had a couple of operations – the first in a 13-year career – that weren't entirely satisfactory. Clearly I wasn't one of Jim McLean's better signings."

The transition back to the world of commerce and industry saw Ally put his former banking expertise to good use in establishing a company of dedicated Independent Financial Advisors operating in Glasgow.

A Glasgow boy born on January 1, 1951, the McLeod post-playing activities still see him operating with an eye for hitting the target.

But now this is conducted at the Glenbervie Golf Club, where you'll find the former St Mirren man battling to reduce a handicap several times a week.

GORDON McQUEEN

THERE is no doubt genes played a major part in the formation of Gordon McQueen's soccer career path. Born in Kilbirnie in June 1952, his father Tom was a goalkeeper of some standing in winning a Scottish Junior Cup medal when the local Ladeside team defeated Camelon 1-0 in 1952 at Hampden before a crowd of 72,000.

Tom eventually turned senior and had spells playing with Queen of the South and Accrington Stanley. Such parental chromosomes also saw Gordon performing between the sticks at school before realising his latent potential might be accelerated as an outfield player, and he went on to earn team selection as a left winger.

At 6'-3", his physique was tailor made for a defensive placement - a role he fulfilled with St Mirin's Boys' Guild, prior to joining Largs Thistle in July 1969 as a 17-year-old.

His emerging central defensive prowess caught the eye of the scouting fraternity and Gordon had trials with both Rangers and Liverpool.

Not surprisingly, his preference was for a future at Ibrox. But an apparent difference of opinion involving Rangers' refusal to buy him a pair of boots led to Gordon joining Paisley's finest, under Alex Wright's tutelage, in time for the 1970-71 season.

Gordon's valedictory game on the Junior circuit wasn't one of his finest. Whether the rankling from that Rangers incident played largely on his mind or not, clearly his concentration wasn't 100 per cent as Largs Thistle travelled to Beith. The local Juniors thumped the seasiders 9-0!

The initial McQueen appearance in black and white saw Saints take on Kilmarnock at Love Street in the 1970 sectionalised League Cup. It wasn't a game readily implanted in the McQueen memory banks. St Mirren lost 3-1, his playing cohorts on the day being: McGann, Murray, Connell, Munro, McLaughlin, Gilshan, Lister, Hamilton, McLeod and Pinkerton. Ronnie Hamilton was the one on target with Saints' sole strike.

Gordon's desire to improve his lot generated a plea to the now St Mirren manager Wilson Humphries to go full-time. Such a request was ironic in that St Mirren were a part-time organisation at the time.

The request was granted, though, with the sole contribution to full-time training being Gordon and Humphries keeping each other company as they pounded round the Love Street cinders.

Regretfully, Gordon's first St Mirren season ended in relegation, Saints accompanying Cowdenbeath to the lower league reaches. What was noticeable in the following Division Two season was the relative frugality in conceding goals. Only 47 counters were picked out of the Buddies' net from 36 league games.

Scouts from south of the border homed in on the St Mirren defensive stalwarts and McQueen was high on their most wanted list. His 77 appearances and six goals from virtually two seasons was an impressive contribution to his CV.

Willie Todd was now club chairman at a time when the transfer system was greatly instrumental in helping clubs survive. Saints were losing £1,000 a week and there was a realisation that an immediate financial input was a must.

Gordon was in the shop window aand Leeds United made an initial offer of £25,000.

The offer was rejected by the St Mirren board as other bids had also been received from Ipswich Town, Celtic and Tottenham Hotspur. Back came the Elland Road club with a reported increased offer of £30,000 plus a rider, giving St Mirren only 48 hours to accept.

St Mirren reluctantly accepted the deal but Todd was taught a salutary lesson - you have to build up a club so that you don't have to sell your top talent!

The lesson was further compounded when Gordon subsequently moved to Manchester United for a then British record transfer fee of £450,000.

Gordon's time at Leeds saw him enter the international arena and he gained his first Scotland cap against Belgium. He would win a total of nine caps while at Elland Road.

At club level, Gordon was on the bench when Leeds lost 1-0 to AC Milan in the 1973 European Cup Winners' Cup. His trophy cabinet was further enhanced with a League winners medal when the legendary Don Revie was in charge.

Now a cult figure at Elland Road, much vitriol was spilled when Gordon moved to Manchester United in February 1978 for that record fee.

The move added to his medal collection as he won an FA Cup badge after Brighton were eventually seen off after their 2-2 draw in the famous "Smith must score" game.

The international cap collection was expanded to 30 while at Old Trafford, with perhaps the 1977 2-1 win over England at Wembley being a major highlight. That game will be remembered for a number of reasons, firstly for a magnificent headed goal from Gordon and secondly, for the memorabilia collectors - the Wembley goalposts were roof-racked up the

M6 as match souvenirs!

The sands of playing time began to decelerate after Gordon's last cap against Wales in 1981. A coaching appointment would be an attractive proposition and he travelled to the Hong Kong club Seiko FC around 1985 as their player/coach.

A return to the UK saw the former Saint take over from Davie Whiteford as manager of Airdrie, only to be succeeded after a short period by Jimmy Bone.

Gordon's hands-on activities at club level ended after a prolonged spell with Bryan Robson at Middlesbrough as Boro's first-team coach.

Latterly a Sky Sports pundit, Gordon caught the eye of football writer Douglas Lamming, who summed up the McQueen virtues as: "A towering presence with weight to match, yet fast moving. Authority in the air was, of course, assured and he worked hard to improve an early weakness in positional play."

And all from an initial two-man full-time training regime!

JOHN McTURK

TO make your mark in the St Mirren sides immediately after the 1939-45 conflict was always a daunting proposition. It was particularly more so if your playing credentials were directed towards the full-back consortiums of the day.

St Mirren were well endowed in their defensive rearguards with Davie Lapsley, Jimmy Drinkwater, Davie Lindsay and Jimmy Mallan, to name but four of the Paisley stalwarts.

The breakthrough for John McTurk was going to be difficult. But he achieved it and his first-team debut was logged onto his CV on March 26, 1955.

The St Mirren inability to regularly find the net on league business in that 54 55 campaign had led to a meagre post-Christmas return of only one win in 11 games. The lack of a proven goal scorer being Saints' soccer nadir. The solution? Send for big Willie!

Willie Telfer, the established Love Street centre-half, was balletic with his style and fluidity and many suggested his true vocation was up front and not shoring up the Saints rearguard. He had also been known to find the net in his occasional role as a rampaging centre-forward.

Hibernian were the visitors that March day to face Paisley's finest. The reshuffled team saw Telfer lead the attack, Mallan move from left-back to centre-half and the then untried 18-year-old McTurk enjoy his first full-back appearance in black and white.

But John said: "I don't know so much about enjoying it – I was pretty nervous and apprehensive. This was the time when Hibs were cocks of the walk, due in the main to their Famous Five forward line of Gordon Smith, Bobby Johnstone, Lawrie Reilly, Eddie Turnbull and wee Willie Ormond.

"Even though I say it myself, I had a great game marking Smith. He didn't get a look in and when we came off the park Gordon wouldn't shake my hand. Jimmy Mallan saw the snub and didn't take too kindly to this lack of political correctness and, as befitting the Mallan character, wanted some retribution. Fortunately he calmed down and none came."

The team shuffle worked. The Hibees lost 4-2, McTurk received his first win bonus and Telfer scored twice.

If John's football niche was destined for a defensive beat, he had early teenage options because of a speed factor that could have earned a place as a pacy frontman.

Born on July 11, 1936, in Lugar – home of the quaintly named Junior club Boswell Thistle – John's athleticism at Cumnock Academy left him with a dual option in the school team. A more than useful sprint man, he was the Academy's 100 yards champion. And his speed was honed for the centre-forward and full-back roles at school, altering primarily to full-back in his post scholastic days.

John recalled: "I didn't stack up any Highers at school.To be honest I was more interested in football. I played a few games initially with the New Cumnock amateur side Glenpark but I wasn't signed by them. Auchinleck Thistle were my next playing port of call before I joined the Juniors with Auchinleck Talbot.

"I had a couple of trials with Partick Thistle before Dan McKinlay, the St Mirren chairman, and the manager Willie Reid persuaded me my football future lay at Love Street."

A member of the 1959 cup squad, John played in the initial second round match against Peebles Rovers at Love Street, Saints logging in a 10-0 return thanks to four from Gerry Baker, a hat-trick from Tommy Bryceland, two from Bobby Holmes and a single strike from Jim Rodger.

For the remaining games in that memorable tourney, Reid's left-back preference was "Cockles" Wilson. But had the substitute syndrome been in vogue in the late 50s, McTurk would almost certainly have been on the cup final bench.

Having faced competition at full-back at club level, John also had international rivalry at Under-23 level but failed to dislodge the resident incumbents of Falkirk's Alex Parker and Eric Caldow of Rangers.

Of all the games played in St Mirren colours by John, and there were 65 in his seven Paisley seasons, perhaps his most frustrating campaign was the 55-56 League Cup competition.

He played in three of the six sectional ties against Kilmarnock, Airdrie and Dundee then lost his place to Jimmy Mallan as Saints went all the way to the final, only to lose 2-1 to Rangers.

In consideration of all the flying wingers he had faced, John's nomination as to his most difficult adversary was undoubtedly Rangers' Willie Waddell.

NcTurk said: "Big 'Deedle' was strong, fast and determined. He was another who never shook my hand at time up. You got the impression that in the eyes of our opponents I was somewhat economical in the tackle but in all honesty I was never booked or cautioned.

"I was taken to task at a function I attended with former Rangers skipper Bobby Shearer. Bobby introduced me to Waddell. 'Do you ken this man?'

'Oh aye', said Waddell, 'He was a right dirty wee b*****d!' Not true, definitely not true."

Life after being released by Reid in 1960 saw John take a circuitous route round a number of Scottish clubs.

Spells with Queen of the South and Morton saw John win promotion to Division One with each club, before taking up playing residences with Stirling Albion and Albion Rovers.

The senior playing activities finally drew to a halt with a return to the Junior scene with Lugar Boswell Thistle and Cumnock.

A joiner to trade, John's has become something of a designer car buff in retirement. In tandem with his wife Joy, they love nothing better than taking to the open road in their Blackpool custom-built psychedelic TVR.

NORRIE McWHIRTER

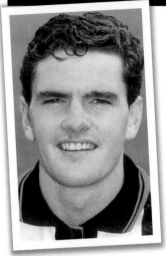

THE literary landscapes of the 16th century saw Robert Bolt portray Lord Chancellor Sir Thomas More as "A man for all seasons".

In more modern times, Norrie McWhirter was another all seasons' man.

His St Mirren debut savoured a weather cocktail with every conceivable season being shoe horned into a 90-minute stint at Pittodrie in March 1987.

Hail, sleet, snow, torrential rain and occasional sunshine blended with a North Sea gale to make ball control a lottery.

Norrie had arrived off the bench to patrol the Saints right-back beat when Tommy Wilson launched a wind assisted up and under to completely deceive Theo Snelders in the Aberdeen goal. That 1-0 win was only one of three St Mirren away wins in that memorable 86-87 season - the goal being a treasured nugget in Wilson's limited scoring collection.

Just 17 on his debut, Norrie was an early starter on the progressive football ladder. He was ahead of his time, playing in Camphill High School third year team when still only in the second grade.

It wasn't surprising that the local youth teams were falling over themselves to harness this burgeoning talent, which was cocooned in a frame Glasgow Herald columnist Willie Hunter once unkindly lampooned as being "a body with the physique of a paper clip."

As the 86-87 campaign progressed, the teenager's taste buds were perhaps marginally soured with Saints' Scottish Cup win.

Norrie explained: "I wouldn't say I was soured with the cup run. Sure, I was on the bench for the semi-final with Hearts, but I was still only 17.

"This was still the era of having only two substitutes and Ian Cameron and Tony Fitzpatrick were chosen in the final. Disappointed? Yes, but in no way disillusioned."

Norrie did make it to a cup final - he was the Saints skipper in the 1993 B& Q Cup final against Falkirk at Motherwell's Fir Park. The weather gurus conspired with the event organisers to site the Saints fans in a sleet and snow laden blizzard on the then open terracing. And the fans' discomfort was no doubt being transmitted to the players, who succumbed to a 3-0 defeat.

There have been many post-war icons serving the Buddies over the years. In a 1998 readership poll for St Mirren's Saints Club Magazine, nominations for the right centre-back slot included Jack Copland, Willie Kelly, Willie Telfer, Brian Martin, Roy Aitken and McWhirter.

Not surprisingly, the McWhirter commitment factor saw Norrie out in front, completing a back four of Davie Lapsley, Gordon McQueen and Iain Munro.

Norrie's selection for that defensive role is all the more remarkable as his vertical yardage only equates to being 5'-10". His prodigious leaping ability to generate lift off the ground to nod away a succession of cross balls was one of his main assets.

However, there were many down points. The recipient of only one Under-21 cap, Norrie came off the bench against Bulgaria in 1999. That match provided a hamstring problem for him, though.

He said: "That injury was only one of an extensive catalogue of fitness problems. I broke my leg in a game against Aberdeen Reserves, ruptured my thigh muscle and even had my ankle reconstructed."

It's only fair to say that subject to a clean bill of health, McWhirter would have had many more contributions to his trophy cabinet to supplement his five Paisley Daily Express Star Saint awards, in addition to numerous Player of the Year accolades from the St Mirren Supporters' Association.

The playing curtain finally dropped at a Reserve outing against Ayr United at Viewfield Park in Lochwinnoch.

Norrie in a customary no holds tackle damaged yet another ankle and if you are aware of the terrain of Viewfield Park, the subsequent stretcher cartage of the Saints captain from the bottom of the dip to the clubhouse, and subsequently to the RAH, was indeed a Herculean haul.

In no uncertain terms, he was told to stop playing. In truth, he should have finished playing a lot earlier as the relationship with manager Tom Hendrie wasn't the most magnanimous.

Norrie admitted: "Tom and I didn't see eye to eye. He didn't like my style and I didn't fit into his gameplan. I wish he'd told me I didn't fit in and I'd have left Love Street a lot earlier."

Fortunately, Norrie didn't leave until he had at least savoured his testimonial match against Kilmarnock on July 24, 1999 - a game enhanced with a pre-match display featuring a St Mirren Legends 11.

A full-time player since his school days, making a career switch away from football to support the needs of his wife Pamela and son Darren posed a job-seeking problem.

You could obviously take Norrie McWhirter out of football but it was a different proposition to detach the football bug from the McWhirter lifestyle.

A coaching contract with the Reid Kerr College for a year partially satisfied the crisis until former Saints colleague Campbell Money took Norrie on board as Ayr United youth coach.

The success of the Ayr youth teams spoke volumes for the Money-McWhirter double act - the combination leading to Norrie's appointment as Campbell's assistant manager.

However, severe financial constraints at the Ayrshire club saw them embark on a policy of having a part-time managerial input, a strategy in no way acceptable to Messrs Money and McWhirter.

Money reluctantly offered his services to the needs of community coaching while Norrie joined a colleague who had his own joinery business.

Intertwined throughout McWhirter's football career was one Paul Lambert. At school together, at Linwood Rangers together, they even joined St Mirren as a duo partnership.

Each was the best man at each other's wedding and if Norrie hadn't had such a regular relationship with the local medical fraternity with his prodigious injury catalogue, who would doubt that he might have at least equalled Paul's international cap haul of 40 Scotland outings.

Even when Paul moved into management the pair couldn't be separated, with Lambo taking Norrie to Livingston as his No.2 at the beginning of the 2005-06 season. Unfortunately, their stay at Almondvale barely lasted six months but whatever happens in the future, it's a fair bet that won't be their last gig together...

JUNIOR MENDES

IT was just after his new baby son had arrived in the London metropolis on September 15, 1976, that Mr Mendes headed off to register the birth. It had been the custom in the Mendes family to have new born sons christened with the father's full name.

However, it wasn't Hillyard Albert Mendes that appeared on the birth certificate, it was simply Junior!

Nippy, with a prodigious turn of pace, Junior's emerging potential was spotted by the scouting fraternity at Chelsea's Stamford Bridge and at the tender age of 13 was taken on board on the back of the Scottish equivalent of an "S" Form.

Mendes' speed was perhaps the major weapon in his armoury. Registering 11.7 seconds for the 100 metres when he was 15 gave thoughts of possibly emulating the iconic Linford Christie on the Olympic stage.

On Junior's own admission, he was more of a pacy hurdler at school than an out and out sprinter – a technique that would prove invaluable in later days as he leapt over countless legs bent on despairing tackles.

Life with Chelsea provided a positive learning base. Playing and training alongside such luminaries as Ruud Gullit, Glenn Hoddle and Graham Rix could only seriously enhance your football health.

Junior retained one major Stamford Bridge memory.

He recalled: "I was selected to play in a testimonial match against Leicester City at Filbert Street. We won and I scored!"

Further poignant memories weren't over plentiful and Junior confided his dearth of playing woes to Chelsea colleague wee John Spencer. "Spenny", whose north of the border playing affinities included Rangers and Motherwell, had the ear of old Love Street friend Kenny McDowall.

Celtic manager Tommy Burns had a need of a warm up match to test the fitness of the recently injured Jorge Cadete and Jimmy Bone obliged, setting up the bounce game at Love Street in the spring of 1996. Included in the Saints line up was the spring-heeled 19-year-old Mendes.

His pace plus the scoring of a goal in that game sent the St Mirren management team scurrying for a registration form, Junior signing on the dotted line on April 30, 1996.

Junior's first encounter with the paying Paisley faithful saw him strut his stuff in McDowall's end of season testimonial match against Morton.

His first competitive outing saw him in the Saints line up taking on Berwick Rangers in the second round of the 96-97 Coca Cola cup, His playing colleagues for that 4-0 win were: Combe, Dick(McLaughlin), Baker, McWhirter, Fenwick, Watson, Hetherston, Taylor, Gillies, Yardley (Iwelumo) and Paul Archdeacon, who came on for Junior late in the game.

To say that Mendes was a laid back character could be classified as being somewhat economic with the truth. In fact, he was so laid back he was on occasion effectively horizontal!

One such laid back embellishment took place on the 1996 Boxing Day fixture. St Mirren were on First Division duty against East Fife at their Bayview home. All three points had been secured and with little festive fayre consumed on Christmas Day the team were anxious to get back to Paisley for the Noel celebrations ASAP.

About a couple of miles outside Methil someone decided to implement a head count on the team bus. One down, who was missing? It had to be Junior!

This was effectively in the pre mobile phone era, and as such connection with the former Chelsea man was out. The directive from manager Bone on the bus was, 'Keep going – he'll get a lift'.

Sports journalist Michelle Evans takes up the story: "I was sitting in my car in the Bayview car park finishing my report for The Sun when there was a tap on the window. It was Junior. Sheepishly, he admitted he had been last as usual and had missed the team bus. Fortunately there was a silver lining for him. I gave him a lift home and managed to beat the team bus back to Paisley."

The sartorial elegance of the young Londoner was never in question. On match days it was black waistcoat, black trousers, white shirt, natty tie, black shoes – but no socks!

He admitted: "It's perhaps more of a London thing. It's the fashion you see? The players down at Chelsea and the people I know all wear these low cut loafers and they never wear socks. Sometimes I just forget to put them on when I'm all dressed up, but you've got to keep abreast of the trends!"

If there was one aspect of Mendes' play that he felt needed improvement it was his goal scoring capability. A total of 28 goals from 127 starts wasn't a disastrous return and, on reflection, every Mendes strike was tinged with quality. Two hat-tricks, against Airdrie and Clyde, gave rise to the consideration that he should be playing in a higher league.

He certainly opened the door to a higher league but in controversial circumstances. After he'd energised St Mirren into the Premier League he opted to join Dunfermline for a reported fee of £20,000 – a move that found little favour with the residents of the Love Street North Bank.

He turned out in only 15 games for the East End Park side and significantly, he wasn't in the Pars line up when they met St Mirren at Paisley in the fourth round of the 2000-01 CIS Cup.

Before leaving for Dunfermline, Junior had a short loan spell with Carlisle United. But his failure to settle in the Kingdom of Fife gave the Paisley management team the opportunity of bringing him back to Love Street to play 20 games in the 2002-03 season.

By now the wanderlust bug had manifested itself, Junior spending time at Mansfield Town from January 2003 to the 2004 close season.

A move to Huddersfield Town followed where he spent more time on the bench than in the team.

Subsequent loan periods followed with Northampton Town and Grimsby Town, as he tried to re-establish his career in his home territory.

The latter stages of the Mendes playing career might not project high quality images. But from a St Mirren standpoint, who will ever forget February 26, 2000?

Saints were on a charge for the First Division title but Raith Rovers at Stark's Park is never an easy fixture. The St Mirren quest for all three points looked like faltering with the score tied at 1-1 – cue Mendes.

A virtual last minute galloping run down the left flank, hurdling a number of despairing outstretched legs ended with Junior smashing the winner past Guido Van de Kamp in the Rovers goal.

Memories are manufactured from such occasions – Junior Mendes orchestrated more than most.

ANDY MILLEN

THERE is a minute left to play. Your team are winning 3-0. A loose ball in the opposition penalty area, one player wants to enhance the scoreline and goes in hard with a possible yellow card in the offing. Such is the enthusiastic epitome that personifies Andy Millen's playing career.

A Senior career that started on September 15, 1984, as a 19-year-old was born as an effervescent nine-year-old in the playing ranks of St Martha's Primary School in Balornock and was still going strong after more than 800 Senior first-team starts against Celtic in the autumn of 2006.

Andy's love for the game saw his defensive and midfield talents on tap at secondary school level with All Saints School in Barmulloch, marrying up that affinity in a teenage association with the much acclaimed Eastercraigs club.

Even after a full playing programme on a Saturday, his thirst for a game was never fully assuaged, efforts being generally made to infiltrate an illicit bounce game on the Sabbath.

The Eastercraigs club were a gold mine for burgeoning soccer talent and seven of Andy's team-mates found favour at Senior level. For Andy, it generated trials with Middlesbrough and Aberdeen before he was offered a peg at Newlandfield Park with Pollok Juniors.

He recalled: "I was 18 when I signed for Pollok but only spent three months with them before Alex Rennie signed me for St Johnstone. Premier Reserve football was my playing diet for a season.

"That was in 1983-84 when the Perth club were relegated. Alex Rennie kept the same team together after relegation, thinking the same squad would get them a quick return to the SPL. It didn't quite work out that way and it took another six seasons to get back up."

Andy's Senior debut saw St Johnstone scheduled to play Forfar Athletic at Station Park in the First Division.

He went on: "Making your first Senior appearance is always a big highlight. The team pool was put up on the notice board on the Thursday night. I was in and was pretty excited.

"The Perth club's chief scout was a lovely guy named Alex McLintock. He phoned me on the Saturday morning to tell me I was in the starting line up. A dream day? It should have been but was slightly tarnished by the fact we lost 4-0."

An 80-game spell with St Johnstone led to a two-year stay at Alloa Athletic, before the Millen playing anchor was securely dropped at Douglas Park, Hamilton.

Andy's time with Accies earned medal space on the Millen mantelpiece in winning the B&Q Cup in successive years, against Ayr United in 1991 and Morton a year later.

Millen said: "While the winning of these two cups was a magical experience, every player yearns to get their hands on a league winners medal. I nearly made it with Alloa in 88-89.

"The Recreation Park side were, in fact, promoted and I was lucky enough to be captain. But it was Albion Rovers who topped the league and there are no medals for the runners-up.

"Another disappointment at Hamilton happened in the 91-92 season when Partick Thistle beat us for the second promotion place by a mere two goals. That was the season when St Mirren were relegated."

These knockbacks were firmly deposited on the Millen back burner when Andy was launched onto the Premier League stage courtesy of an invitation from Tommy Burns and Billy Stark at Kilmarnock.

He explained: "I had worked with Billy Stark at Hamilton. He was a regular guy and I'm deeply grateful for the opportunity Billy and Tommy gave me to play at the top level. I spent two seasons at Rugby Park, followed by a couple of terms with Hibernian, before moving to Raith Rovers."

Andy continued to add to his club collection, enjoying a spell with Ayr United, where he had his first taste of the coaching cake.

He said: "I had great memories at Somerset Park. Hibs won the 98-99 First Division and Ayr were third. It was great to play with the likes of Andy Walker, John Davies and Gary Teale. Iain Munro and Gordon Dalziel were good enough to let me take the Reserves but any serious coaching only started when I reached Clyde."

In between Ayr United and Clyde, Andy experienced the tempestuous atmosphere of playing for Morton against Saints. It was a unique club that he joined with other such luminaries on the roll as Alex Linwood, Billy Steel, Rowan Alexander and Neil Orr, who had all played on both sides of the Renfrewshire divide.

The willingness to play anywhere has earned Andy the nom de plume of Mr Versatile. This approach has seen him fill virtually every outfield position. He was even press ganged into being a stand-in keeper when Hibs custodian Jim Leighton was sent off at Easter Road.

So what were the circumstances that led to Andy's arrival at Love Street?

He explained: "I had a phone call from Gus MacPherson telling me he was taking the St Mirren job around Christmas 2003. He asked me if I would be interested in joining him. I had no hesitation – I needed a change.

"You do serve a time and a purpose and my time was up at Clyde. They were just surviving when I joined them at the start of 2000. When I left they were top of the First Division."

An emotional man, Andy's feelings were on full view at the 2005 Bell's Cup final against Hamilton at Airdrie's Excelsior Stadium. He'd taken off his jersey at the end of that meritorious win and with tears in his eyes was searching the crowd for daughter Paula and son Ross for a congratulatory hug.

As the celebrating fans returned to their coaches, one busload saw a delighted Ross with an ear-splitting grin proudly wearing his dad's sweat-soaked jersey.

One further emotional occasion came a pre-Christmas match with St Johnstone in 2005. Andy had just registered 800 starts in senior soccer – a remarkable statistic. MacPherson made the point if there has to be a presentation, do not, repeat do not, make it on the pitch.

The advice was accepted with the full squad and directors making the presentation in the boardroom after the game.

Of particular satisfaction to Andy on that occasion was a hand written fax from his former Hibs boss Alex Miller. In the hard grind that is synonymous with the English Premiership, Alex – the assistant manager at Liverpool – had taken the time to offer his personal congratulations.

A fabricator/welder to trade, with a four-year apprenticeship and City & Guilds certification for back up, Andy is of a mind to stay in the game and body swerve any return to engineering.

Keen to tread the future coaching paths, he has his full alphabet of SFA coaching certificates and has made inroads into the full UEFA qualification.

Which brings one to the record-breaking Scottish exploits of Graeme Armstrong. Graeme, in a 15-year Senior career, cobbled 909 first-team appearances, embracing time at Stirling Albion, Berwick Rangers, Meadowbank Thistle, Stenhousemuir and Alloa .

Is there any likelihood of Andy equalling that record? The answer was an emphatic: "No!"

Andy did however establish one further record, a testament to his amazing fitness level. On August 12th 2006 against Celtic at Celtic Park with his age at 41 years and 63 days he became the oldest outfield player to compete in the SPL. Only the madcap goalkeeping antics of one John Burridge is ahead of Andy on that particular statistic.

ALISTAIR MILLER

IMMEDIATELY after the Second World War, many would argue the point that The Boys' Brigade's Glasgow Battalion had the largest number of youth leagues in the country. It was considered the career path of many an aspiring player that an a.m. outing for their school to be followed by a p.m. appearance with their BB Company was the way to soccer success.

Alistair Miller was one who set out on this particular walkway. A pupil at Bellahouston Academy, his scholastic soccer was welded to a playing affinity with the 129th Glasgow Company – a BB unit who can also boast Alex Ferguson as an ex-member.

Those with a BB heritage would claim that the BB method never leaves you. Alistair was one who was deeply entrenched in the Sure & Stedfast movement and gave many hours in return in his later years as an officer with the 1st Elderslie Company.

Willie Ralston, the BB Captain of that 129th Company, was one of those dyed in the wool Third Lanark supporters. Keen to do the Cathkin club a favour, he recommended the Miller inside forward talents to Hi-Hi manager Alex Ritchie, with Alistair putting pen to paper for the Crosshill club in 1953.

Playing Third Lanark icons of the time were the robust but fair Matt Balunas, the leggy Ally McLeod– later of St Mirren and Scotland fame – and the diminutive pocket dynamo Harry Mooney.

Miller's one regret in arriving at Cathkin Park was never managing to play alongside the elegant wee Jimmy Mason. Mason, a brush salesman whose swivel hip routines sent many an adversary careering off in the wrong direction, had retired the previous year.

A mandatory perquisite of these times demanded the fit, the hale and the hearty devote a couple of one's formative years in support of Queen and Country. The Royal Scots took a liking to our Mr Miller, offering him employment in a khaki dress mode in support of the country's National Service needs.

Jimmy Millar of Rangers striking fame, the aforementioned McLeod and Partick Thistle's strong-going wing half Davie Mathers were Miller contemporaries enjoying those military manoeuvres.

Demobilisation and a return to football's civvy street brought Alistair into conflict with Bill Hiddlestone – the Third Lanark chairman generally credited with the Cathkin club's financial downfall.

A free transfer emerged from their ensuing tete-a-tete, with Alistair suffering minimal withdrawal symptoms on learning that St Mirren boss Willie Reid wanted to acquire the his skills for a certain club in Paisley. He duly signed on at Love Street on August 18, 1957.

Halcyon days for Alistair in a black and white strip were prominent on St Mirren's 1958-59 Scottish Cup run. Relatively clear cut wins over Peebles Rovers, Motherwell and Dunfermline in the early rounds preceded Celtic in the semis. But a Celtic side with the redoubtable Bobby Evans, the Irish blarney of Bertie Peacock, plus the strong going Johnny Divers up front seemed a particularly insurmountable hurdle.

It wasn't. This Saints team were destined to be no pushovers, taking the Hoops to the cleaners in knocking in four goals without reply – three of them before the break! Miller, from his left wing beat, scored two of them.

Aberdeen in the final, with future Saints boss Jim Clunie in the heart of the Dons defence, provided the opportunity to avenge that fortuitous 1955 League Cup final result.

The record books will highlight it was Miller who netted the third and clinching goal in St Mirren's well merited 3-1 win over the Pittodrie men.

As Alistair remembered: "It wasn't the greatest of goals but in terms of importance, possibly the best.

"The ball arrived in front of the Aberdeen goal where an almighty stramash ensued. Big Jim Clunie, keeper Fred Martin and wee Tommy Gemmell were all involved. The ball broke across the face of the goal and all I had to do was tap it over the line."

For those who know him, Alistair was never one for the single word, with his phraseology being generally thought provoking in the extreme. Such verbal fluency found him in trouble in the following season's Scottish Cup run.

Saints had drawn Celtic in the second round. A 1-1 draw at Love Street preceded a 4-4 replay at Celtic Park – a result all the more galling considering St Mirren were 4-2 ahead at one point. Another draw, another replay, with a flip of a coin taking the second replay back to Parkhead.

The legendary Jack Mowatt was in charge of the refereeing proceedings and in Miller's judgment was determined there would be no further replays!

He said: "All of a sudden the linesman had his flag up. Mowatt beckoned me over. 'Another word out of you and you're off'. Honestly, I never opened my mouth and Jack Mowatt got his wish – we lost 5-2."

After five seasons in black and white and 153 appearances yielding 30 goals, pastures new beckoned. Willie Reid, who had moved on to manage Norwich City, remembered the precocious Miller talents in Paisley and Alistair moved to Carrow Road in May 1962.

A three-year stint with the Canaries saw Miller match his skills against England's best.

One outstanding memory was Stoke City arrived at Carrow Road with a forward line reading Matthews, McIlroy, Mudie, Violet and Ratcliffe.

The star-studded line up must have suffered from travel sickness, though – they lost 5-0.

John Charles, on his return from Juventus to Cardiff City, was another worthy adversary, as was Jimmy Dickinson at Portsmouth and Eddie McCreadie, the Glasgow born full-back at Chelsea.

North of the border, Hearts' Terrible Trio of Conn, Bauld and Wardhaugh, the Ancell Babes at Motherwell and the Famous Five at Easter Road were other prime opposition candidates of note.

A return to the Caledonian climes saw the Miller expertise being paraded at Berwick Rangers, then at Dumbarton, before the boots were finally jettisoned after a short spell with Hamilton.

Part time on his return to Scotland, Alistair's commercial interest centred round a garaging business, before he entered the catering industry, supplying sustenance to the schools and the teaching profession.

A family man, Alistair and his wife Jean had three daughters in Karen, Gillian and Amanda.

Away from masterminding the family fortunes, the Miller golf handicap was constantly under review at the Old Ranfurly course, while the winter months provided competitive solace with the roaring game at the Greenacres Ice Rink.

Never one to catch the selectorial eye, Alistair Miller was the complete professional journeyman with those 1959 Scottish Cup successes deeply impinged on many ageing Paisley memory banks.

ARTHUR MILNE

THE measurement of a player's goal-getting ability is invariably assessed by comparing goals scored against appearances made. A goal every game is dreamland territory. A goal averaging out to every second game played slots one into the super striker category. A goal every third game is not just more realistic, it too is an impressive return.

Arthur Milne, in his immediate post-wartime with St Mirren, is neatly pigeon-holed into the latter category, with 33 goals from 97 black and white appearances.

With "Li'l Abner" the charismatic comic character of the day, it wasn't surprising that Milne's diminutive stature soon had the fans fondly referring to him as "Li'l Arthur".

Small he might have been, but stocky and competitive with it. His other prominent physical feature was undoubtedly his centre parting, conceivably one of the widest in the football business!

Born in Brechin in 1915, Arthur's tentative football steps were taken with the local Juvenile side Brechin Victoria. Invited down to Chester for trials, he was more successful on his return to Scotland with his hometown team Brechin City. The run out became a run in as Dundee United took him on board for the 1934-35 season.

A barrowload of goals were then logged onto his Tannadice CV in his spell with the Tangerines, although in those days the sartorial elegance of the home garb was black and white. News of the Milne striking expertise was such that he was soon invited down to Merseyside for trials with Liverpool.

The time was now 1936-37 and Arthur was the central figure in an amazing registration fiasco. Both Dundee United and Liverpool had failed to place him on their retained lists, which left Arthur as a free agent.

Hibernian manager Willie McCartney was the first to recognise the signing opportunity created by the registration faux pas, taking the striker to Easter Road in time for the 37-38 season.

Milne – a player with a prolific scoring record – was another whose football career suffered thanks to the Second World War. He only played three post-war matches for Hibs and became somewhat disenchanted at being displaced as the Hibees' regular centre-forward.

Arthur made his displeasure known and posted a request for a transfer.

Saints manager Bobby Rankin had a void to fill with the departure of that scoring legend Alex Linwood to Middlesbrough. Milne would seem to be a ready replacement and an approach to Hibs for his transfer was made on September 9, 1946.

Hibernian wanted £2,000 to seal the deal but the sweet-talking Mr Rankin secured his man for £1650 – the figure being reported as approximately one third of the fee received from Middlesbrough from the Linwood move.

Ironically, Arthur's playing comfort zone wasn't satisfied in his St Mirren debut game – his first appearance saw him operating on the left wing.

Rangers at Ibrox on league business is never an easy fixture and his colleagues on that debut day – September 14, – 1946 were Newlands, Telfer, Lindsay, Smith, Drinkwater, Scott, Crowe, Stenhouse, Aikman and McLaren, who all succumbed to a 4-0 defeat.

In the latter stages of that game, Arthur did take over from the former Hearts centre Archie Aikman, the Press extolling great virtue to the change.

Arthur didn't do much better in his second outing for Saints. He was back at Ibrox, this time in a League Cup match, and again lost 4-0. But on this occasion he started and finished as the Saints frontman.

The best Milne scoring run occurred in the 1948 Scottish Cup. Two against Shawfield Amateurs in the first round and one against East Stirling in the next round was followed by a couple against Clyde in the third round, with all three ties being played at Love Street.

However, the run was terminated at the quarter-final stage, Milne's former club Hibs putting paid to any St Mirren thoughts of cup glory with a 3-1 success.

Arthur was given a free transfer at the end of the 49-50 season and he went on to play a number of games for Coleraine in the Irish League.

He died in Edinburgh in May 1997.

CAMPBELL MONEY

TO be given a nickname by your team-mates generally signifies acceptance of your playing credentials. The degree of insult in arriving at the nom-de-plume christening usually relates to some outstanding likeness or physical characteristic.

In Campbell Money's case, his striking resemblance to Officer Dibble in Hanna-Barbera's Top Cat cartoon series earned him instant recognition - the endearment "Dibble" following him throughout his playing, coaching and managerial career.

Campbell was an Alex Ferguson signing, with the ink of his signature drying out on the recruitment form on June 8, 1978. Campbell was only at Love Street for a month and disclaimed any responsibility when Ferguson was sensationally presented with his P45, to be succeeded by Jim Clunie.

The Money debut game for Saints is painfully remembered by the then young keeper.

He said: "I remember it well. It was a pre-season friendly against Southampton at Love Street and we drew 1-1. In particular, I remember having gathered the ball and the Southampton frontmen had turned their backs on me expecting a punt up field.

I rolled the ball out to one of our defenders. It was short. Ted McDougall must have had eyes in the back of his head. His predatory instincts told him here was a possible scoring chance and I had to dive to smother the ball. But he didn't hold back in making contact and I tell you it was painful!"

Performing for his school saw Campbell only occasionally in goal, as playing in midfield generated a comfort zone with greater satisfaction and involvement in the game. Such were the playing options on offer at the Ayrshire boys' clubs of Whittlets and Carrick Colts.

Campbell didn't play in goal on a regular basis until he was 15. And it was Dailly Amateurs, operating in the South Ayrshire Amateur Leagues, who conditioned the transition from midfield to last line of defence. Campbell then joined St Mirren a few weeks before his 18th birthday.

At Love Street, he went on to generate almost 400 St Mirren outings - 392 to be precise - with the undoubted highlight being that 1987 Scottish Cup final against Dundee United.

As Campbell reminisced: "Even if I'd played in a full international for Scotland, it wouldn't have surpassed the feeling of winning that cup. The 50,000-plus crowd was the biggest I'd ever played in front of."

You won't find a full cap in Campbell's locker, but he did play for the national Under-21 squad on three occasions, his membership of the team being as a permitted over age player. On one occasion, he was presented with the captaincy and a 1-1 with the Norwegians in Scandinavia followed.

Five outings with the Scotland Youth team plus one "B" international cap completes the Money honours List.

A further cup final in a playing capacity came his way in December '93. The League Challenge Cup - then in its infancy and known as the B & Q Cup - featured St Mirren and Falkirk at Fir Park in conditions to test the hardiest, with torrential rain interspersed with driving sleet and snow.

The Motherwell ground was then undeveloped and the Saints fans apportioned the open terracing. Needless to say, many returned to Paisley suffering from the early throes of acute pneumonia, not to mention severe depression after a 3-0 defeat.

Goalkeepers generally don't feature on the scoring charts but Campbell did his best to repair that statistic. St Mirren were drawn to face Brechin City at Glebe Park in a second round League Cup tie in 1991. After extra-time and with neither team able to snatch a winner, the dreaded penalty shootout reared its ugly head. Campbell was on hand to crack home one of the spot-kicks to give the Buddies a 5-4 passage into the next round.

Money's thirst for goals went on to produce two further succcesfull penalties in the 92-93 season - the first coming against Cowdenbeath on December 2, 1992, the same match that Ricky Gillies made his senior scoring debut.

They say old goalkeepers never die, they just, well... there are many options to complete that piece of custodial nonsense.

In Campbell's case, an opening into coaching materialised when Jimmy Bone appointed both Kenny McDowall and Campbell as joint St Mirren coaches during the 95-96 season.

A managerial vacancy at Stranraer subsequently came on the market and Money topped the applicants' list at Stair Park, registering himself as player-manager for the start of the next campaign.

For a player who played under eight St Mirren bosses, that considerable experience was about to face the litmus test.

The integrity factor shone brightly in Campbell's assessment of his early Stair Park performances.

He said: "The real problem was combining playing and managing. It might have been different if I'd only been coaching. And although I never played a first-team game for Stranraer, playing in the Reserves I felt with my performances I wasn't contributing enough. I certainly wasn't offering enough to be considered for a first-team berth. I felt I had to concentrate on one or the other and obviously the management side came first."

But very well did he perform from the dugout. In his first full season. the League Challenge Cup, arguably Stranraer's first ever piece of national silverware, was won and promotion to the First Division arriving the following year.

Perhaps the greatest Money managerial achievement was the selling of central defender Mark Campbell for a considerable transfer fee to Ayr United.

It was that ability to discover, rear, develop and produce top quality players that sent Ayr United on a recruitment quest down the A77 to head hunt the Stranraer manager to front line the Somerset Park youth policy.

A continuation of the Money success followed him to the Ayrshire club. Following the 98-99 season, United featured as winners or runners up over a three season period in the Reserve League West. But what was more encouraging for the Honest Men was the success of their Under-18 youth side in winning back-to-back championships over the same period.

With financial constraints shackling clubs in funding big money transfer deals, a successful youth policy with guys like Campbell Money at the helm is clearly the way of future advancement.

That way forward became a major highway in the Money career when he succeeded Gordon Dalziel as United manager during the 2002-03 season.

Although he parted company with Ayr United, active football is a drug for many – Campbell Money more than most. He was involved for a while with community coaching but that didn't assuage his football thirst. A double headed assignment fulfilled the need with Campbell operating as Head of Youth Development with Stenhousemuir during the working week and at the weekends managing the fortunes on the Junior scene with Cumnock.

IAIN MUNRO

JOB satisfaction in a football environment is not long term, it only exists on a week to week basis.

These prophetic words from Iain Munro oversaw a playing career of nomadic proportions followed by a taste of management that was, on occasion, sweet and sour in the extreme.

The youngest in a family of four, with three sisters to effectively mother him, the precocious teenager with considerable talent took the well worn path to Drumchapel Amateurs, where that doyen in the art of discovering football prodigies, the venerable Douglas Smith, took Iain under his almost paternal wing.

Success was instant, with Iain an integral cog in the winning of the 1968 Scottish Under-18 cup, the colours of Bellfield Boys' Club being lowered on the back of a 5-3 scoreline.

Iain had previously turned down the possibility of a billet at Coventry City but parental guidance advised the need for further academic attainment before embarking on a rollercoaster soccer ride.

Munro said: "Drumchapel Amateurs were probably the best organised and had the best facilities of any youth team around at the time. If you failed to get a foot on the senior soccer ladder with The Drum, there was clearly a deficiency in your soccer make up.

"That Under-18 final was played at Love Street and wee Bobby Bell, who was the St Mirren physio, saw me play. The result was an invitation to meet Saints manager Alex Wright. At that meeting in 1968 I signed a provisional form.

"The following year I had a cartilage removed and didn't sign professionally for St Mirren until December 1969."

Nostalgic memories of senior debuts can be embellished with derring deeds of fabulous goals, goal line clearances and of possible goalkeeping athleticism. In Iain Munro's case, the theatre was biased more to a pantomime plot.

He explained: "It was a 1970 Ne'erday holiday match against Airdrie at Love Street. I came off the bench for about the last five minutes, got one kick at the ball and received in return a clutch of kicks up the backside from Derek Whiteford & Co!"

A managerial chain reaction then set in, with Wilson Humphries succeeding Wright and spending some 15 months in charge before the once perky Tommy Bryceland took over.

Humphries had moved eastwards to take up a coaching post at Easter Road, his knowledge and recommendation as to Munro's capability being enough to secure Iain a peg with Hibernian.

After a three-year spell with the Hibees, Jock Wallace arrived on the scene to take centre stage in the Munro profile. His Ibrox need was to recruit a left winger. Munro apparently fitted the bill ,with Ally Scott and Graham Fyffe forsaking Rangers as the make weight pairing in the transfer deal.

The Rangers experience raised doubts as to the exactitude of the Munro playing comfort zone.

The player recalled: "Jock Wallace tried to make me an out and out outside left. If you play with Hibs and St Mirren, you play a little deeper. With Rangers or Celtic you're a lot further forward. It was then I realised I wasn't a left winger. I didn't have the pace, I was simply a committed up and down runner."

Failure to establish himself in Wallace's playing jigsaw saw Iain move back to St Mirren in November 1977, with his halcyon days on the senior circuit arguably spent during his second stint at St Mirren. Topping the memorabilia listings were the acquisition of seven full Scottish international caps which, in tandem with Billy Thomson, makes him St Mirren's most capped player.

Iain said: "My first cap was against Argentina at Hampden. That was just a year after the 1978 Argentina World Cup debacle. That was a tremendous experience for me to play against the likes of Maradona. He was so strong and had great pace married to some fantastic skills."

If any examples of the impecunious nature of football finance were required, they arrived when Iain left St Mirren for Stoke City in October 1980. Saints had signed him from Rangers for £25,000 but Stoke manager Alan Durban forked out £160,000 to take him to the Victoria Ground - a nice little earner for St Mirren!

Further wanderlust then took over in establishing sporadic stopovers at Sunderland, Dundee United and again at Easter Road. Season 1985-86 finally confirmed the football adage that recovery from injury in later life becomes exceedingly long term.

Iain said: "At the start of that season I had a severe knee injury, a culmination of all the playing wear and tear. Some folk would suggest it was all those years of standing on my right peg! A specialist told me I was finished and if I didn't haul down the curtains I could be destined for a future in a wheelchair."

Some scholastic back up to a football career had been conceived with a teacher training course at Jordanhill College's School of Physical Education. Under the tutelage of the redoubtable Hugh "Bomber" Brown, Iain had graduated as a PE teacher - but his thirst for active soccer participation hadn't been fully assuaged.

A move to management is a progression in the game and Iain took up a coaching appointment with Jim Leishman's Dunfermline ide in 1987.

Incremental steps to assistant manager and then joint manager followed. But a fall out with Leishman was well chronicled and Iain moved on to take charge at Dundee in October 1991.

Life in the Dens Park hotseat was minimal as an appointment at Hamilton Academical was more geographically acceptable in commuting from his Uddingston home.

It was at Douglas Park that the realism of management life came home to roost.

Munro said: "After taking the morning training, I'd finish at lunchtime, then perhaps drive down to say Birmingham to take in a game. I'd be back home between one and two in the morning then up in time to take the next day's training. All in all you ended chasing your tail!"

A further step in the Munro management progression followed with the term ignominious being an appropriate classification.

In a cost-cutting exercise at the start of the 1996-97 campaign, St Mirren dispensed with the services of coach Kenny McDowall. So incensed was manager Jimmy Bone with the decision that he immediately resigned in protest.

In stepped Munro on Monday, September 9, to take up the challenge in a deal brokered by former TV commentator and Celtic chief executive Jock Brown.

What seemed an acceptable return for the St Mirren prodigal was torn to shreds 24 hours later as the deal hit the terminal buffers, much to the embarrassment of the St Mirren board.

A Munro move to Ayr United followed with a series of administrative tasks fulfilled under Gordon Dalziel's jurisdiction.

Once the Somerset Park routines had been concluded, Iain returned to teaching with his last visit to St Mirren Park being to record a TV interview in support of his first football mentor - Drumchapel's Douglas Smith.

CAMMY MURRAY

HIS mum would call him Cameron and his school teachers addressed him likewise. But to all in his immediate football fraternity. he was just plain "Cammy".

Born in Blantyre and generally brought up in the Clyde Valley, Cammy Murray's early days were spent on the hoof. His father was a policeman and the the daily dustings with those of a villainous disposition necessitated the setting up of a number of homes in the Lanarkshire area.

Once the Larkhall homestead had been established, the 14-year-old youngster turned out for the local Larkhall Strollers, then his brother stepped in.

Cammy explained: "My brother George had signed for Aberdeen and it was through his auspices that I managed to get a trial with Drumchapel Amateurs.

"They were a marvellous side and in the team that I played in, 10 of the 11 turned senior. These included Alex Willoughby, Jim Forrest and Martin Ferguson, Alex's brother."

Willie Reid was the Saints manager who recognised the Murray potential and signed him as a possible successor to Rab Stewart and Red Campbell.

Initially a centre-half, Cammy couldn't oust Jim Clunie from his residence in the central defensive department, with his conversion to a full-back role being the acceptable alternative.

Ironically, Cammy never played under the Reid jurisdiction as Bobby Flavell took over. Cammy went on to out see the management overtures of Jackie Cox, Doug Millward, Alex Wright, Wilson Humphries and Tommy Bryceland, before financial necessity reared its ugly head.

He recalled: "Tommy Bryceland gave me a free transfer and I was really upset. I had been 10 years at Love Street and played nearly 500 games for the club. I thought I was at least worth a testimonial but they said they had no money. However, that didn't stop them going out to sign Ian Ure from Manchester United. I was more than a bit peeved at that turn of events."

Cammy's first outing in a St Mirren jersey for the reserve side saw him compete alongside some illustrious Love Street icons, with former Hearts and Kilmarnock man Jimmy Brown in goal, Willie Fernie, Albert

Henderson, Tommy Bryceland and Tommy Gemmell all contributing in the second string line up.

His first-team debut was altogether a much less conspicuous occasion.

Cammy said: "My first ever game was in the Renfrewshire Cup against Morton at Cappielow and I got an absolute roasting. Their left wing triangle of Eddie O'Hara, Dougie Cowie and Archie Robertson were three superb players. I never managed a kick at the ball!"

Murray did achieve maturity and the likes of John Hughes and Bobby Lennox of Celtic and Rangers' Willie Johnston all failed to subsequently outwit the Saints full-back.

If the Murray trophy cabinet isn't the most voluminous in housing sporting mementoes, pride of place will surely go to the medal Cammy gained for Saints in their promotion-winning season of 1967-68.

Some 26 appearances plus one substitute outing, together with a three-goal contribution, all combine to endorse the value of that much treasured gong.

Being in the right place at the right time is a prime perquisite for international recognition. Capped for the Scotland Under-18 youth squad - they lost 4-2 to England at Peterborough - and a stand by replacement for the Scottish League, Cammy's cap collection was extremely threadbare. He was obviously in the wrong place at the required time, as it was Dundee's tow-haired Alex Hamilton who regularly caught the selectorial right-back eye.

The fitness fanatic that was Roger Hynd took Cammy to Motherwell after the termination of his Paisley playing days, and his time at Fir Park preceded a five-year spell at Arbroath.

As Cammy remarked: "Playing at Gayfield meant a fair bit of travelling but it was like going on your holidays every fortnight."

Support away from football in supplying the necessities of life for his wife Ray and sons Alan and Stewart revolved around a market gardening business in the Clyde Valley, with the picturesque Murray abode over looking the River Clyde at Kirkfieldbank. However, life as a market gardener can seriously damage your football health.

He said: "I was in the business for 11 years but it was really hard going and it didn't help the football cause. I used to get up between four and five in the morning, load the van for market and then head for training.

Clyde Valley growing is a dying industry and I could see me eventually working away for nothing."

If such a lifestyle was never going to provide complete job satisfaction - despite the attractions of the salmon fishing rights at the bottom of the garden - Cammy was made of sterner stuff. He had amassed a number of Highers from his school days and went on to take additional Highers as a mature student at Motherwell Technical College.

His academic success provided an entrance to the Scottish School of Physical Education at Jordanhill College, with a subsequent educational appointment as a PE teacher being attained at Lanark High School.

It was fortunate the Murray soccer prowess gleaned over a 16-year career wasn't totally binned, as Tommy McLean, then masterminding Motherwell's fortunes in the First Division, took Cammy on board at Fir Park.

Murray said: "They had a few part-timers and I was involved with them. I also helped out with the youth side. I ran the rule over potential new players and did match reports for Tommy.

"When Motherwell were promoted to the Premier League, the reserve matches were on a Saturday, so I was asked to take the reserve side. That was my remit for the next nine years."

Ask Cammy for a career highlight and he'll veer away from a personal playing occasion.

He said: "Top of the heap was being involved with Motherwell when they won the Scottish Cup in 1991. I remember Tom Wharton telling me the highlight of his career was being on the same pitch as Pele. That's how I felt about that cup campaign.

"I was even given time off from my school duties to be involved in the cup build up. It was quite simply a memorable showcase occasion for me."

The physical wellbeing of local Lanarkshire youth continued in the capable hands of the former St Mirren man - although the youngsters at Lanark Grammar went on to be groomed not only in the practical subtleties of football, but also in coming to terms with a host of other sporting spheroids.

HUGH MURRAY

IT was one of those football evenings at the Glynhill Hotel. The gastronomic delights of the St Mirren Annual Dinner were peppered with numerous soccer anecdotes, some with fictional origins, others being less fanciful and more factual.

Featuring in the latter category was a report from Stewart Gilmour, in his pre club chairman days, of St Mirren heroics at the summer Colmschate Youth Tournament in Holland. Emanating from the Dutch delights, he eulogised at length on the outstanding potential of one Hugh Murray.

The skill factors of the young midfielder had to be harnessed to the St Mirren cause – they eventually were, but not before Master Murray had made the rounds of the Lanarkshire Youth Clubs.

A pupil at St Augustine's Primary School in Coatbridge, he graduated to Boys' Guild football before heading for Fir Park and the Motherwell Boys' Club.

Interspersed while wearing the claret and amber of the then Steelmen, Hugh spent some time with his secondary school mates in furthering the ambitions of the local Wolves Boys' Club.

Shuggie explained: "I spent two to three years at Motherwell with the St Mirren Youth Development Officer Joe Hughes watching me on a regular basis. I was invited down to Sunderland for a week's trial and I also trained with Hearts and St Mirren before being asked to go down to Chelsea. However, I didn't make it to Stamford Bridge as it clashed with a family holiday."

It was the Coatbridge connection that sealed Hugh's St Mirren destiny.

He went on: "My dad knew Joe Hughes, who also lived in the town. The thought of getting an early chance with St Mirren was a big incentive as Ricky Gillies, Brian Hetherston and Gary McGrotty had all received early debuts so I signed for Tony Fitzpatrick in January 1997. Mind you, the chance of a free lift with Joe to Paisley each day for training was perhaps the clinching feature."

Hugh's tentative start to the senior game came at Love Street as an 18-year-old when he came off the bench to face East Fife in the third last game of the 96-97 season. Saints won 1-0 thanks to a Jim Dick goal.

He had to wait for the opening league fixture of the following season for his full debut. St Mirren were at Broadwood tackling the nomadic Airdrieonians side, the 3-1 scoreline in Saints' favour being particularly memorable for a superb Junior Mendes hat-trick.

International recognition came at Under-16 level in the European championship when both Hugh and Gavin Galloway travelled to meet both Finland and Iceland.

Under-18 honours evaded the industrious midfielder but Under-21 possibilities now beckoned.

Capped in the millennium year against France, Northern Ireland and Wales, Hugh was also earmarked for a venture to face Bosnia Herzegovina and Estonia. Saints, however, were on track to land the First Division title and manager Tom Hendrie was not a happy chappie at the thought of losing his midfield kingpin for an important league encounter.

Scotland manager Craig Brown and Under-21 boss Alex Smith were verbally bludgeoned into releasing Hugh from these Under-21 duties. It was conceded it was unlikely he would play so he was released and the Coatbridge man rattled in a couple of crackers against Airdrie at Love Street.

While these goals were important, nothing compared with the scoring drama at Stirling Albion's Forthbank ground on May 2, 1998. The relegation equation was simple – the side that lost would most likely be relegated. As it turned out, Saints stayed up thanks to a stunning Murray belter that zoomed into the postage stamp top corner to ease the pressure on Fitzpatrick and Joe Hughes.

However, that goal doesn't head the pecking order of momentous Murray strikes. Top of the heap came in an 8-0 thrashing of Clydebank at Love Street, when a couple of balancing headers on the run preceded a cracker of a drive that almost burst the net.

Always up for a laugh and a modicum of mischief, it was reported the Saints team were unhappy with their strips – they tended to itch. The solution? Have the St Mirren black and white stripes painted directly onto your torso. The ploy involving Hugh and Steven McGarry only became clear with a glance at the date. It was April 1.

The penultimate game of the 1999-2000 campaign, a defeat of Raith Rovers at Love Street to land the First Division silverware, looms largely in Hugh Murray's memory banks.

He said I: "It was a magical experience. I was only 20 at the time and would like to experience it again just to take it all in."

So when did the possibility of promotion enter the players' minds?

Shuggie added: "It was as early as pre-season. We were being tipped as second favourites for relegation, which really stirred up the hackles. We started well with pre-season wins over Blackpool and Rangers and after the 6-0 win at Kirkcaldy we were all quietly confident of doing well."

There is a well stocked mantelpiece of trophies in the Murray homestead. That promotion-winning medal and a Bell's Challenge Cup gong are surrounded by the St Mirren Young Player of the Year in 1998 and the Bell's First Division Player of the Month for September 1999, with the attendant gallon bottle of whisky still being under lock and key at his mum's home.

The Match Magazine readers voted him as the First Division Player of the Year in 1999-2000 and there lies a tale.

Hugh said: "The award was a bit of a mix up. The trophy was presented to me by the St Mirren Programme Editor but when I looked at the inscription on the award it was Jackie McNamara's award for his SPL efforts that year. We eventually managed to sort it out and make the exchange."

Never categorise Hugh Murray as a ladies' man but he does have the family backing of three sisters and his mum Louisa. Louisa is never best pleased when the Paisley fraternity refer to her favourite son as Shuggie.

She might not be particularly pleased with the nickname but she would be a proud lady when a local pundit in the main stand pronounced, When Shuggie Murray plays well, St Mirren play well'.

That pride factor has been further enhanced when, in tandem with Fitzpatrick, Campbell Money and Gillies, Hugh was one of the first inductees to the newly established St Mirren Hall of Fame.

One further record is a major contribution to the Murray career profile. He is the only St Mirren player ever to win two League Championship medals thanks to his title-winning efforts in 2000 and 2006.

At the start of the 2006-07 season and in no doubt in recognition of his sterling St Mirren service Hugh was granted a Testimonial Year.

JACKIE NEILSON

A CONSIDERABLE number of UK players have temporarily emigrated in the past to Italy in search of footballing fame. The financial inducements of Serie A have enticed such as Dennis Law, Graeme Souness, Paul Gascoigne and John Charles to earn a slice of football's good life in pasta land.

Jackie Neilson could have been one such emigrant. In fact, he could have been number one!

Just when his football career was about to take off, having served a valued apprenticeship which embraced Newbattle School, Newtongrange Bluebell and the renowned Mid Lothian Junior side Newtongrange Star, the two-year call to arms in the shape of National Service with the army kicked in.

While many derided the value of military service, it was the making of Jackie Neilson.

He spent a year stationed in Gibraltar before being posted to Italy. There his football ability earned him daily training sessions and regular outings with the British Army team.

The Neilson prowess certainly caught the eye of those with football know how and he was offered £3,500 to stay and play in Italy. Seriously big money in the immediate post-war days.

A bout of Scottish stubbornness then took over. Delighted at having such recognition thrust upon him, Jackie's innermost feelings demanded that he take up the challenge of playing senior soccer in Scotland.

Even then the Italian interest wasn't assuaged. Demobbed at Aldershot, the Italian agents followed him home to the coal-mining domain of Newtongrange but failed to effect any modification to the Neilson career path.

Hindsight is a precise science and looking back at those early days Jackie might just harbour a thought that perhaps he might have made a mistake in opting for the Scottish fayre.

St Mirren manager Bobby Rankine knew all about the Neilson footballing faculties. Playing as a right-back at school, retaining that berth at Newtongrange Star, his British Army position was as an inside right. It was

Rankine who converted the Neilson talents into prime wing half material.

The mists of time added to a touch of romance clouds the exact details of the Neilson St Mirren debut. He said: "I can't remember much about it, other than I remember getting married on the Friday and playing Falkirk in Paisley the following day."

In Jackie's estimation, Rankine was a players' man.

He explained: "Bobby would take time off to come through to Newtongrange just to see my mother. He would even come over occasionally to see me playing tennis.

"I always had a soft spot for the Hearts because two of my brothers played for them and was always anxious to find out how they'd got on. Bobby used to provide the information. Big Willie Telfer and I would be soaking in the post-match bath when Bobby would come over. Willie was completely confused with the Rankine tic-tac. It was simple - thumbs up they'd won, thumbs down meant gloom and doom down Gorgie way."

By virtue of taking home a winner's medal from the 1959 Scottish Cup, it was anticipated that match against Aberdeen would figure prominently in the Neilson nostalgia ratings.

He said: "The final was a great occasion with a smashing atmosphere but to be truthful, I got more pleasure from the semi-final when we beat Celtic 4-0. The Parkhead manager Jimmy McGrory came into our dressing room after the game and congratulated us. He told us that was the finest display of football he'd seen in years.

"I was extremely lucky to play with a lot of good players who never won a medal with St Mirren, so my heart goes out to the likes of Willie Telfer and Bobby Holmes."

Married life for Jackie saw him move west to Paisley. When Willie Cunningham was transferred to Leicester City, Jackie fell heir to the Cunningham abode and went full-time for two years.

One aspect about the Neilson character, he calls a spade a spade and is never short on honesty.

He admitted: "Being full-time with St Mirren was a farce. You had too much time on your hands. Your mind wasn't fully occupied so I ditched the so-called full-time structure and got a job in the office with Pressed Steel. I stayed with them until I left St Mirren and went back to Newtongrange."

They say you can take the man out of football but find it mission impossible in taking football out of the man. Such was the Neilson dilemma.

No longer a player, he yearned for some hands-on work and landed a two-year contract to coach in South Africa.

He failed to last the pace, didn't take to either the climate or the standard of football on offer and returned to his Midlothian roots after only a year to take on the responsibilities of an office manager.

Never fortunate enough to be offered a full Scotland cap, he did play in three Scotland B internationals, all against England. Jackie also turned out on four occasions on Inter League duty.

Wing halfs were not normally prone to fire in a multitude of goals. Occasionally they were on offer and Jackie's favourite was one against Celtic.

He recalled: "It was reminiscent of a Barnes Wallis production. We were playing Celtic and beat them 6-3. The luckless Frank Haffey was in the Parkhead goal and I hit a drive from about 25-yards. It was like the Dambusters scenario. Haffey dived and the ball bounced and bounced and eventually bounced over him. It was pure theatre."

A one club man, Jackie spent 12 seasons with St Mirren and is in no doubt as to the playing differences between his day and the current era.

He said: "We had more ability. They might be fitter nowadays but it all depends on yourself. If I were playing today, I would walk through a game. Mental dedication is what it's all about and I had it!"

MALCOLM NEWLANDS

NOT far from downtown Dumfries stands what was at one time the mining village of Allanton. Perhaps not too many luminaries have emanated from the Dumfries & Galloway settlement but Saints' immediate post-war goalkeeper, Malcolm Newlands, was born there on March 28, 1925.

The Newlands family of three brothers and four sisters were eventually domiciled in the Lanarkshire township of Newmains, Malcolm being educated at the local primary school.

The Boys' Brigade played a large part in Malcolm's formative years. A regular player with the 1st Newmains Company, a favoured memory was his appearance with his BB colleagues in a PE display at the 1937 Empire Exhibition in Glasgow's Bellahouston Park.

While the current image of youth football conjures up a multifarious jungle of ever enlarging boys' clubs, the accepted career progression of the 1940s was fashioned with a Secondary Juvenile placement, followed by a toughening up process on the Junior circuit.

Malcolm followed that well-worn path with spells at Law Villa and Carluke Rovers.

He derived a degree of playing satisfaction at these levels but the thought of appearing in the higher echelons of the Senior game frightened the living daylights out of the young Newlands.

He recalled: "In truth, I wasn't over keen on the Senior football business and when I heard that Dave McCrae of Hearts was coming to the house to sign me I was off and out the back door like a shot. It was my father who was the driving force that eventually brought me to my senses.

"The following week, St Mirren's Willie Fotheringham came to the house. He took his jacket off, complimented my mother on the cooking aromas coming from the kitchen and was happy to take a plate of stew and tatties. That put me at ease with him, so I signed for St Mirren."

That was 1943 and a year later generated a particularly satisfying St Mirren memory.

Malcolm said: "It was January and a bitingly cold day at Ibrox. There had been some doubt as to the game going on but we played and beat Rangers and I'm told that was the first time we'd beaten them on their own patch for 35 years."

Malcolm's introduction to residence between the St Mirren sticks saw the Buddies take on Aberdeen at Pittodrie.

He went on: "This was another bleak day and not only had we to face the prolific scoring of Aberdeen's Matt Armstrong, we also had to face a barrage of sleet and snow showers. No light cotton tops in those days, the heavy woollen jerseys simply stuck to us and had to be cut off with scissors at time up!"

The lure of financial security via a transfer fee, no matter how modest, was a post-war attraction for most club treasurers. Such an approach from Preston North End sent Malcolm down to Deepdale and the St Mirren exchequer into raptures, with manager Bobby Rankin then having to secure the services of another keeper.

Five seasons with Preston and having the pleasure of playing alongside the legendary Tom Finney yielded 80 league appearances for Newlands. One particular memory was firmly embedded in the Newlands memory banks.

He explained: "We were playing Stockport County in the English FA Cup. Jack Connor, a very good friend of mine, was in line to record an English league record of four hat-tricks in successive games. He missed out in our game, he only scored two, and I must confess I had mixed feelings for him in being instrumental in dumping his possible record."

Any interview with a goalkeeper will invariably generate the obligatory question as to their most memorable save. In Newlands' case, his save could possibly be a future candidate for What Happened Next!

He said: "After my time at Preston, I moved on to Workington on the Cumbrian coast. Workington play at Borough Park and were members of the English League until 1977, when they were replaced by Wimbledon.

"Workington were playing Doncaster Rovers in a reserve match. Joe Harvey, the old Newcastle United player, was the Workington manager and in the course of play I badly damaged my hand in making a save, This prevented me from clutching the ball.

"These were the days before the introduction of substitutes, so I was taken out of goal and played on the wing. There must have been some thoughts on a possible playing career switch as I went on to score a hat-trick!

"I've often been asked who had the hardest shot I ever faced in the game. I think that particular prize would fall to Andy Fyffe of Morton. Andy had a ferocious shot and in one derby game at Cappielow he drove in a pile driver from a free-kick. I managed to get my body behind it and was nearly pole axed. Even Andy came up to see if I was okay."

Goalkeepers are renowned for their dead ball kicking expertise but clearing one's lines from a moving pass back can cause some custodians a problem or two.

Malcolm recalled: "Pass backs were before my time but they wouldn't have been a problem for me. When I was training I never played in goal. I always played out and that would have given me all the confidence in the world to deal with a moving ball."

The core of Newlands' post-war playing career was spent with Workington. Some might denigrate the club as being located in the soccer sticks and a favoured back water in the game but to Malcolm, it was the happiest time of his football life in playing for a great family club.

He hung his boots up in 1962 after eight seasons and 250 appearances for the club. He went on to manage a pub in Cockermouth before returning north to Newton Drive in Newmains.

Malcolm died in 1996 and was survived by his wife Betty, a son and a daughter.

BOBBY PINKERTON

BY any stretch of the imagination, Bobby Pinkerton's route to playing for St Mirren was a tortuous path in the extreme.

Initially, after Bobby had checked in at the Bellshill Maternity Unit on February 19, 1941, the Pinkerton family established firm roots in Hamilton. Beckford Street Primary was the first to appreciate the Pinkerton soccer skills, Bobby captaining the school team and earning representative recognition on a couple of occasions with the Lanarkshire Schools side.

A short spell at Rutherglen Academy preceded a career switch for Bobby's father, with the family's move to Ayr almost bringing the guillotine down on young master Pinkerton's embryonic soccer development.

Bobby explained: "I went to Ayr Academy and on the Tuesday afternoon games period we went over to the old racecourse pitches. What was on offer nearly deflated me – only rugby balls and no footballs!"

Rugby and cricket were the Ayr Academy team pursuits and notable Pinkerton scholastic contemporaries were Ian Ure – later to join St Mirren – and Mike Denness, who found fame as a prodigious batsman with Ayr Cricket Club, before going on to play for and captain the full England side.

Despite the rugby, Bobby was still mad keen on the round ball code and Ayr Albion Youth Club satisfied the Pinkerton craving. Ayr Albion enjoyed a similar status to Douglas Smith's albeit more famed Drumchapel Amateurs. The two sides never clashed on league duty but were regular combatants in the Scottish Cup.

Cumnock Juniors were the next Pinkerton port of call but there were a number of trial options on offer.

Bobby recalled: "I was invited down on trial with Aston Villa for a week. I also had another trial outing with Kilmarnock when Willie Waddell was their manager before I eventually signed for Queen of the South.

"My Palmerston debut was intriguing. The Saturday after I'd signed we were set to play Falkirk and who was also making his first appearance for Queen's? None other than the former St Mirren stalwart Willie Telfer, who had gone to the Dumfries club from Rangers."

After 18 months with Queen of the South, Bobby found himself the recipient of a mid-season free transfer, his Palmerston report card reading "Young, Enthusiastic and Inexperienced!"

That P45 from Queen's found him in football's no-man's land as the timing of his release rendered reinstatement to the Juniors impossible – at least until the start of the next season.

A chance meeting with former Airdrie stalwart Willie "Cowboy" McCulloch saw the pair embark on a game-finding mission. And they eventually persuaded Newton Stewart in the South of Scotland League into giving them a game. In Bobby's words, "We had a whale of a time!"

He added: "I still thought I could make it in the Senior game but was content at the time to join Craigmark Burntonians for a couple of seasons. My time at Station Park saw players such as Alex McAnespie and Sam Goodwin performing for Craigmark and the club reaching the Scottish Junior Cup semi-final."

Bobby's dream of a positive career in the Senior game demanded some positive action. He had dabbled in journalism, writing scraps on the Junior game for the local tabloids. Conceivably, it was his writing that triggered a solution to his soccer craving.

He explained: "I wrote to Motherwell and Partick Thistle for trials but it was my letter to St Mirren that bore fruit. Doug Millward had just joined St Mirren as manager. I was invited up from Ayr to play in a closed door friendly against Greenock Juniors.

"I thought I played reasonably well and was a bit concerned at being taken off at half-time. However, it was to my benefit because Doug offered me signing terms."

Pinkerton's meandering route to Senior soccer had now encountered an acceptable terminus.

A league encounter with Hamilton Accies at Love Street on December 18, 1965, was a pleasing first game in Saints' colours for Bobby, a single Tommy Robertson strike earning a seasonal Christmas win bonus for the side.

Six seasons at Love Street saw Bobby branded as a brainy inside forward acting as a provider for the frontmen. Indeed, in the promotion-winning side of 67-68, he helped to provide the free-scoring Jim Blair and Peter Kane with a 21-goal return each.

Fortunate to have a mainly injury-free career, Bobby missed only two games in that memorable campaign, going on to be posted absent only once the following league season.

The Pinkerton St Mirren stats reveal he played a total of 167 games, netting 25 goals in the process. Three of that tally came in a league match against Albion Rovers at Cliftonhill in 1968. But there is one special counter that tingles the Pinkerton memory cells.

He said: "Games against Morton always create a volatile atmosphere. We were playing them in October '68. The score was one apiece and we were in the last minute. One last foray upfield and I managed to hook one in from all of 25 yards. It screamed into the postage stamp top corner and not surprisingly, the fans erupted. So did I!"

Career highlights for Bobby were simple. He went on: "Just playing for St Mirren was reward enough but strutting your stuff at Ibrox and Parkhead was the icing on the cake."

Memories of beating Rangers were always memorable, a single goal from Hugh Gilshan on November 16, 1968, at Love Street brought a smile to the Pinkerton countenance.

He said: "Val McNaughton, the St Mirren chairman at the time, took us to the Brabloch Hotel for that pre-match meal. Talk got around to bonuses and Val promised £50 a player if we beat Rangers, knowing full well his money was safe – or so he thought!

"You've never seen such a financial sprachle as the proverbial piggy bank was broken open to honour the bonus promise."

It was Alex Wright who sanctioned a free transfer for Bobby that enabled him to join Stranraer to further enhance the existing affinity between Saints and the Stair Park club.

Still the Pinkerton playing thirst hadn't been quenched and Bobby went on to achieve major honours with Irvine Meadow.

The pride of Ayrshire's Junior sides reached the Scottish Junior Cup final with Bobby on board. But it took three games to dispose of Cambuslang Rangers in 1973 before Bobby landed his coveted cup winners medal to accompany his league championship gong. They added to the prized Rotary watch he won in the 67-68 season as St Mirren's Player of the Year.

Never full-time, Bobby was at one time the sales manager for the Marley Tile Company, specialising in the roofing side of the business. Latterly, for around 25 years, he was the Scottish sales manager for a Ready Mix Concrete firm.

Would he like to play in the modern climate?

He replied: "Definitely. Players nowadays receive more justified recognition for their efforts. I was only ever interviewed once. The Daily Record came down to see me for a feature. My football thoughts were sought with me astride a roof top in my Marley days!"

Such is the current media and player progression…

GERRY QUEEN

FOR a youngster to be born within the shadows of Ibrox Stadium, Govan, Montrose Hospital to be precise, the setting suns might have implanted a warmth to eventually appear in the light blue of Edmiston Drive.

Regretfully, within the sectarian shenanigans of the West of Scotland, those recipients of scholastic tuition at Lourdes High School in Cardonald were never invited to autograph a Rangers recruitment form.

Such was Gerry Queen's start in life. A start that saw him employed in the Rolls Royce drawing office at Hillington, the precision engineering company nurturing a much respected Under-17 Juvenile side.

Gerry recalled: "We were playing against Neilston and in their side was a Scottish internationalist. I managed to score two goals against him and on the strength of that performance Willie Reid signed me for St Mirren. I was then farmed out to Johnstone Burgh.

"My first game for Saints was a reserve match against Airdrie. We drew 2-2 and for a 16-year-old it was a satisfactory start."

However, St Mirren's start to the 62-63 season wasn't clouded in glory. An opening 3-0 cuffing at Ibrox was followed by 4-2 defeats by Kilmarnock at Love Street and Falkirk at Brockville. Certainly full points had been taken off Motherwell and Raith Rovers, but the St Mirren attack lacked sparkle.

Saints sought to remedy the deficiency by introducing Gerry at inside left, with Tommy White leading the attack supported by George "Dandy" McLean at inside right.

Aberdeen at Love Street provided the stage for the St Mirren rejigged attack and the then 17-year-old Queen made his senior debut on October 6, 1962. The match ended in a 2-2 draw.

Gerry said: "When you are a young player running down that tunnel and ontothe pitch for the first time, the atmosphere is something very special.

That day against the Dons I was up against George Kinnell, a favourite Pittodrie son, who was actually a cousin of Jim Baxter's.

"Kinnell was a player of some standing and I think I acquitted myself quite well against him. At the end of the game he came over and shook my hand and for someone playing in his first senior game that was a totally memorable experience."

Gerry's first senior goal came six games later, popping in the equaliser against Airdrie at Love Street.

He was in the St Mirren line up when wee Archie Gemmell, at 17, made his senior debut against Dundee United at the home of Paisley's finest on October 3,1964. But it was a match the previous season at Ibrox that Gerry rates amongst his most memorable.

February 8 was the date and the final scoreline of 3-2 in Saints' favour firmly etched into the Love Street memory banks.

Gerry added: "We had a superb young team. Tommy Robertson was at outside right, his namesake Jimmy, later to move to Tottenham Hotspur on the back of a £25,000 fee, was on the other wing. Tottie Beck led the attack with Jim Clunie marshalling the defence. All in all it was an excellent young and well-balanced team.

"When we played Rangers that day, Willie Henderson was in their team. He was in his heyday at Ibrox and a veritable genius. But even with Willie marauding on the right wing we trounced them 3-2.

"We even had two goals chalked off, so we actually fired five past the Ibrox keeper - a more than satisfying win for what was a young and inexperienced team.

"If we had managed to hold onto that team and build on it, who knows what we might have achieved. I was a couple of years behind George McLean, who signed for Rangers.

"Two years later I signed for Kilmarnock. Archie Gemmell went to Preston and then Gordon McQueen went south. That was the way of St Mirren - they always seemed to sell a major player every other year - effectively and regretfully the economic facts of football life in Paisley."

Queen's last game in black and white was against Dundee United at Tannadice on January 15, 1966.

Malcolm MacDonald, at one time the most elegant purveyor of defence splitting passes at Celtic Park, was now the Kilmarnock manager and in need of increasing the quality content at Rugby Park.

Queen was made to measure and made the transition from Paisley - the move weighted with Ronnie Hamilton leaving the Ayrshire club plus an undisclosed financial figure enhancing the Love Street coffers.

Gerry's Kilmarnock stay lasted three seasons, with one outstanding memory being a 3-3 draw against Rangers at Ibrox. The game was etched into the memory banks as the Soviet Premier Kosygin took in the game and was introduced to the players.

Other days of distinction at Rugby Park embraced successful campaigns in the Fairs Cup, the predecessor of the current UEFA Cup.

A first round 8-2 aggregate turnover of Antwerp with a couple of strikes from Queen in the 66-67 tourney, took Gerry's game to a more mature level.

After Rugby Park, a move down south to Crystal Palace at Selhurst Park followed. And this allowed the newspaper fraternity to enjoy one screaming headline - Queen scores at the Palace!

Gerry's first outing with Palace couldn't have been tougher as the South London side matched their strengths against Manchester United in a 2-2 draw, the Old Trafford side being richly served with Messrs Charlton, Best and Law.

Gerry recalled: "Life with Palace came abruptly to an end when it was known that the showman Malcolm Allison was en route to Selhurst Park.

"Believe it or not, 10 players, two coaches and the secretary Peter Barnes were all transferred to the Orient - as in the Leyton Stadium in East London and not the Far East."

Thoughts of life after football began to kick in and former Morton and Rangers full-back Kai Johansen enticed Gerry out to South Africa. He went initially on holiday but went on to stay for a number of years and finished his playing days there.

Through his South African contacts, Gerry embarked on a project recruiting players for the embryonic soccer environment of America.

He explained: "I was meeting a number of parents who were asking all about football in the States. I'd never been there so I went over with opportunities arising to coach and coaching is something I love. That became a full time job."

Few would advance the theory of romance being rampant in football. It is in Gerry Queen's case!

He said: "I met Rosemary when she was eight. I delivered newspapers to her home. We grew up together in Penilee and saw each other in our school days but then lost contact.

"In addition to my coaching activities in the States, I also had some business interests there. On one occasion a lady mentioned to Rosemary, now over in America, that the guy over there has the same accent as you.

"She came over to speak to me in this tiny US town. An amazing instant recognition followed and romance blossomed in Florida."

Now back in God's country, Gerry, still keen to enter the coaching business in Scotland, was content to ply the property magnate in nearby Johnstone.

BOBBY REID

AYRSHIRE has had its share of notable ploughmen who have grafted hard in pursuing the straight furrow syndrome. The immortal Robert Burns was one, Robert Reid's dad was another.

And while youngsters will happily submit to paternal leanings, young Robert generated an emotion that was sheer laugh or cry material for his father.

He explained: "After life on the farm, my family established their home base in Irvine. As a teenager I'd played a couple of trials for Junior teams, one of which was Irvine Meadow, who were enjoying the fervent support of my dad.

"He was heartbroken that the Meadow Park club didn't sign me and even less pleased when I joined Kilwinning Rangers. However, worse was to come. My second game for the Buffs was against Meadow. We won and my dad didn't know whether to cheer my efforts or go off in the sulk."

Born in Kilmarnock in October 1955, Robert was educated at Bank Street Primary, where the accepted format was school football in the morning and playing for the Boys' Brigade in the afternoon.

By the time he had celebrated his 15th birthday, Robert had departed the BB football stage in favour of the youth club game, turning out for the Ayr Albion Under-16 team.

By the time Robert had settled in the Kilwinning side, a number of senior teams including Motherwell, Rangers, Hamilton and Dumbarton had expressed an interest in the defensive performances of this strapping teenager.

The St Mirren scouting team were also in the picture and sent back glowing reports to Love Street, where the sweet-talking Irish brogue of manager Willie Cunningham was sufficient in persuading Robert that his football future lay with the Buddies.

Saints had just implemented a major player clearout at the end of the 1972-73 season. Some seven or eight had left and new blood was required, with Robert signing on his 18th birthday. He had been Robert for 18 years but this immediately changed to Bobby when he walked through the Love Street portals.

January 12, 1974 was the Saints debut day for Bobby. A cold, wet and windy day at Ochilview Park wasn't in enhanced any by the local Warriors, Stenhousemuir giving no mercy to their Paisley visitors, dishing out a 3-1 defeat.

Never a full-time player, Bobby's salary earning future was destined for a career in law. By this time, Alex Ferguson had succeeded Cunningham and Fergie's friendship with Dundee United's Jim McLean secured training facilities at Tannadice while Bobby studied at Dundee University for his law degree.

A lynchpin in the St Mirren 1976-77 defence, Bobby was a key player in the promotion-winning team, contributing 39 league appearances topped with a 10-goal tally.

Playing colleagues during that title-winning campaign included Billy Stark, Tony Fitzpatrick, Lex Richardson, Frank McGarvey and Jack Copland, to name but a few.

This upturn in St Mirren's fortunes wasn't lost on the national selectors and Scotland manager Ally McLeod in particular. Under-21 call ups subsequently arrived for Bobby in the 1977 matches against Wales, Switzerland and England, plus a seat on the bench in the match with Czechoslovakia.

Bobby revealed: "I had to turn down the chance of going to the European Under-21 championships due to my law studies. They wanted me to go as one of the two over age players. I suppose on reflection I would have preferred a career in football with law in the background, but common sense ensured a reversal of this."

Asked as to who his most difficult opponents were, Bobby was forthright in his assessment.

He said: "I used to use Jimmy Bone as a benchmark in my handling of the opposition. Jimmy was a strong player and didn't hold back in the challenge. Steve Archibald, when he was up at Aberdeen, was another difficult opponent. Big defenders always enjoy playing against robust attackers and in this respect I regularly enjoyed my jousts with Rangers' Derek Johnstone."

Five seasons with St Mirren and then disaster.

Bobby went on: "I was selected to play for the Scottish League against the Highland League up at the Telford Street ground in Inverness in the 77-78 season. It was, in effect, an annual fixture. During the game I simply stuck my leg out to knock the ball down with my studs. Nobody tackled me and my right knee simply exploded.

"I was carried off, returned to the hotel for a meal, went to bed and in the middle of the night my knee had swollen to balloon proportions.

" I went straight to the Victoria Infirmary when we returned to Glasgow and was embedded in plaster from hip to ankle for a number of weeks. It was the end of a promising career.

"I've no regrets and I'm not bitter in any way but it took me another two years to appreciate that football was finished for me."

Now a resident in Inchinnan with wife Elizabeth and daughters Carol and Gail, Bobby still has a thirst for athletic activity. He is happy to run a few half marathons each season, which demands he runs in a straight line with no twists or turns en route. A spot of horticultural maintenance in the Reid garden plus a round of golf also find a small niche in Bobby's leisure activity programme.

Occasionally a visitor to Love Street on match days, the now well established solicitor's last venture at St Mirren Park was to manage the St Mirren Legends at Kenny McDowall's Testimonial match in May 1996.

Bobby Reid for so long in the football firmament, the solicitous former Saint has gone back to his early days, professionally now known again as Robert Reid.

WILLIE REID

IT is perhaps one of the more difficult transitions in working life in making a move from effectively the shop floor to a sedentary position of management. Difficult in commerce and industry and perhaps even more so in a football environment.

Willie Reid was one who managed such a move and achieved fame and success on both sides with St Mirren.

One of a family of six, Willie was born a Buddie on February 6, 1917. As with most players of his day, an apprenticeship in the Junior game was a prerequisite to mounting the Senior stage. Willie's Junior days saw him in an Ashfield strip, winning a medal in the 1936-37 Maryhill Juniors Charity Cup competition.

An engineer to trade, Willie's day job as a shipyard welder with John Brown's of Clydebank saw him contribute to the building of both the Queen Mary and the Queen Elizabeth. The job went on to be classified as a reserved occupation during the Second World War, thus enabling him to pursue his football energies in his off duty hours.

His senior career started with Cowdenbeath before he moved to Dumbarton and earned media praise as a "polished, hard playing half-back with legs of teak."

These physical attributes greatly interested Saints manager Bobby Rankin, who made Willie his first St Mirren signing on May 21, 1945. Dumbarton's coffers were substantially enriched to the tune of £430.

During a seven-year post-war playing career, the Reid polish was applied to 163 St Mirren outings in all major games, with 12 goals added as a sweetener.

His debut game for Saints saw the Buddies travel to Shawfield on August 11, 1945, to take on Clyde in a league encounter. Saints won 3-2 thanks to a couple of goals from Stewart and one from McKenna.

For anyone with aspirations in supporting St Mirren, life in the Love Street fast lane generates feelings of rollercoaster proportions. As a player, Reid was subjected to a number of such physical sensations.

One memorable occasion in the euphoric category was a 1948 first Round

Scottish Cup tie against Shawfield at Love Street. Saints' 8-0 winning margin was momentous for Alfie Lesz and Gerry Burrell, the diminutive wingers running amok with a combined four-goal contribution.

Equally palatable was the league demolition of Dundee, also at Love Street, in March 1949. The roads and miles back to Dens Park were seemingly considerably longer thanks to a 6-1 thumping by Saints.

Not quite so fruitful an entry in the Reid CV was a 1953 visit to Bayview Stadium to take on East Fife on league business. With such renowned goal-getters as Henry Morris, Charlie "Legs" Fleming and Davie Duncan on call, defensive trouble ahead beckoned. The travelling Paisley support were severely chastened by the 7-0 scoreline.

Eddie Blyth was a playing colleague of Reid's and has fond memories of his wing-half expertise.

Eddie recalled: "Willie was perhaps the oldest player in the team and we used to address him as 'Faither'. He was well built, had great balance and was the proverbial ball winner.

"I had no indication he had any management potential and when he was approached to become the St Mirren manager it took me completely by surprise."

St Mirren boss Rankin was not in the best of health in the early 1950s. His physical wellbeing became a matter of concern for both his family and his football club, so much so that Reid was appointed as assistant manager to provide positive back up for the ailing gaffer.

After undergoing a serious operation from which he never fully recovered, Bobby passed away in the Royal Alexandra Hospital in Paisley on August 25, 1954.

The Rankin-Reid relationship was further cemented two days later when Willie, in tandem with Willie Telfer, Willie Johnston and Jackie Neilson, carried Bobby's coffin into the Woodside Crematorium.

A managerial successor was required and who better to fill the vacancy than Reid. His appointment was confirmed at a board meeting on August 31, 1954.

Willie's first team selection for the League Cup match the following day against Raith Rovers at Love Street snatched a 3-1 win. The team in action was Lornie, Lapsley and Mallan, Holmes, Telfer and Johnston, McMaster, McGill, McGrory, Gemmell and Callan. The goals came from wee Tommy Gemmell with two and a single strike from John McGrory.

Playing success in the Scottish game can generally be measured by cup success or the simple logging in of positive results against the Old Firm. But, more particularly with St Mirren, against our neighbours along the A8.

Willie never managed to be in a winning St Mirren side against Rangers as a player but he overcame that deficiency as a manager. His success rate was a mere two wins in 14 confrontations, winning 3-1 at Ibrox in October

1959 and 2-1 at Love Street five years earlier.

However, it is St Mirren's Scottish Cup win in 1959 which Reid expertly orchestrated that remains a treasured memory.

Tommy Bryceland was a member of that cup-winning side and extolled the Reid virtues at length.

He said: "Willie was a great tactician and made a point of knowing everything pre-match about the opposition. A quiet man, he wasn't one for bawling or shouting at you. He left St Mirren in 1961 to join Norwich City. He preceded me to Carrow Road and was probably instrumental in advising Norwich about my capabilities prior to my going south to East Anglia.

"Perhaps Willie's biggest problem at Norwich was similar to my own – the Norwich folk had great difficulty in understanding our accents!"

Another former Saint from the Reid management era was full-back John McTurk.

John said: "Willie was a great manager and a great organiser. Quiet and laid back, he wasn't a bouncing up and down type of boss.

"As a player, he was perhaps a bit of a rough diamond in that he was a no holding back type of guy who operated a 'Thou shall not pass' policy."

As a manager, Willie was widely respected for his tactical knowledge and brought innovative ideas on the training grounds.

Having succeeded Archie Macaulay at Norwich, Reid spent two seasons at Carrow Road before being replaced by George Swindin as manager in 1962.

Willie's return to Scotland saw him relinquish any full-time football activities, although he did act as a scout for St Mirren for a number of years. He returned to Troon and continued his early career as a welder at the local Ailsa Shipbuilding Company.

Willie passed away in 1975 in Troon at the premature age of 58.

LEX RICHARDSON

IT'S an intriguing nomination. Lex Richardson's rating as to his most difficult opponent was the fiery Gordon Strachan during the ginger-haired one's sojourn at Pittodrie. Both had a socks to Brylcreem measurements around the 5'-7" mark, while both tipped the scales in the 10 stone region.

In truth, both were cast from the same mould and were undoubtedly pocket dynamos with Herculean work rates.

The charging up of Lex's in-built dynamo was triggered at St Luke's school in Barrhead, where his playing role was centred around the old fashioned right-half slot.

Born in Barrhead, the Richardson non-stop style wasn't lost on his home town team, with the Dunterlie Park hierarchy quick on the draw to recruit him to the Arthurlie cause. For a while, the local boy "done good", until the now defunct Blantyre Celtic upped the pleasantries to entice Richardson to David Livingstone country.

Alas, the grass is not always as green on the other side and Lex returned to Arthurlie in his early 20s.

Lex's final appearance for the Barrhead club was registered in a West of Scotland cup tie against Lesmahagow. Arthurlie were 3-1 down before Lex inspired a dramatic fightback to win 4-3, with the winner being fashioned direct from a Richardson corner.

Saints manager Alex Ferguson was by now in receipt of a sheaf of glowing reports of the dynamic Mr Richardson's exploits at Junior level. It was now time to tread a higher stage, the 22-year old arriving at Love Street a week after that cup tie.

Lex's memories of the Ferguson management techniques were firmly etched in his mind.

He said: "The recollections were magic, particularly of a man who was regularly fired up to blast boots and other missiles at the wall. Outwith that, he was a superb motivator, which helped to produce a promotion-winning side as well as upping the Love Street attendance levels to between 12 and 13,000."

The 1975-76 First Division was a truncated affair, as the 14 clubs played each other only twice and the league programme being completed by the end of February.

As a fill in till the end of the season, a Spring Cup was introduced and the new tournament provided Lex with a debut appearance against Meadowbank Thistle at Love Street, St Mirren winning 3-0. Lex failed to score but one drive sent the crossbar into a severe vibratory spasm.

Goals for the Richardson scrapbook eventually became a plenty. A 1982 League Cup tie against Ayr United saw Lex bag all three in the 3-1 win - the match ball taking pride of place in the Richardson trophy cabinet.

But perhaps a more satisfying scoring achievement came with the visit of Rangers to Love Street on March 28, 1981. Lex was the scourge of the Light Blues with both goals in the 2-1 win, the first being a 25-yard rocket.

It was perhaps Lex's versatility factor that prompted Jock Stein to consider the midfield maestro for higher honours. Lex regularly pulled on the No.10 shirt but took up permanent residence in the No.4 jersey to orchestrate proceedings when Tony Fitzpatrick migrated south to Bristol City.

Two Scottish League caps followed and Richardson took on the team captaincy in a match against the Republic of Ireland League in Dublin.

Three further Under-21 honours followed, with Lex being allowed in on the back of being a over age player in games against West Germany and England twice.

Fortunate to escape serious injury, he missed out on only one game in the 1976-77 Division One championship-winning season. And he was particularly forthright as to who were the stars of that competition.

Lex beamed: "We had a great midfield. It was outstanding with Tony Fitzpatrick, Billy Stark and myself, of course!"

The Richardson memories of St Mirren's European exploits in the early 1980s are still paint fresh. Elfsborg in Sweden was only bettered with two games against St Etienne, complete with Michel Platini, in 1980. Two years later, it was Feyenoord, with the charismatic Ruud Gullit, in the UEFA Cup.

Eight seasons at Love Street meant it was perhaps time to move on. But the St Mirren faithful were none too happy with the proposed transfer of Lex to Dens Park in exchange for Eric Sinclair. Mutterings in and around the Paisley watering holes seemed to indicate Dundee had the best of the deal.

Almost three terms in the City of Discovery preceded a return to the western seaboard and to Morton in particular.

Lex said: "My family roots were still in and around the west of Scotland. However, the pelters I received from the St Mirren fans on my return to Love Street wearing a Morton shirt seemed to indicate my move to Cappielow wasn't my best piece of judgement."

If perhaps the energy bank wasn't quite yielding the same dividends, the

Richardson creativity factor was still offering a bonus - one cashed in by Jimmy Bone and John Young in taking Lex to Arbroath for a spell.

It was Davie Provan, in his assistant managerial role at Love Street, who was rated by Lex as being his major mentor in the game. Not surprisingly therefore, Lex's post Arbroath activity should find him ending his senior career at Albion Rovers, when Davie Provan was the manager at Cliftonhill.

The senior slice of his playing days might have terminated but the Junior fields beckoned and Carnoustie Panmure were quick to engage the Richardson talents.

We asked Lex as to the origin of the name Panmure. He didn't know but Tom Johnston, secretary of the Scottish Junior FA, proffered a thought that the name originated from a local landowner's estate going back to the time of the 18th century Jacobite rebellion.

Richardson added further history to the area with a 10- year contribution to the Carnoustie cause - five as a player and five more as the manager.

Lex wasn't in charge when the Panmure club scaled the heights of the Scottish Junior Cup, losing to Renfrew on penalties in 2001 and beating Tayport three years later. But he did provide serious vocal support!

Prior to going full-time with Saints, Lex could be seen behind the wheel of a fork lift truck working for a Love Street construction company. And in his working life after football the Richardson income was generated as the store supervisor with a Carnoustie company.

Lex's last appearance at Love Street was in the St Mirren Legends squad at Norrie McWhirter's Testimonial game. And although now virtually in permanent soccer retirement, he occasionally turns out in charity games for the Dundee United All Stars.

IAN RIDDELL

"I HAVE been very fortunate in what I achieved in football. There were numerous players far better than me, with greater skill, who never got the opportunity to play at the highest level."

These were the words of self assessment of Ian Riddell, one of St Mirren's resolute full-backs in the late 50s and early 60s.

Tracking Ian down to ascertain his Saints career was tortuous. Listening to the irreverent outpourings on the car radio of Stuart Cosgrove and Tam Cowan in "Off the Ball" one Saturday revealed an interview with guest Derek Riddell. Derek is a thespian by profession with numerous TV appearances carded on his CV and he let slip that his dad, Ian, played for St Mirren.

Thanks to the perseverance of BBC producer Martin Dowden, we were able to trace Ian to his home in Bishopton.

A "Doonhamer" by birth, Ian's teenage days were spent at Dumfries Academy, where he captained the side that won The Scottish Schools Shield in 1956. His football progression gathered as he went on to play in the Scotland-England Schoolboy confrontation at Stamford Bridge, the Scots losing out by a one goal margin.

A clutch of Highers in his academic pocket gave him entrance to the Scottish School of Physical Education at Jordanhill College, the Alma Mater of all aspiring gym teachers.

Allied to the studies came further football with the College team under the supervision of Roy Small, who would later become the SFA's Technical Director, prior to Andy Roxburgh's reign.

Roy well remembers the Riddell attributes. He said: "Ian was a very able player – sharp, incisive and knew when and where to pass the ball. Definitely a player of above average ability. He was also capped for the national amateur league side when he was at Jordanhill."

Ian pulled on the dark blue of amateur Scotland on two such occasions – both against Northern Ireland, once at Cappielow and the other in Belfast. Further fame enveloped the Riddell student career when he assisted the College team to gallop up the amateur league structure from the sixth to the first division in the space of five seasons.

The principal of the Jordanhill College PE spectrum was Hugh Brown, the father of former Scotland manager Craig. Hugh was a bosom Buddie of St Mirren manager Willie Reid and one their get togethers precipitated an invitation to Ian to play a trial for St Mirren.

Ian recalled: "I first played in a Reserve match against Hearts at Tynecastle. Apparently I performed to the coach's satisfaction and played a further trial at Love Street. Willie Reid seemed suitably impressed and I signed for St Mirren in the late autumn of 1958."

Only a couple of weeks in the Love Street front door and Ian was tasting first-team football, with his debut against Hibs at home. Coincidently, November 22, 1958, was also debut day for Gerry Baker, Gerry scoring in the 2-1 win.

Ian's remit in that inaugural Saints outing was simple – stop Gordon Smith! Known as the "Gay" Gordon in the 1950s, one shudders to think of the ramifications such a nickname would induce in today's conversational parlance.

Ian explained: "Gordon was a thoroughbred player who was very athletic, fast and well balanced. Hibs played in a 4-2-4 formation as opposed to the accepted 2-3-5 of the day. Eddie Turnbull played behind the front four with me taking on Gordon. I was a bit overawed but more than happy to take home a win bonus."

While Smith was a regular thorn in the sides of most left-backs, he didn't cause Ian as much trouble as Rangers' wee Willie Henderson.

Riddell added: "Willie was fast and direct while Celtic's Jimmy "Jinky" Johnstone also gave you a heap of trouble but always gave you a second bite of the cherry. I wasn't the fastest player in the world, I relied on reading the situation and moving before it happened."

Ironically, Ian never appeared in any of the 1959 Scottish Cup-winning ties – he couldn't oust the resident duo of Messrs Lapsley and Wilson.

He did, however, play in one momentous cup tie.

He explained: "It was 1961, the year Dunfermline won the cup. Saints played the East End Park side in the semi-finals on April 1 at Tynecastle. A nil-nil draw meant a replay four days later, again at Tynecastle, and St Mirren went down to a right flukey goal. Perhaps a perverse situation in remembering a defeat, but the magic of playing in the cup made it all the more memorable for me."

While at Love Street, Ian caught the eye of the Under-23 selectors and went on to collect two caps – both against England, one at Ibrox and the other at Middlesbrough.

Riddell said: "The Middlesbrough game deserves particular mention. The previous Saturday St Mirren had drawn 3-3 with Third Lanark in the Scottish Cup. The replay went on at Cathkin the following Tuesday evening when that tremendous 8-0 win saw big Jim Rodger net four of the best.

"Tommy Bryceland, Third Lanark's Dave Hilley and myself were in the Scotland squad meeting at 10am the following morning at Queen Street station in Glasgow for the train to Ayresome Park. We won 1-0 but I reckon I lost half a stone with three games in five days."

Ian logged in 158 appearances for Saints in an eight-season stay, finally being freed by Bobby Flavell and going on to join Berwick Rangers.

January 28, 1967, was another major entry in the Riddell soccer diaries, with Glasgow Rangers meeting Berwick over the border in the first round of the Scottish Cup. A 1-0 win for the Shielfield Park side thanks to a Sammy Reid goal also saw Ian at left-back once again confronting Henderson – this time successfully!

Never a full-time player, after Berwick Ian concentrated on his PE teaching career, encouraging youngsters onto the wall bars at St Mirin's Academy and the Reid Kerr College.

In his leisure time, Ian continued to have an eye for a ball, performing with credit at the Erskine Golf Club, where he became Club Champion twice, County Champion once, as well as Club Captain.

His golf expertise matched his days in professional football – "I don't like losing!"

JIM RODGER

THE Lanarkshire township of Cleland was once famous as a productive coal mining community. In football terms, it was also highly productive in fashioning right wingers blessed with a touch of pace. The incisive incursions of Jimmy Delaney of Celtic and Manchester United fame was one, while dear to St Mirren hearts, Jim Rodger was another.

The legendary Bill Shankly was accredited with the utterance to one wayward wannabe, "All your brains son are in your feet!"

Fortunately for Rodger, all his essential grey matter was secured in the correct geographical location.

After Jim's early educational standings had been cemented at Cleland Primary, he moved on to Wishaw High School, where he was a member of the successful Wishaw High side who won the prestigious Scottish Schoolboys Shield. Further scholastic attainment was generated by entering the portals of Glasgow University to sit a BSc degree in mathematics.

In tandem with his studies, Jim played as a 17-year-old for his university team prior to joining Cumnock Juniors. It was while he was operating at Townhead Park that a scout recommended the Rodger talents to Ibrox, with the taskmaster that was Bill Struth signing the young Lanarkshire winger.

Jim explained: "I was at Ibrox for just over three years when Scot Symon took over as manager. His player policy was full-time or nothing. Eight or nine of us were either serving apprenticeships or at university. No way was I prepared to interrupt my studies, so I was given a free.

"Fortunately, just before the axe fell, I'd had a good game for the Rangers reserve side at Love Street. Willie Reid saw that game and, hearing that I was being released, signed me for St Mirren. That was in May 1955.

"I've often been asked who was my most difficult adversary. Simple? Jimmy Mallan. The ex-Celt was playing for Saints in that reserve match. The Ibrox reserve team coach was Bob McPhail. His game plan was elementary. Ralph Brand had been told to chip the ball over Mallan's head and let me run on to it. Jimmy was finding it hard to keep up with me which provoked a veiled aside, 'Go easy son if you want to walk off the park!'"

Like many of his era, Jim's post university credentials were requisitioned by Her Majesty - a two-year National Service spell with the colours was a mandatory requirement and the RAF secured his services.

He never flew into the wide blue yonder as his BSc degree earned him a commission and Flying Officer Rodger donned a scholastic mantle to teach mathematics at the RAF Apprentices School.

Such was his liking for teaching that on his demob, Jim took a teacher training course at Jordanhill College, going on to provide an insight into algebra and other related subjects for generations of Scottish youngsters.

Two hugely influential post-war events in the summer soccer calendar were the Glasgow Police sports meeting at Hampden and Rangers Sports at Ibrox.

Both contributed to the pre-season build up with their eagerly awaited 5-a-side competitions.

Jim explained: "St Mirren always did well in these abbreviated tournaments. I enjoyed playing with Willie Telfer, Jackie Neilson, Davie Lapsley and 'Togo' Johnstone - four old heads and me. The game strategy was fundamental. They kept the ball and when they saw a chance, as I could run a bit, they gave me the ball and I'd put it in the net."

The Rodger debut in St Mirren colours was a League Cup tie against Airdrie at Love Street, in August 1955. The 3-2 scoreline was a satisfactory start, Tommy Gemmell notching a brace and Brian Callan netting the other.

The "Wee Prime Minister", erstwhile Ian McMillan, scored twice for The Diamonds.

The 1959 Scottish Cup campaign holds special memories for St Mirren's galloping winger. The 4-0 slaughter of Celtic in the semi-final was a particularly pleasing day out for the underdogs. But Saints' build up for the final was remarkable.

Jim said: "Willie Reid realised that we had probably peaked in the Celtic game and there was every likelihood we would be off the boil for the final against Aberdeen.

"Three days before the Hampden final, St Mirren played India of Inchinnan in the Renfrewshire Cup. Normally it would have been either the second or third teams that would have played but Willie put out the entire cup final side, less Jack McGugan, who had tonsillitis. I think the final score was something like 35-0. You had to believe it fired up our boilers."

While that 1959 winners medal provides tangible proof of a great Hampden excursion, the St Mirren-Jim Rodger folklore file wouldn't be complete without reference to the cup campaign two years later.

He explained: "We were extremely lucky to draw with Third Lanark in the third round at Love Street, with a last minute goal from Rab Stewart giving us a fortuitous replay.

"The following Tuesday we were over at Cathkin for the return match. They had a galaxy of quality players - Dave Hilley. Alex Harley, Matt Gray and wee Joe McInnes, to name but four. But the Gods shone on us that night. We were two up at the interval and it finished 8-0. I was fortunate and managed to score four of them."

A seven-year spell at Love Street ended amid managerial confusion. Reid opted to join Norwich City and Bobby Flavell arrived to mastermind the Paisley Saints.

However, the Flavell appreciation of the Rodger style of play was somewhat low key, with Jim being subsequently transferred to Hearts for a three-year stay at Tynecastle.

But Jim still speaks fondly of three people who made an enormous contribution to his Paisley performances. The first was Reid, whose wise counsel and steadfast support were crucial in Jim's early days with the Saints.

The second was his former adversary, Mallan, who took the young lad under his wing and taught him how to get the better of many of the hard-tackling full-backs of that time. The third, to use Jim's own words, was "that prince of inside rights", Tommy Bryceland, whose precision passes and wonderful skills opened up many defences for his Buddie on the right wing.

With the Rodger boots being finally pegged in 1966, the winger of mass destruction became a headteacher of mass instruction at Portree High School in Skye.

Now living in Symington in Lanarkshire, the nearby golf course at Lanark demands much attention. And on the horticultural front, Jim and his wife Jessie have proverbial green fingers in tending that blaze of colour that is their garden.

SAM SMITH

ANY aspiring player born in and around the 1920s was always scheduled for a major hiccup in fulfilling a potential football career. Sam Smith was one who felt the full impact of the Second World War.

A resolute character with considerable drive and determination, Sam was a Shawlands Academy pupil. This was a scholastic establishment that catered for both codes of football, Sam preferring the round ball version.

Playing for the school in the morning was supplemented by Saturday afternoon matches with Nitshill's 265th Boys' Brigade Company. Indeed, BB football gave Sam a taste of representative activity when he was selected to play for the Glasgow Battalion against their Belfast counterparts at Lesser Hampden.

A centre-half-cum-right-half in those teenage days, Arthurlie offered him a trial and the Junior club secured his signature in 1937.

Sam recalled: "I played for a month at Dunterlie Park and then had an offer from Blackburn Rovers of £5 a week plus a £90 fee to sign on. I almost assumed ersatz millionaire status, particularly in the light of a weekly wage of 12/6 (or 62.5p in today's currency) as an office junior."

It was the maternal guidance of Sam's mother who put the proverbial boot in and quickly dispelled any thoughts on a move south to Ewood Park.

The young Arthurlie defender was still attracting attention at home, with interest from Celtic and Clyde now paramount. An approach from the Parkhead club saw Sam sign for manager Willie Maley for the princely sum of £2 per week.

But he revealed: "I never kicked a ball for Celtic. They wanted me to go full-time. I thought it was a precarious occupation for me and was summoned to meet Maley in his Bank Restaurant in Queen Street. The ultimatum was simple, 'Go full-time or leave'. I left.

"But Sammy Blythe signed me for St Mirren in time for the 1938-39 season. There was a mass exodus from Arthurlie at that time, with eight of the team going to the Senior ranks.

"I made my debut for the club in a reserve match against Rangers and they didn't field a particularly star-studded line up. I was up against Davie Kinnear and he was ably backed up by Bob McPhail, George Brown and big Jimmy Smith."

Adolf Hitler's hopes of world dominance made it inevitable that numerous calls to the colours would follow and Sam's army destination was initially scheduled for the Argyll & Sutherland Highlanders. That was before an input from his former BB Captain re-directed him to the Royal Signals unit at Catterick.

Nearby Darlington were always on the lookout for khaki-clad players to bolster their north of England efforts, particularly so when the Garrison side at Catterick went on to rout the then Feethams-based team by a 10-0 margin.

Sam explained: "It was certainly financially handy to play in the English league. Fourteen shillings a week from the army didn't go far. The additional thirty bob from Darlington generated a near Midas touch for me."

Six and a half years in the army took Sam from Lance Corporal to the Officers' Mess, with three pips on his shoulders signifying Captain status.

On his demob, his first post-war outing for Saints was a match against Rangers at Ibrox. But the Love Street side of Newlands, Smith, Lindsay, Cowan, Roy, McKenna, McIntosh, Stenhouse, Linwood, Moffat and Gillies went down 3-1.

Some 78 post-war outings in black and white followed but there was only one goal to spice up the Smith soccer CV.

He remembered it well: "It was in a league match against Celtic at Love Street. I hit a 30-yard left foot pile driver at Rolando Ugolini in the Celtic goal that simply screamed into the net. It was a once in a lifetime strike. The Sunday Post's Jack Harkness suggested 'Smith would be a happy man in his palmist of days!'"

So who topped the Love Street popularity polls when Sam first appeared in a St Mirren jersey?

He said: "Alex Linwood was one man I wouldn't have enjoyed playing against. He was nippy, fast and, boy, did he have an eye for goal. Willie Reid was a great left-half and, of course, he went on to manage Saints.

"Big Willie Kelly was arguably the most dominant centre-half in the Scottish game at that time but unfortunately he fell foul of officialdom and collected a lengthy suspension for his troubles."

After leaving St Mirren in 1949, Sam went on to spend a season with Forfar Athletic – a move destined to be interwoven with his future business, social and family life.

Deep farming instincts were instilled in his character, and these were manifested in his initial employment as an office junior with a firm of livestock auctioneers. He rose to become chairman of that Forfar-based company.

With Sam's home now established in the Angus township, his early footballing pedigree wasn't lost on the locals and he donned the managerial yoke for the Loons in 1954. He eventually joined the board at Station Park and only stepped down as chairman in 1991.

A family man, Sam and his wife Nessie are the proud parents of Graham, Carol and Elaine, with Elaine inheriting her father's sporting genes and being undefeated as the Scottish Women's Table Tennis champion for 10 years.

Charismatic, ebullient, enthusiastic, the adjectives are never ending in assessing Sam Smith's larger than life contributions to Scottish football and agricultural horizons.

These horizons were subsequently chronicled in the early 1990s when Sam produced his autobiography – Four Fields. So what prompted him to commit his Paisley and Forfar foibles to print?

He explained: "I wrote it for the family for fun. I'm a blethering type of chap – perhaps being an auctioneer you're supposed to have the gift of the gab! I hope you enjoy the read."

DOUGIE SOMNER

LOOK at yourself in the mirror and try to evaluate your job skills and strengths. Are you truly honest with your assessment?

Dougie Somner was. He said: "I was a penalty box player and a deadly finisher from all of two inches! I had no great pace but had good anticipation of what was about to happen and made sure I was in the right spot at the right time."

Honesty at its best.

Dougie was, in essence, a late starter in the game. Born in Edinburgh, he grew up in East Kilbride, with Murray Primary and Duncancraig Secondary providing the educational necessities in furthering the three "Rs".

He was selected to play for an East Kilbride Schools team before joining the Juvenile side Glasgow United. United had both Kenny Dalglish and Vic Davidson, later to perform with Celtic, in their line up and being an undersized 5'-4" 16-year-old, it was difficult for Dougie to have his name penciled onto the team sheet.

He recalled: "I took a year out of playing in the afternoon to concentrate on my education and was only involved in schools football.

"I eventually had to earn a living and got a job as a civil servant at the National Engineering Laboratory in East Kilbride. They had a works team and persuaded me in the summer of 1968 to start playing again."

So well did he perform that he soon caught the eye of the Brockville hierarchy. Former Saints full-back Willie Cunningham was the Falkirk manager at the time and Dougie signed a full-time contract, making his Bairns debut against Hibernian at Easter Road in October 1971. It wasn't a particularly memorable occasion - Falkirk were thrashed 6-0.

Playing contemporaries during his four-year spell at Brockville were two later Scotland managers in Alex Ferguson and Andy Roxburgh. However, despite having such a prominent back up, the new Falkirk boss, John Prentice, was a difficult man to please. And Dougie soon recognised that life with the Bairns was about to hit the buffers.

A subsequent move to Ayr United under the legendary Ally McLeod provided Dougie with one of the most traumatic times in his developing career.

He said: "That was in June 1974, the year Mary and I were married. I came back from our honeymoon to find I had no job and virtually no money. All in all, it wasn't a great start to married life!

"I went part-time and got a job on a farm to supplement the family income. I spent 12 weeks at Somerset Park but life was a bit of a drag. I was in and out of the first team and never settled."

In Dougie's early teenage days he had been training at Firhill under Jimmy Davidson and Davie McParland. The Jags youth coaches had remembered his youthful exuberance and untapped talent and persuaded Bertie Auld, the Partick manager, to find a peg for the Somner hat in time for the 74-75 season.

Dougie explainend: "My career really took off at Firhill. Bertie got me fit, managing to take a stone and a half off me in a few weeks.

"And I spent five very successful years with Thistle - I was their top scorer every year."

The statistical count makes for an interesting analysis. Some 16 goals in the 1976-76 campaign saw Dougie placed second top in the First Division scoring charts. Two years later, and with the Jags now in the Premier League, he was fifth, and the following year he advanced to fourth place with 11 strikes.

It was this success rate that sparked an interest from Saints boss Jim Clunie. He was seeking a possible replacement for Frank McGarvey and the Somner deal was duly sealed in 1979.

Dougie's first season in St Mirren's black and white was nothing short of sensational. He was the Premier League's top marksman, with the lethal hitman bagging a magnificent 25 goals.

The following season, 1980-81, saw a further 13 goals deposited in the opposition onion bag and Dougie also claimed St Mirren's first ever goal in Europe in the 2-0 win against Elfsberg in Sweden in the UEFA Cup.

He said: "I spent five great years at Love Street, but you'd have to say that scoring goals was relatively easy when you saw the calibre of players we had. Committed players like Peter Weir, Billy Stark, Jimmy Bone, and Frank McDougall, to name but a few, provided a core of excellence that made St Mirren a great side.

"While we didn't manage to claim any silverware on the domestic front, we did win the Anglo-Scottish Cup in the 1979-80 season, beating Bristol City over two legs. What was particularly edifying was scoring two goals in that final."

With the Somner reflexes becoming not quite as sharp in the mid 80s, manager Rikki McFarlane sanctioned a move to Hamilton. The sojourn at Douglas Park lasted a mere 12 months before a strong maternal interest developed.

Dougie exaplained: "My mother lived in Montrose and when the local Links Park boss Ian Stewart asked me to join them, I jumped at the chance. I spent two years with the Gable Endies, which gave me the chance of seeing my mum almost every weekend. However, that was the playing swansong. I retired in 1986 when I was 35."

With such a galaxy of goals to contemplate, finding one particular Somner strike that was that little bit special was difficult. And it wasn't achieved on a Scottish park, but over in Italy.

Somner takes up the story: "I was fortunate to be picked for a scratch Under-23 league side to play the Italian League equivalent in Verona in 1978. The side were made up of players from teams at the lower end of the Premier League and was under the direction of Ally McLeod before the infamous Argentina World Cup finals debacle.

"We managed to watch the Italians training the night before the game and were a bit awestruck at their skills, touches and finishing. Perhaps it wasn't surprising when we learned that we were watching the likes of Cabrini and Paulo Rossi.

"We also heard that a representative from Cuba had been sent to cast his eye over this Scottish side, believing it was the full Scotland team. We managed to draw 1-1 and I had the satisfaction of scoring the Scottish goal with a header.

"I got a lot of satisfaction from that goal and added to the amount of red wine on offer from the socialising side, it was a pretty memorable trip."

Life goes on after playing and Dougie did contemplate management.

He added: "When I left Hamilton, Partick were looking for a player-manager.

I was one of six that were interviewed but Benny Rooney got the nod, no doubt down to his greater experience. In retrospect, it was a blessing in disguise - management can be a pretty precarious living."

That living requirement was finalised with an eventual appointment with the Renfrewshire Enterprise organisation based in Paisley, and the affable Mr Somner's skills were put to good use on training and educational issues.

His interest in football never abated, with some partial satisfaction being registered in the running of the Rolls Royce team in East Kilbride.

As they say, you can take the boy out of football but taking football out

of the boy is a different proposition. Dougie quipped: "I just loved the banter of the dressing room!"

GARDNER SPEIRS

IT'S important. Make sure you get the spelling right. It's "ei" and not "ie" and as for Mr Speirs' Christian name, he is greatly indebted to his grandfather for the extension of the family's heritable lineage.

Precocious might be an apt description, he was certainly energetic and was well charged with high octane effervescence in his youthful days. Never one with a physical presence to blunt the aspirations of a rampaging frontman, Gardner was ideally suited for more creative duties.

In his heyday at St Mirren Park, a wide left midfield role was his accepted comfort zone.

While in his early learning days - initially at Golfhill Primary and, latterly, at Airdrie Academy, where he played alongside former Rangers youth coach John McGregor - he was essentially a hard-working inside left in the soccer parlance of the mid seventies.

Promise of a career with some potential was emphasised with selection for the Scottish Schoolboys Under-14 team and later playing with the Under-18 side when he was a mere 15.

One of the hardest working of the backroom staff at Love Street was Jack Gilmour, uncle of Saints chairman Stewart Gilmour. Jack's scouting programme took in a Saturday morning schools match with Airdrie Academy and Speirs taking on a Paisley school.

Impressed with Speirs' latent ability, young Gardner, only 13 at the time, was invited to participate in a series of Monday night training sessions at St Mirren Park.

Holding the managerial fort at that time was a certain Alex Ferguson. He was also equally impressed with the skill potential on view and duly had an "S" Form autographed by the 16-year-old Airdrie-born player in 1979.

Gardner explained: "I actually left school to go full-time with St Mirren and went on to spend 10 seasons at Love Street. They say you learn something from each of your mentors and I was lucky to have the experience of learning under Alex Ferguson, Jim Clunie, Rikki McFarlane, Alex Miller, Alex Smith and Tony Fitzpatrick.

"Each contributed something to my game but if pushed I'd have to say Rikki McFarlane was the biggest influence on my career. He had the ability to read the game well and knew exactly where the pressure points were."

Gardner's experiences in his initial outings for Saints could be generously categorised as being sweet and sour in the extreme. December 1980 saw him come off the bench for the last 10 minutes to face Partick Thistle at Love Street. A 1-0 win created sweet music for the Paisley faithful.

However, on from the start for the first time some three months later saw Saints at Parkhead and Celtic administering one of these regular 7-0 drubbings.

Better times were on the horizon, though, with none more satisfying for Speirs than playing against Feyenoord, with Ruud Gullit and Johan Cruyff in their line up, in the 1983 UEFA Cup. However, the experience came at a cost - the 3-0 first round aggregate score leaving Saints and Gardner to ponder what might have been.

Goal scoring midfielders are at a premium these days and Gardner's peak season arrived in 1985-86, when he topped St Mirren's scoring charts with seven.

He said: "I suppose I was lucky when we had the likes of the three Franks around - it was Messrs McGarvey, McDougall and McAvennie who normally saw to the team's scoring needs. But one goal in particular has special memories for me. We were playing Dundee United at Love Street and there hadn't been any scoring. In the last minute the Tannadice keeper Hamish McAlpine and Frank McGarvey had a wee altercation or stushie if you like. Net result was a penalty and I scored with the last kick of the game."

The time came to move on and Gardner enjoyed a spell at Broomfield with Airdrie, before hopping across the North Sea to spend some playing time in Denmark. A return to the Caledonian climes saw him play out a short spell at East Stirling, prior to taking a playing curtain call in the Junior ranks with Bathgate Thistle.

With full-time football in a playing sense now a fast receding memory, the proverbial crust had to be earned to support Gardner's wife Lynne and their two youngsters Greg and Rachel. Providing a taxi service for the wilds of darkest Lanarkshire was the financial salvation - a lifeline that was sold when former boss Alex Smith came calling.

Gardner said: "I always had a great respect for Alex, having worked with him at Love Street, and when he asked me to help out at Broadwood with Clyde's young kids, I jumped at the chance. From there I progressed to taking the reserve team before becoming the Bully Wee's assistant manager."

There comes a time when managerial input achieves a saturation ceiling and the hot seat incumbent is unable to take a club any further. That was Clyde's dilemma. Smith and Speirs had performed wonders with limited resources at Broadwood but a makeover was required and Allan Maitland

and Ronnie McDonald stepped up from a Junior environment to take charge.

Fortunately, Speirs' expertise wasn't entirely lost and Aberdeen employed him as Pittodrie youth coach in 1998. The Dons were progressing under a Scandinavian influence. The likeable Ebbe Skovdahl was at their helm with Tommy Moller Nielson his right-hand man.

When Moller Nielson decided to return to his home shores, Gardner was upgraded to Skovdahl's assistant - a position he held until Pittodrie's Great Dane returned to Copenhagen.

Aberdeen started looking for a high-profile replacement and, regretfully, Gardner didn't quite fit the Pittodrie mould. After a few games in temporary charge in the winter of 2002, the dynamic duo of Steve Paterson and Duncan Shearer upped anchor from Inverness to mastermind football in the Granite City.

Once the Speirs children had completed their scholastic terms at Aberdeen, the family returned to their roots in Carluke, with Gardner ever hopeful his agent could steer him into another soccer channel, as opposed to spending his working day behind the wheel of a taxi.

Now, he is highly thought of with the SFA, and youth supremo Ross Mathie regularly calls on his services to supervise a number of coaching sessions both here and on the continent.

Need a qualified full-time coach? Telephone number available on application!

BILLY STARK

BILLY'S early days were centred round the Anniesland district of North West Glasgow. Temple Primary was his first educational home but, regretfully, they never fashioned a football team.

However, the local Temple Parish Church did through their nourishment of the 116th Glasgow Life Boy team, with not only the BB officers looking after the coaching duties, but Billy's Dad also lending a helping hand.

In truth, Billy owes a great deal to the patriarch of the Stark family, his father closely following his son's career fortunes, which were pleasurable in playing and more minefield-minded in management.

With the termination of scholastic studies at Knightswood Secondary School, a wage-earning career had to be negotiated.

A five-year apprenticeship as a draughtsman with Baird's Structural Steelwork Company in downtown Anniesland provided an insight into the geometric field of angles and measurement, required attributes for any player contemplating a midfield career in football.

The Anniesland area was notorious for housing numerous red blaes pitches.

Generally accepted as a good playing surface for those with a penchant for spraying accurate passes around, they were equally diabolical in making a tackle, which resulted in blaes encrusted knee caps and other severely lacerated anatomical areas.

Anniesland Waverley was one such club that spawned players of quality from these ash surfaces. Billy was creating quality ripples with the amateur side, so much so that St Mirren scout "Baldy" Lindsay was salivating big time at the thought of Billy joining Saints.

Stark revealed: "Baldy seemingly fancied me as a player. He was on the phone every night, banging on the door and brow-beating both me and Saints manager Alex Ferguson into my joining up at Love Street.

"Anniesland Waverley actually played at Love Street on one occasion and I missed out on a close family wedding to play in a trial game for the club.

"I played in a 1975 pre-season game for St Mirren against Selkirk and had a nightmare of a first half. Perhaps I played a little better in the second period because Fergie signed me as an 18-year-old on the team bus on the way home."

With St Mirren having a mediocre time in the 1974-75 campaign, the restructuring of the league format to encompass the embryonic Premier League saw Paisley's finest downgraded to compete in Division One.

Billy's league baptism saw him thrust straight into the 75-76 opening match with Queen of the South at Palmerston Park, and Peter Leonard scored twice in a 2-2 draw. Intriguingly, Billy never played reserve football - he was a first-team regular right from the start.

If the start was 75-76, the finish was 82-83 and, in a black and white jersey, he amassed a prodigious 75 goals, making him St Mirren's top post-war scoring midfielder.

A member of St Mirren's 1979-80 Anglo-Scottish Cup-winning side, Billy played under three managers at Love Street - Ferguson, Jim Clunie and Rikki McFarlane.

Stark's career was in need of revitalisation and it was McFarlane who was instrumental in negotiating Billy's transfer to Aberdeen in 1983.

The Stark trophy haul is substantial, with considerably more medals than Scottish caps. In fact, he only represented Scotland in one Under-21 match against Iceland in 1985. Was there some disappointment, if not frustration, at not achieving further national recognition?

Billy said: "I don't have a chip on my shoulder. I've enjoyed great job satisfaction in playing at club level. You have to be realistic and when you consider Graeme Souness and Gordon Strachan were ahead of me in the midfield pecking order, you can understand breaking into the Scotland team was going to be difficult."

Top league marksman with the Dons in 86-87, Billy had three final experiences at Hampden with the Granite City team.

A winner in the 1985 League Cup final, he was on the scoresheet in the 3-0 victory over Hibernian. Prior to that triumph, he had been on the bench on Scottish Cup duty, earning a winners medal in beating Celtic (2-1 in 1984) and against Hearts (1-0 in 1986).

At 31 and with great experience in the game, it was Celtic who secured his signature and a further three seasons were spent with the Hoops.

Two other Scottish Cup medals came his way while sporting green and white - one as a winner and the other a loser. Dundee United were beaten in the 1988 final but his former team Aberdeen triumphed against the Celts two years later with an amazing 9-8 penalty shootout success.

Two seasons at Rugby Park and a final fling with Hamilton brought the curtain down on Stark's illustrious playing career. Even at Hamilton, the medal collecting business was still on song, the Ducal Town team winning the 91-92 B&Q Cup with Billy on board.

With the boots destined for permanent hibernation, a career switch with soccer undertones was a desirable option.

It came with a call from Tommy Burns at Kilmarnock, who was in need of an assistant manager in time for the 93-94 season. The pairing lasted a year at Rugby Park before they left to take over at Celtic Park - the move generating high acrimony together with a degree of legal confrontation in the Killie environs.

The dust eventually settled with Messrs Burns and Stark overseeing the fortunes of Celtic for a three-year spell.

Club management has never been or will ever be a cradle to grave job and when Celtic eventually dispensed with Burns' services, Billy was on his own at Parkhead until Wim Jansen took over to end Rangers' nine-in-a-row SPL championship run.

With the iconic status that Allan McGraw enjoys down Greenock way, his deteriorating health problems demanded he step down from active management at Morton and Billy was invited to step into the Cappielow hotseat in time for the 98-99 programme.

Two seasons with the Cappielow club were followed by a similar spell with St Johnstone. Regretfully, the need for success from club chairmen, demanding directors and frustrated fans took its toll when the Tayside team were relegated in 2002.

Billy was left to pick up the pieces, but even he couldn't put the Perth Saints back together again and chairman Geoff Brown handed Billy his P45 towards the end of the 2003-4 season.

A Stark future in the game - it's either a new start in the volatile cauldron of pro soccer or it's back to the drawing board! Fortunately neither materialised although for pro soccer read amateur soccer with Billy succeeding Kenny Brannigan as manager of Queen's Park.

GEORGE STEWART

AN assessment of St Mirren's leading post-war marksmen reveals that George Stewart's 44-goal tally clearly places him in the club's top 20. As such, George undoubtedly rates an unqualified mention. But, living in Buckie on the Moray coast, would we be able to locate him for an interview?

Cue the local Information Bureau housed in the magnificent architecture of the local library. The young lady was more than helpful as we asked for directions to the Stewart homestead.

She said: "I know that address, it'll be George and Anna you're after. No 12 - just ring the bell!"

We didn't have to. George was on the doorstep at the appointed time. A man born in Buckie, raised in Buckie and still living in the fishing port was clearly an icon in the eyes of the local community.

But we were here to talk football and not the price of fish, although from George's former job as a fish salesman, he no doubt would have given you a fair price for some haddock.

Football at the local Buckie Primary School was virtually non existent until George reached the educational boundary of the qualifying class.

He said: "We had a new teacher at that stage who was football daft. It was only then that, thanks to him, we started playing against other schools."

As a teenager, George showed considerable aptitude as an out and out goal getter - so, surprise, surprise, he signed for his hometown team Buckie Thistle, operating then and, to this day, in the Highland League.

Word of a striker with some potential soon spread to the central belt and George was persuaded to take up digs in the City of Discovery and join Dundee. He didn't quite set the Dens Park heather on fire and was sent out on loan but George was extremely secretive as to who the loan club was.

Dundee United perhaps?

St Mirren's Bobby Rankin was anxious to find a replacement for the injury-ravaged Alex Crowe and also for L'll Arthur Milne, who had been given a free transfer.

And 23-year-old George stepped into the Paisley breach and made his debut in a League Cup match, ironically against Dundee, at Love Street on September 2,1950.The Buddies won 3-1.

The first of the Stewart 44 goal count came a fortnight later in a a 2-0 win over Falkirk at Brockville.

Playing contemporaries of George's in his four-year stay at Love Street were those mercurial and somewhat diminutive wingers in Gerry Burrell and Alfie Lesz.

Stewart's accent is a rich north coast dialect but even he had difficulty in understanding the verbals when the Saints gameplan took a wobbly.

Gerry's Belfast broadsides and Alfie's Polish protestations occasionally rendered the need for the services of a language translator.

Asked about a particularly memorable goal from his collection, it was assumed George's sole St Mirren hat-trick against Queen of the South at Love Street in the 52-53 season might have topped his ratings.

However, with the mists of time hazing the memory banks, we are indebted to the Paisley Daily Express, who were in no doubt as to the most momentous Stewart strike.

Partick Thistle at Firhill at the backend of August 1952 was the setting with the Paisley tabloid full of striking admiration.

It read: "George Stewart, running in, stumbled, fell and roly pollied like a youngster going down hill. A McGill cross came over, struck one of Stewart's flying boots with the ball soaring past Tommy Ledgerwood in the Thistle goal."

Goal of the season? Perhaps not - but great theatre!

George's last game for Saints saw him again involved with Partick at St Mirren Park, only on this occasion, March 24, 1954, the Jags spoiled the Stewart departure with a 3-1 win.

That Love Street exit saw George head south for a short stay with Worcester City. However, climbing the managerial ladder at that time was one Walter Galbraith. Walter had earned his playing spurs with some galloping full-back performances with Queen's Park and Clyde.

Walter was now at Accrington Stanley and having had first hand experience of the Stewart expertise at sniffing out goals, brought him on line at Stanley's Peel Park ground.

It was during George's five years with Accrington that he earned his sole representative honours. At that time the English League format consisted of Division One and Two plus Divisions Three North and South.

Each year composite teams from geographical spreads of the Division Three clubs met each other in representative combat, Stewart being twice selected for the Northern Division.

Always a full-time player, George left Accrington and signed for Coventry City, before the Highfield Road club sold him to Carlisle United.

The playing career completed its full cycle with George eventually returning to Buckie Thistle.

Would the affable Mr Stewart enjoy playing in the current soccer climate?

He said: "To a point, yes. Certainly from a financial point of view. In my days, the wages we got were washers. I've still got my contracts to prove the point. It was £7 a week plus £1 a point bonus money. The money being dished out nowadays is beyond a joke - it's stupid money."

George's wife Anna is a Buckie lass and supported her husband in all of his soccer endeavours. They were married while George was at St Mirren.

No doubt their family of three sons and their families contributed greatly to their Golden Wedding celebrations. But for George's immediate Buckie cronies, it was conservation of their liquid assets at their best.

He joked: "I felt thirsty and met up with five of the lads and went to the pub. I stood them all a beer and thought - no, I'd better give them a dram as well. 'Here's to you lads, I'm married 50 years today!'"

They celebrate in some style in Buckie!

Tracking George and Anna down was the result of some prime investigative journalism.

A Saints fan, Steve Boyd had organised a first aid training course on the Cormorant Alpha oil platform. One of the course students, Ewan Addison, had some subsequent practical experience on hand when he was called on to treat an elderly gentleman who had taken a bad turn at a funeral in Buckie.

The elderly gentleman was George Stewart. Then the St Mirren grapevine went on overdrive with Messrs Boyd and Addison, in contact with the Paisley paper, the common denominator being the St Mirren connection.

Fortunately, the Stewart health problems were soon cured and George was happy in the knowledge his heart attack will in no way prevent him from starring once again on his local bowling green.

WILLIE TELFER

IT was with some irony that Willie Telfer found his international career stymied by the main residents of the Rangers "Iron Curtain" in George Young and Willie Woodburn.

Ironic in that Telfer's controversial £10,000 transfer from St Mirren to Rangers in November 1957, as a mature 32-year-old, was, in fact, to replace the then ageing Mr Woodburn.

The national selectors did manage to harness the Telfer defensive skills for the 1953 match with Wales at Hampden, although the 3-3 draw spoke volumes for the strikers on duty as opposed to those at the back. Only one full cap, but four Inter-League outings featured on the Telfer CV, England and the Republic of Ireland supplying the opposition.

International selection almost came Willie's way pre-war. As a developing schoolboy at Glengowan Primary and later at Larkhall Academy, he was selected for six Scottish Schools Trials. But further scholastic soccer recognition hit the buffers when a certain Adolph Hitler went on the rampage in a quest for world domination.

The now defunct Burnbank Athletic took the Telfer teenage talents in hand, until Willie Reid signed the 17-year-old for St Mirren in 1943. The going rate at the time was £2 per game plus a win bonus of £2.

The possibility of a cup winners medal almost came Telfer's way in the 1955 League Cup final. Aberdeen provided the opposition but Lady Luck clearly domiciled in the Dons dugout and an own goal plus a fluke from Graham Leggat took the trophy to Pittodrie on the back of a 2-1 result.

Playing in an era of the traditional 2-3-5 formation, as opposed to today's multifarious arithmetic combinations, would Telfer have relished playing in the current climate?

His response was typical: "I'd have loved it. In my playing days everybody attacked and everybody defended. Nowadays, teams attack with sometimes two and occasionally only one up front. Taking the ball off them would be like taking toffee off a wean!"

Willie developed a sure-footed athleticism that was balletic on occasion and when married to a degree of footballing arrogance, he generated a confidence factor that saw off many a burgeoning centre forward.

Top strikers in his day included the legendary twosome of Lawrie "Last Minute" Reilly and the uncrowned King of Tynecastle Willie Bauld.

Of the "Auld Reekie" double act, Reilly's delicate touches and lay-offs were designed never to savour a physical encounter. Such subtleties at times infuriated Telfer, who much preferred the call to arms in confronting the Hearts man. As Telfer confided: "Bauld was one who could handle himself."

The introduction of the teenage Telfer to the senior scene was as a goal scoring centre-forward, But it was as a mobile centre-half that manager Reid saw his future career path.

There were occasions when the St Mirren net finding capability was found wanting. Sign a new centre-forward? No, just shift Big Willie up front - he'd do the business. He did, with perhaps his most memorable contribution being a hat-trick against Queen of the South.

Telfer was always seen by the Paisley faithful as having black and white blood in his veins. So when Scot Symon came calling on behalf of the Ibrox regime to seek a central defensive replacement for the man the Rangers fans dubbed "Big Ben", those with heritable St Mirren roots assumed a state of unbelieving shock.

At 32, Willie's best years were arguably behind him and yet his athletic maturity earned him a Scottish League winners badge with his newfound Ibrox colleagues in 1959.

European football was generally in an embryonic state as Willie's shelf life was reaching termination, yet the record books will highlight sterling performances against AC Milan, Anderlecht and Bratislava in early European Cup campaigns.

While full-time football came late in the Telfer career, a crust had to be earned in providing wife Mary and sons Douglas and Bobby with an acceptable lifestyle. It was the Larkhall abattoir that generated the financial clout to fund the family grocery bill.

Not surprisingly with Willie's flamboyant performances on the field, where 50-50 confrontations generally finished 60-40 in his favour, his civilian job in the slaughterhouse earned him the nickname of "Killer".

It must be a Paisley form of endearment as former full-back colleague Davie Lindsay also earned a similar accolade for his robust style.

Once the boots had been pegged, Symon utilised the Telfer know-how in operating as a scout for the Govan citadel. A hankering to try management emerged along with an invitation to oversee the fortunes of Albion Rovers.

Two seasons with mid-table league placements for the Cliftonhill club ended any thoughts of securing a permanent managerial seat.

Always having an eye for a ball, Willie switched to bowling, turning out for the Reploch Bowling Club in hometown Larkhall. Despite a hip replacement operation, he was still able and fit enough to assist in the winning of the Lanarkshire Bowling League title.

Born on October 25, 1925, Willie died on November 12, 1995.

BILLY THOMSON

IT was, for many years, a Mecca in terms of Glasgow's outstanding retail establishments. Lumley's of Sauchiehall Street was a haven for the supply of strips, balls, boots and every conceivable type of sporting accoutrements.

Billy Thomson was one who made the pilgrimage - but not as a potential purchaser.

After leaving Linwood High School, a living had to be earned and thoughts of selling stock to the sporting wannabees a possible career highway. That highway became a veritable cul-de-sac, as the disillusioned Mr Thomson failed to log in a minimal sales return.

But many in the great game will be glad Billy turned his back on a retail career.

One of a family of three, Billy's brother also featured on the football front. He played Junior with Benburb, Yoker Athletic and Johnstone Burgh.

A trial with Tottenham Hotspur was on offer until a festering mastoid curtailed a promising future in the game.

Billy's playing route was more productive, though. A left sided midfielder in his school days, it was only when the school's resident keeper went AWOL that Billy was drafted to begin a life between the sticks.

Glasgow United were one of the top youth teams in the country, bursting with latent talent. Dozens of scouts attended every game and Billy's goalkeeping strengths attracted considerable attention, particularly in downtown Maryhill.

Former Partick Thistle winger Davie McParland and then manager of the Jags, together with ex Rangers chief Scot Symon, were the guiding influences at Firhill.

A goalie was on the Thistle shopping list and Billy answered their need in 1973. Six years were spent at Firhill, in which time a sartorial trend in goalkeeping dress sense was developed by the new Thistle No.1 - he always wore trackie bottoms!

Billy explained: " I did wear shorts on occasion. You have to remember goalkeepers aren't as active as the outfield players. There are times when the temperatures can plummet to Baltic proportions!

"I first wore shorts that stopped just above the knee. They were reasonably comfortable, then I was given a pair that finished just below the knee.

They were so lightweight and even more comfortable. That led me on to wear the full tracksuit bottom.

"I used to take a lot of verbal slagging from my team-mates but I was comfortable wearing them - even on hot days!".

No doubt some of the dressing room banter was on offer at Love Street, for it was Jim Clunie who persuaded Billy to join the black and white brigade at St Mirren Park.

The Thomson St Mirren debut came against Dumbarton in August 1978 in a League Cup tie at Love Street, the hosts winning 2-0 thanks to a double from Jimmy Bone.

Billy's memories of life in Paisley are vivid.

He said: "I spent six superb years with St Mirren and the highlight was getting into Europe and playing against the likes of Feyenoord with Gullit and Cryuff.

"What was particularly pleasing was taking third place in the Premier League in 79-80, which was a magnificent achievement for what some misguided people are prone to call a small club.

"There were a great bunch of lads around at that time, such as Jack Copland, Iain Munro, Alex Beckett and Andy Dunlop."

Billy's heroics earned him the top spot in a poll to establish St Mirren's greatest post-war team.

The Scottish selectors were also impressed. Alan Rough and George Wood at Everton were the national team keepers in contention, with Billy's international debut taking place against Northern Ireland in 1980.

He went on to win a further six caps, making him, in tandem with Munro, St Mirren's top capped all-time player.

Tannadice beckoned and Billy was persuaded that life with the Tayside Tangerines, under the redoubtable Jim McLean, was a way of life not to be missed.

Irony then crept in and Billy and his United team-mates faced St Mirren in the 1987 Scottish Cup final. Not surprising, Thomson had mixed feelings at facing his former club.

Saints fans need little reminding that it was an extra-time goal from Ian Ferguson that sent the Paisley decibels into overdrive, Billy being comprehensively beaten at his near post with the Ferguson drive.

Around that time, United made a habit of appearing in Scottish Cup finals, but were equally remiss in capturing any of the silverware on offer. After losing to Saints in '87, the Arabs again arrived at Hampden the following season to face Celtic. Surely this was the occasion to break the

Tannadice cup final hoodoo?

It wasn't, with ex-Saint Frank McAvennie knocking the ball past Thomson twice to take the cup to Parkhead.

Come the 1991 cup final, Billy had been relegated to being back up to Alan Main as United faced Motherwell at Hampden.

Hero of that encounter was Fir Park keeper Ally Maxwell, who sustained a ruptured spleen in an aerial challenge with John Clark but managed to finish the match despite suffering excruciating pain.

But a lengthy period of recuperation, plus a contractual disagreement with Motherwell boss Tommy McLean, meant Maxwell never played for the Lanarkshire side again. They needed a replacement keeper, cue Billy Thomson to take up the challenge.

And there was a considerable challenge to convince the Motherwell fans, who didn't take kindly to Maxwell's successor.

The cup final hero had become a cult figure at Fir Park and some banners proclaimed "THOMSON MUST GO", almost but not quite undermining Billy's confidence.

Periods with Rangers and Dundee followed but as his playing career eased towards the buffers, Billy was anxious to sample the trials and tribulations of coaching - there being a distinct shortage of goalkeeping experience in the Scottish soccer scene.

Dens Park gave Billy his first coaching appointment before Dick Advocaat lured him to Ibrox.

The initial Thomson remit in the light blue camp was to work with the established first-team men. However, since Alan Hodgkinson opted to return south to his English roots, the entire Rangers goalkeeping fraternity prospered under the tutelage of the former St Mirren man.

Billy never had any thoughts on management but was clearly on track to boost the country's goalkeeping potential.

JIM THORBURN

IT had all the credentials of a vintage Keystone Cops farce.

Saints had drawn Raith Rovers in the third Round of the 1962 Scottish Cup at Kirkcaldy. Thanks to a goal from former Celt Willie Fernie, St Mirren managed to scrape a 1-1 draw to take the replay back to Love Street.

Jim Thorburn was the Stark's Park keeper at the time and knew the St Mirren players well. Being a West of Scotland man and given permission to forego the tenuous travels to the east coast for midweek training, all his training sessions were undertaken at Love Street.

That Tuesday evening replay saw the Rovers keeper in an altercation with Saints flying winger Jim Rodger. The severe clout on the Thorburn cranium rendered him unconscious, necessitating an ambulance being called. To label the paramedic driver as being a little precocious was clear understatement in the extreme.

Straight through a set of red lights, he collided with a car and then ploughed into a Paisley china shop with fragmented pottery in flying abundance.

By sheer coincidence, the first policemen on the scene was Thorburn's father-in-law, who arranged the requisite onward transportation for the injured keeper to the Royal Alexandra Hospital.

In waking up from his concussed state the following morning, Jim was amazed to find cuts in virtually every area of his anatomy - a consequence of his rattling around the stricken ambulance. The proverbial ping pong ball in a tumble dryer sprang readily to the Thorburn mind.

What was bad for Jim was exceedingly worse for the errant driver - he finished up sustaining a fracture to both legs!

Born in Lanark, it was at nearby Biggar High School where the Thorburn soccer development was initiated. Originally a right half with some potential, the absence of the regular custodian conditioned Jim's transition to goalkeeping greatness.

A teenage trial for the Douglasdale club against Carluke Rovers was taken in by a Leeds United scout, culminating in a visit to Elland Road.

The media coverage generated interest from a number of clubs, not the least of which was Manchester City. However, it was Raith Rovers who won the day, offering a senior recruitment form, and Jim spent seven years with the Kirkcaldy club.

Having served an apprenticeship with the Govan firm of Fairfields, conceivably the move into the shipbuilding firm's drawing office, involving the profusion of angles, curves and straight lines, fashioned the clutch and cutting out of numerous goalkeeping cross balls.

However, his seven-year stay at Stark's Park created minimal highlights for inclusion in the Thorburn diaries, although reaching the semi-final of the 1963 Scottish Cup was one special occasion. Losing out 5-2 to Celtic at Ibrox wasn't the predicted score in the Rovers' script, though.

It might be fair to say that Jim's self confidence factor was limited.

Indeed, it was Jim who made the point: "It took me a long time to believe in myself."

A degree of self -belief materialised when Ipswich Town were in need of a new last line of defence and Jim answered the Portman Road call.

Three years were spent with the Suffolk club before Doug Millward - the St Mirren manager at the time and former Ipswich player - heard of Jim's wish to return north and welcomed him to Love Street for the start of the 1965-66 season.

As the new Saints keeper, he was following a long line of successful No.1s, with Campbell Forsyth, Pat Liney, Davie Walker and Jimmy Brown conceivably doyen members from the goalkeeping Hall of Fame.

The fame factor didn't last, and neither did Millward. Alex Wright succeeded him as boss and Saints, with Thorburn in goal, were relegated to Division Two at the end of the 1966-67 campaign.

Wright re-jigged the team, Thorburn kept his place and St Mirren regained their Division One status the following season. The Saints keeper's contribution to the championship-winning side was prodigious. Some 36 games played, only one defeat and exactly 100 goals scored. But more important from a goalkeeping point of view, only 23 goals were conceded, with 19 shutouts recorded.

Now he believed in himself! Jim stayed on at Love Street until 1970, after which he turned out on a few occasions for Albion Rovers.

Many a set of goalkeeping fingers have been well warmed by the ferocity of some rocket style howitzers. Jim has first hand experience with a couple.

He recalled: "Don Emery was one crack shot. He was originally around in the 1960s with Aberdeen before ending up at East Fife. A burly full-back turned centre-forward, there was one occasion he drove in a free-kick that crashed off the cross bar and rebounded well beyond the penalty box.

"Davie Lapsley was another. His technique in penalty taking was unique.

One of his team-mates would spot the ball for him, with Davie starting his run up from his right-back beat!   Invariably his spot-kicks ended up in the net but one time he nearly carved a route through my rib cage!"

Jim and his wife Sheena latterly lived in the Ralston area of Paisley, the close proximity of the local golf course encouraging Jim to hone down his nine handicap - and with some success.

Early in his career, Jim had assumed doubts as to his undoubted ability - but Saints fans had no qualms.

One particular save spelt out their confidence. Jim Kiernan was the St Mirren centre-half and when a cross came in he miscued his clearance, the ball ricocheting off the side of his head. Jim went for it at full stretch, managed to pin down the wayward ball with one hand and prevented a crucial own goal.

That particular save clearly confirmed the supporters' belief - and it was justified.

GUNI TORFASON

CHECK out the Collins English Dictionary. Check out the word CULT. The definition given is a person arousing great devotion, or, intense interest in and devotion to a person.

Gudmundor Torfason, or "Guni" to his footballing friends, was clearly a cult figure during his three-year spell in St Mirren colours.

Born in December 1961 in the West Mann Islands - a community with a population of some 5,000 in the south of Iceland - travel to and from the country's capital Reykjavik could be a tortuous journey, with a 20-minute inter island flight providing the necessary transportation.

While, not surprisingly, Icelandic is the local language, Guni's impeccable English provided an insight into soccer life, and without in any way being derogatory, in the country's lunar type wastes.

He explained: "Obviously, because of our geographical location and the fact that daylight is minimal during the winter months, we can generally only play outdoors from May through to October. But don't be fooled thinking it is a short season. We have a number of quality indoor arenas and this provides us with the facilities to play the whole year round."

Taking his playing career to a greater stage necessitated Guni leaving his home pastures and he touched down early in Austria to play for Rapid Vienna.

Belgium and KSK Beveren were next on the Torfason soccer itinerary, before he joined KRC Genk.

St Mirren were in the market for a striker and manager Tony Fitzpatrick persuaded the board to fund the Torfason removal costs in bringing him to Love Street in August 1989.

However, it was touch and go for Guni as to whether or not he would make the journey to downtown Paisley.

He explained: "There had been the possibility that I might have gone to Celtic but the Parkhead side opted to sign Dariusz Dziekanowski from Legia Warsaw and I was recommended to St Mirren."

At 6'-1" and 13 stones plus, the playing physique augured well for a successful spell at the home of Paisley's finest.

Guni didn't let The Buddies down. He made his debut in the memorable opening league game of the 1989-90 season. Against Rangers at Ibrox, Saints won 1-0 but Guni didn't score - Kenny McDowall did - his challenge introducing keeper Chris Woods to an undignified position on the grassy Govan sward, much to the ballistic outpourings of the Light Blue battalions.

The first black and white Torfason goal came three days later in a League Cup trip to Shielfield Park, Saints defeating Berwick Rangers 2-0 and gaining a passage to meet Motherwell in the third round.

What was remarkable about Guni's scoring ability was the quality of his strikes. Never a mundane tap in, they were virtually all fashioned from the spectacular mould and brought the Love Street fans out in full throated approval.

Guni's first season for Saints saw him top the club's scoring charts with 12 goals from 29 league outings - a return that might have been further enhanced bar for injury.

All in all in his time as a Buddie he hit 24 goals, giving him a strike rate of one in every three games - a ratio generally accepted as good going for any goal getter.

One particular goal?

Guni said: "I have so many memories of my time in Scotland, I can't really pick out one spectacular goal. What I can vividly remember is the visit to Celtic Park in April 1990. St Mirren won 3-0. Now that creates a piece of sheer unadulterated pleasure."

Not surprisingly, the Icelandic authorities, ever eager to strengthen their national pool, took the Torfason skills on board, Guni enjoying a well-earned 56 international call ups.

However, life at Love Street had reached the soccer cross roads and Fitzpatrick had resigned, to be replaced by David Hay.

Guni explained: "I was out of contract and, as so often happens in football, I was looking for a modest salary increase. But the finances of the club were such that they couldn't offer me a deal.

"St Johnstone could, and I went there for a couple of seasons. I only played 40 games for them but the goal count wasn't as great as at St Mirren Park. I would also have to say I didn't quite gel with the Perth fans in the same way I did in Paisley."

At the age of 33, Guni returned to Iceland and joined First Division club Fylkir. And as the ageing process began to manifest itself, the former up and at 'em striker became a tidy stopper in his later years.

Guni wasn't the first Icelander to don a Saints jersey. Many will remember the goal potency of Theorolf "Tottie" Beck. Guni remembered him well, too.

He said: "Beck was a player long before my time. He was a hero to all

Icelanders but I didn't get to know him very well - he was a very private man."

With such an experienced playing background, enhanced with a detailed knowledge of the game, it wasn't surprising that a management appointment opened up.

Grindavik were the lucky club and Guni renewed his association with St Mirren and Fitzpatrick when the club came over to play an pre-season game in March 1997. The match was played with bounce game speed and activity, with Steve Watson netting the only goal.

No St Mirren game, whether on the competitive or friendly stage, is ever legitimised without the support of arguably the club's most devoted fan - Jimmy McIntosh.

The man affectionately known as "Toshie" was determined to see this particular game and rekindle the Torfason association. Striding expectantly across the car park, the out of breath Toshie demanded: "When's the kick-off?"

Fully expecting a 7.30 pm reply, he was more than a little chastened to find the game was over courtesy of a 4pm kick-off!

Guni and his wife Jakobina have three of a family but paternal oversight is possibly somewhat minimal with Guni's post football progression of activities. In addition to taking a course in Business Studies at the local university, he is also on hand providing sports opinions and analysis on the local television channels.

ROBERT TORRANCE

A CONSIDERABLE number of strikers are blessed with minimal physical proportions, their centres of gravity being in close proximity to terra firma. As such, a slight nudge in the penalty box and many an attacking front man has earned a highly questionable spot-kick, generating copious outpourings of wrath from the stands and terraces.

Some forwards have tended to the milk the situation and have been re-christened as inveterate divers.

Robert Torrance - Robert at home and Bobby in a football environment - was a confirmed diver. However, we hasten to add that while Bobby occasionally snitched a perhaps dubious penalty, his prime claim to diving fame was passing his certification as a recreational diver.

Scuba diving in Loch Long and along the Ayrshire coast provides the diminutive Mr Torrance with the necessary accreditation to propel himself into deep water.

Bobby would make the point that his friendship with the opposition penalty area was conditioned during his early learning curve days with the High Schools of Woodfarm and Eastwood. He was hallmarked as a nippy striker with an eye for goal - the eyes of the Scottish Schoolboy teams selecting him for national duty while resident at both educational establishments.

The excellent scouting system of the famed Drumchapel Amateurs side brought Bobby under the protective wing of Davie Moyes - father of the Everton manager - who guided the team to Scottish Amateur Cup success in back-to-back years.

But Bobby was destined to play for St Mirren. He explained: "I was associated with the club from 13 years of age, when Tommy Bryceland and Willie Cunningham were in charge. And I spent 11 years at Love Street, from being a young teenager until my early 20s.

"From St Mirren I went to Hibernian, then to Partick Thistle, followed by Stirling Albion, Brechin City, Arbroath when Jimmy Bone was the player-manager and, lastly, Alloa, under Dom Sullivan.

"Despite playing with so many other clubs, I have to say that St Mirren were always my core club."

It was Alex Ferguson who brought Bobby on to the senior stage for the 1976-77 championship-winning season. The Torrance contribution to that First Division title was nine starts and 13 substitute appearances, these outings yielding a 12-goal return.

Bobby said: "There probably isn't a better feeling in the football business than making your senior debut. The good vibes and butterfly feelings came to me on September 25, 1976, at Gayfield when St Mirren were playing Arbroath. It was a league match, we won 2-0 and the icing on the cake was me scoring both goals."

While full international honours never found favour with the Torrance household, Bobby was called into the national pro youth match selections on a couple of occasions, against Belgium and Yugoslavia.

As to a career scoring highlight, Bobby will happily confirm that while he has a soft spot for St Mirren, his soccer allegiance is centred around a certain ground in downtown Govan. That affinity necessitates a weekly pilgrimage with sons David, Andrew and Robert to provide support of a Light Blue hue.

With this association of all things Rangers, it was understandable that Bobby's 21st birthday celebrations were gelled with mixed feelings. Saints were due at Ibrox on league business and Bobby scored against his true love.

Full-time for many years, once the part-time contracts came home to roost, additional family income had to be generated.

He explained: "I joined a friend who was employed in the travel industry, working with him a couple of days a week. I quite enjoyed the experience of arranging travel and holidays during the day and football training at night."

Keen to extend his travel options, Bobby bought out the International Travel Company in Glasgow and proceeded to plan, book and direct a multifarious number of football related interests.

One such interest was providing a travel itinerary for the famous or, in some cases, infamous Dukla Pumpherston charity side. Essentially, an old crocks side, they have been spuriously labelled as a "Drinking side with a football problem!"

In the mid-1990s, a Dukla overseas trip to the USA and Canada was completely organised by Bobby's company.

Torrance said: "We played two games, won the first 2-1 and were beaten 2-0 in the second. The latter game wasn't against a comparable old crocks side, their line up was full of young guys in a game played in an oven baking temperature of 85 degrees.

"It wasn't easy for the golden wrinklies, but the result didn't matter.

What was important was the chaff and banter and when you have guys like Chick Young, Tony Roper, Tony Higgins, Jimmy Bone, Gerry Collins and Alex MacDonald around, you'll understand the hilarity stakes were high."

Pondering on his Saints career, Bobby was at great lengths to highlight Rikki McFarlane as having had a great influence on his time at Love Street.

He said: "Rikki spoke a great deal of sense to me. He had that great attribute of providing positive man management. He was very knowledgeable about the game and gave me great encouragement."

In essence, Bobby Torrance didn't need to rely on dodgy penalties. The skill back-up that surrounded him in his early Love Street days made goal scoring a much easier occupation - Frank McGarvey, Tony Fitzpatrick and Billy Stark saw to that.

TOMMY TURNER

OCTOBER 19, 2002, was a momentous day in Tommy Turner's career. Not many players manage to clock up 500 league appearances but Tommy did just that as a Gretna player against Elgin City in a 0-0 draw at the Borough Briggs Stadium. Conceivably, with such a spread of playing activities encompassing six senior clubs, the Gretna officials might have been regretfully unaware of the historic occasion.

While that highlight might have been unfortunately posted in the low key tray, Tommy did enjoy a couple of celebratory promotion-winning occasions.

He recalled: "Morton's Tommy McLean signed me in 1984 and three years later we won the Division One title and promotion to the Premier League. In the last game of the season, we only had to draw to pip Dunfermline for pole position. The game was against Montrose at Links Park and we won 4-1. We went up but Montrose, unfortunately for them, went down!"

A striker for most of his early days, it was the legendary Allan McGraw who converted Tommy into an attacking midfielder. Once the ageing legs became less elasticated, the midfield beat can readily be readjusted to that of a quality sweeper.

That was the Turner role, as well as club captain, when St Mirren won the millennium First Division championship in 2000.

Tommy reasoned: "That was surely the pinnacle of my entire career. Everyone thought we would blow it in the run in after the New Year celebrations. We didn't, and to win the title at Love Street against Raith Rovers most certainly produced waves of emotion."

There was, however, emotion of a different kind in his early days. Tommy had joined Kilmarnock as a teenager only to be given the heave-ho by the Rugby Park management.

He recalled: "I was down in the dumps but owe my future in the game entirely to my dad. He gave me the proverbial kick up the backside and told me to get on with it.

"Arthurlie and Pollok were keen to sign me but I wanted to enjoy the game with guys of my own age, so I went and joined Glentyan Thistle."

Tommy was 20 when he re-entered the Senior scene at Cappielow and was immediately pitchforked into the atmosphere of a Renfrewshire derby. That Senior debut was against St Mirren at Love Street in the quarter-final of the 1984 Scottish Cup, although Saints winning 4-3 did nothing to placate the Turner temperament. He hated to lose!

After six seasons with Morton, the Turner talents headed for McDiarmid Park as St Johnstone manager Alex Totten forked out a reported £100,000 for his services.

The Perth Saints were hardy customers and difficult to beat at home. The 1990-91 season saw Aberdeen thrashed 5-0 at McDiarmid Park, to be followed by a 3-2 Christmas turnover of Celtic. That victory was made all the more pleasurable at that festive time as a Turner 25-yarder arrowed into the postage stamp.

The Turner homestead, as well as his birthplace, was located in Johnstone, and the daily training trek up the A9 to Perth became a bit of a grind. Partick Thistle's John Lambie solved the problem by offering the energetic midfielder a peg at Firhill, Tommy spending a further three seasons with the Harry Wraggs.

Tony Fitzpatrick, in his second spell in charge at Love Street, needed a degree of experience in his team's boiler house to supplement the talent of his youthful Saints, and the craggy Turner countenance was deemed to be just the face to instil some confidence and drive at Love Street.

However, the confidence factor faded when Tommy lost his place and he found semi solace in a loan deal with Queen of the South at Dumfries.

With Anthony Charles Fitzpatrick's demise at St Mirren, enter Tom Hendrie who, in his time as manager with Berwick Rangers, fondly remembered a number of staunch Turner displays while at St Johnstone.

Tommy was retrieved from Palmerston Park and provided St Mirren with 129 league outings along with eight goals. Perhaps the most outstanding of this goal tally was a sliced header that proved to be the winner in a 3-2 home win over Raith Rovers in the league-winning season.

The quiet but forceful man who paraded 32 Premier League games for Saints the next term went on to coach the Buddies reserve side. What followed was calamitous, Tommy receiving the dreaded P45 wrapped in a free transfer package at the end of the 2001-02 season.

With Airdrieonians heading for oblivion in 2001, a replacement team was required to make up the league numbers. And Gretna, formed in 1946, won the nod for Scottish League selection. A galaxy of established players joined the Raydale Park club, not the least of whom was one Thomas Gibson Turner.

Just 20 league outings for the border club generated thoughts that the Turner energy banks were becoming slightly overdrawn. Tommy didn't think so and, at 40, joined Johnstone Burgh for a season with the Juniors.

Dealings finished with the Burgh, he went on to enjoy the Ayrshire ozone with Largs Thistle for the 2004-05 campaign.

Clearly Tommy has a particular mission in sight. The renowned Stanley Matthews was 50 when he hung up his boots, while new Brighton manager Neil McBain blew out a record 52 candles on his birthday cake when he stopped playing in England. Scotland manager Ally McLeod played in a Reserve match at Love Street when he was 61.

What price Turner breaching one of those records?

With the latter Turner playing days reverting to a part-time capacity, income support away from football had to be earned to support his family of wife Suzanne and their two youngsters, Kyle and Erin. A glowing reference from St Mirren helped to provide a job with Aviance as a Ramp Operator at Glasgow Airport. However, the salary on offer wasn't equally glowing and Tommy moved to take up a post as an operator at the Edrington Group whisky bond near Drumchapel.

An avid golfer in his spare time, the Cochrane Castle course provides a regular examination of Tommy's 12 handicap which, on St Mirren golf outings, was generally sustainable in out-driving his Love Street colleagues.

While one unfulfilled ambition in Tommy's locker was to score 50 league goals – he only managed 49 – he left a legacy that will forever be reminder of his playing days at St Mirren Park

He said: "I like to think I'm now a strict disciplinarian. There were times in my early days when the fuse was on the short side. However, I think I've mellowed in my later years. I like to win games and I like to win with some style.

"I always liked to instil in the young boys I've coached a confidence factor in having them believe they are better than the opposition. You've got to believe in your own ability."

The gospel according to Tommy Turner can't be faulted!

DAVID WALKER

THE year was 1960. The spectacle of the Olympic Games had arrived in Rome and the mercury readings provided exhaustive conditions for the competing athletes.

It was Armin Hary of Germany who took the Blue Riband of the sprinting events, winning the 100 metres title in 10.2 seconds and so establishing an Olympic record.

Peter Radford of Great Britain took the bronze, only 0.1 of a second behind the winner and second placed David Sime of the USA, who also shared in that record.

David Walker would have homed in on these times with a feeling of frustration.

Campbell Money and the goalkeeping trade union are generally not noted for their speed and acceleration in guarding their domain - but Davie was fashioned from a different mould. He was a speed merchant, having regularly clocked 9.5 seconds and occasionally at 9.4. over 100 yards.

With these times, he was clearly destined to top his achievement of twice crowned British sprint champion.

However, the drawback to Davie's athletic progression was the fact that he ran professionally at Edinburgh's Powderhall Stadium. And in the 60s, those who had been paid for their athletic prowess were automatically barred from national or Olympic consideration.

With that door firmly shut, Davie turned to football and joined the famous Edinburgh nursery club Hutcheson Vale.

Davie recalled: "The club had a rather unique style of administration - they were managed by a lady - the redoubtable "Ma" Bryson. And Ma Bryson and her colleagues had developed a practice of unearthing quality keepers.

"I learned my custodial skills there, as did Tommy Younger of Hibs and Liverpool, who went on to win 24 Scotland caps, while George Farm in his Blackpool days was selected for duty on 10 international occasions."

Airdrie were in search of a keeper and the young man born in 1935 in Edinburgh filled the bill nicely.

Ironically, it was the former St Mirren boss Willie Fotheringham, then managing the Broomfield club, who brokered the deal. Davie was a mere

16 at the time when he made his Diamonds debut at Broomfield Park.

Being in the right place at the right time is a mandatory perquisite for success in life, and Walker's geographical location was spot on when St Mirren had a goalkeeping crisis in 1959.

He had made his Saints debut against Third Lanark at Cathkin Park just prior to Christmas 1958, but his big moment came the following February.

The resident St Mirren keeper, Campbell Forsyth, was honest enough to declare himself unfit just prior to the 1959 Scottish Cup run.

In all honesty, Campbell would admit that he could have played but the thought of having to come off during the game would be irresponsible to his playing colleagues.

Manager Willie Reid wasn't taking any chances and opted for the former Airdrie No.1, with Davie playing only his second Saints match against Peebles Rovers in the second round of the Scottish Cup - February 13 being the date for the archivists.

No disrespect to the good people of Airdrie, but being catapulted out of north Lanarkshire into a Scottish Cup run that earned Davie a winner's medal was the stuff that soccer dreams are made of. And a measure of the Walker goalkeeping skills was highlighted by the fact he only lost four goals in five cup ties that campaign.

Davie went on to spend three and a half seasons with The Buddies before a season at Gala Fairydean.

Sourcing Walker's whereabouts for an interview was problematical. Rumour had it he had emigrated to Australia. But Davie was quick to correct the fallacy.

He said: "I've never been to Australia. The misunderstanding possibly arose when my colleague and trainer opted to head for Oz."

David's home base was finally located through a wedding in Edinburgh. Former St Mirren midfielder Ian Ross was a guest at the celebratory nuptials, with St Mirren dealings, past and present, becoming the conversational common denominator.

Sufficient to say that Davie was in position to join the rest of his Scottish Cup-winning colleagues at the St Mirren 125th birthday celebrations in October 2002.

A qualified accountant, Davie aspired to become the secretary of a Coatbridge engineering firm and in his later working life became managing director of a small engineering offshore company.

Always a goalkeeper? Well, nearly always!

He recalled: "On one occasion we were playing Third Lanark in a reserve match at Love Street. I was injured and couldn't continue in goal. These were the days before substitutes were sanctioned. I had to hobble on the wing but was in the right spot, again at the right time, to score one of St

Mirren's goals!"

One other accolade from the Walker sporting sphere arrived from Davie's passion for golf. Much of his leisure time was spent in chasing birdies, eagles and the occasional albatross with the Royal Burgess Golfing Society - one of the oldest clubs in the world. And Davie was eventually installed as club captain.

Widely travelled through his engineering interests, he suffered a personal setback on one trip to Brazil.

Davie explained: "I was in Rio de Janeiro on business and was attacked and mugged. One of my prize possessions was my St Mirren J&P Coats watch which was a presentation when we won that Scottish Cup. That was all that was taken from me, so conceivably someone on the famous Copa Cabana beach is regulating his lifestyle courtesy of my timepiece!"

Davie unfortunately lost his wife but has two sons to provide solace, comfort and some pointed family wit.

His cup final jersey is still in his loft and when taken out for mutual admiration and inspection, one sibling was heard to utter: "How on earth did you ever get into that, dad?"

JOHN WILSON

WITH no disrespect intended towards those having a name affinity with Clan Wilson and accepting that "John" as a Christian name is in common use, it conceivably follows that having the name John Wilson imprinted on your birth certificate may not initially signify moments of soccer grandeur. However, interpolate the nickname "Cockles" into the equation and a whole new football scenario opens up.

John "Cockles" Wilson was a West Kilbride lad. His family are reputed to have operated a fish shop in the town and to supplement the shop's seafood stock, John's early days were spent raking the local seashore sands in search of fresh supplies of shellfish. The resultant nickname rubber-stamped John for life.

He was an energetic young man and his early footballing days were spent as a burgeoning centre-forward knocking in goals on a regular basis for Ardeer Thistle.

Like many of his day, the immediate post-war years necessitated a two-year spell with the National Service colours, John being earmarked for the RAF with and his major base posting being in Germany.

He did manage back to the UK in March 1955 and was invited by St Mirren to take part in a friendly against Reading.

Few people will remember his debut game, for he appeared under an assumed name and had to be stretchered off after only three minutes with a broken collarbone. Cockles appeared as a trialist and in these days so called trialists were listed on the team sheet as A.N. Other, or they appeared under an assumed name. Cockles' playing nom-de-plume on this occasion was Alan Robertson – no one knowing who had provided the pseudonym.

Despite the anonymity and his premature departure from the game, the St Mirren authorities were sufficiently impressed to offer him signing terms and the 19-year-old Wilson became a St Mirren player on April 20, 1955.

At the time of that trial, Cockles' RAF duties in Germany meant his early St Mirren appearances were somewhat sporadic. His full first-team debut was in a League Cup tie against Queen of the South, when he appeared as a centre-forward. The Doonhamers from Dumfries were also the opposition when he made his first league appearance in black and white.

He flitted in and out of the team before reappearing as a left-back in a Scottish Cup fifth Round tie against Partick Thistle in 1957.

St Mirren's occasional lack of scoring fire power meant the services of the former centre turned full-back were always on ready call. That call was answered in a league match against Airdrie at the old Broomfield Stadium, Saints winning 4-3 thanks to a Wilson hat-trick, Davie Lapsley chipping in with the fourth.

Undoubtedly the 1959 Scottish Cup final was the jewel in the Wilson soccer crown, his winning medal from that 3-1 win over Aberdeen claiming pride of place in his memorabilia collection.

In total, John contributed to the St Mirren success rate on over 350 occasions, with another highlight coming at the end of the 1961-62 season when he was voted as the Saints Player of the Year.

A serious foot injury brought a premature end to an illustrious career, although he had one last outing, captaining Saints in a bounce game against Millport Amateurs in August 1966.

An inspector with the Rolls Royce Engine Plant at Hillington, the debillitating motor neurone disease ultimately kicked in and John's untimely death after a sustained long illness came on February 23, 1985. He was just 49. His dependents were his wife Agnes, son John and daughters Rosemary and Wilma.

As a mark of respect, a minute's silence was observed at St Mirren's next home game and the 2-1 win over Hibernian was dedicated to his memory.

Many tributes have been paid to the popular Saint.

Former playing colleague Jim Rodger remembers him well.

He said: "I played with John both at Love Street and against him when I went to Hearts. One of the quickest full-backs in the business, he had two good feet and his tackling was as clean as a whistle. He never achieved international recognition as the 'establishment' seemed to prefer Eric Caldow of Rangers.

"I particularly remember the quarter-final the year we won the Scottish Cup. We were playing Dunfermline at Love Street and were one down at the interval. I managed to score the equalizer and it was John who was first to congratulate me. I'll never forget his ecstatic outburst – 'Ya big champion!'"

Ian Brown, manager of the Paisley Engineering Company, ran a Saints supporters' bus for many years.

He revealed: "It was at the time of the 1987 Cup Final. Looking back at the 1959 winning side, Cockles was the only one missing due to his early death and as a tribute to him we renamed our supporters' club the Cockles Wilson St Mirren Memorial Supporters' Club. We felt it was a small but fitting tribute."

Bob Money, St Mirren's Safety Officer, eulogises Cockles in a completely different light.

He explained: "I had taken over as The Boys' Brigade captain of the 3rd Paisley Company. We needed a guest of honour for our annual display where the boys would show off progress in their various activities.

"I had approached Jim Clunie but he already had a commitment to another BB company function for the night in question. He recommended Cockles and John arrived resplendent in his club blazer, tie and flannels. He addressed the boys superbly and stayed for the entire evening chatting to the parents and the boys. He was a splendid ambassador for St Mirren Football Club."

Former St Mirren chairman Willie Todd was full of praise for the man. He added: "He was one of the most wholehearted players St Mirren ever had. You couldn't have met a nicer guy."

A memorial dinner was held in the Glynhill Hotel on Monday March 25, 1985. Chaired by comedian Mr Abie, the guest list included broadcaster Ian St John, comedian Hector Nicol, the ecclesiastical wit of the Rev James Currie and journalist Alex Cameron.

Not many St Mirren players will have earned the accolade of having such a dinner held in their honour. John Wilson did.

TOMMY WILSON

HOW much do you reckon you're worth?

Substantial? Minimal? Par for the course? In Tommy Wilson's case, the variance in his apparent soccer value in moving from St Mirren to Dunfermline in November 1989 was semi astronomical!

After seven years at Love Street and Fraser Wishart's arrival from Motherwell, Tommy's quest for a contract extension was heading for the buffers. Tony Fitzpatrick couldn't, or wouldn't, go along with the Paisley-born full-back's request, with a freedom of contract release - or P45 in modern employment terminology - being the net result.

Jim Leishman was the man who signed Tommy at East End Park but not before severe ramifications resulted in determining the financial compensation package.

Tommy takes up the story.

He said: "St Mirren demanded a settlement fee of £300,000. The Pars only offered a paltry £30,000, which on the face of it was a bit of a blow to your football ego. Apparently it was the biggest variation in the asking and offering fees in the history of the transfer tribunals.

"The tribunal eventually settled on £71,000 plus VAT. Looking back, it was a bit of a laugh but it wasn't particularly funny at the time."

If his mid football life crisis was clouded in controversy, Tommy's formative years were more streamlined.

While born a Buddie, Tommy lived most of his days as a Glaswegian, with his scholastic days spent at Mount Vernon Primary and Bannerman High School in Garrowhill.

He said: "I didn't manage to make any of the select teams but was given a regular game with Gartcosh Boys' Club. The club were in the throes of being disbanded and as Queen's Park had a team in this particular league, a number of us were invited along for a trial at Hampden.

"I was only 16 at the time and didn't hear from Queen's Park again. Being bold, bloody and resourceful I took the bull by the horns, phoned Hampden and got a game playing for their Under-18 side.

"Shortly after, I was promoted to the reserve side and then made the full first team. It was a fairly meteoric rise for a 17-year old."

Full-time football is a no-no for any Queen's Park player. A living had to be earned and Tommy served an engineering apprenticeship with the Caterpillar organisation.

The planning and administrative experience gained working at the Lanarkshire plant would prove invaluable in Tommy's later organisational activities with the SFA. However, the Caterpillar work schedule meant probable shift work and a possible fond farewell to football. Fortunately, St Mirren came on stream.

Tommy recalled: "A possible university degree course might have been an alternative solution, but it was when I was watching the 1982 World Cup finals in Spain on TV that I received a telephone call from St Mirren.

"It was an invitation for me and my dad to come to Love Street to meet Jack Gilmour, one of the directors, and manager Rikki McFarlane. That meeting resulted in a full-time contract being signed for Saints in 1982."

The move from the black and white of Hampden to the identical colours of St Mirren provided a sense of awe for the new Saints rookie.

He added: "There was I, 21 and meeting up with such St Mirren icons as Lex Richardson, Jack Copland, John McCormack, Frank McDougall and the other Frank - Mr McAvennie."

Tommy's early games saw him turn out in a pre-season friendly against Leeds United. But he rates playing against an Isle of Man select side in the Manx Island's pre-season tournament as being his main debut appearance.

Life at Love Street generated numerous highs and lows. On the up side was clearly the 1987 Scottish Cup final against Dundee United, with the Saints defence on acute tenterhooks until Ian Ferguson's winner.

The major downside was the last day of the 85-86 season. Hearts needed a single point to clinch the Premier League title. They went to Dens Park and lost 2-0.

Celtic, playing at Love Street, needed to win by a substantial margin to take the championship on goal difference. A 5-0 victory saw mission impossible become a raging reality.

Tommy said: "It was abject humiliation in losing that game. As a professional, it was hard to take. Many questions were posed about our commitment and effort, but in all honesty Celtic were by far the better team on the day."

Not known for his goal scoring prowess, Tommy was more adept at keeping a tight control on his club's "goals against" column. But one net finding occasion burns brightly in the Wilson logbook.

Aberdeen's Pittodrie Stadium is only a good going free-kick from the North Sea. As such, many of the Dons' home games find opposition battling against the elements.

Occasionally, seasonal weather produces snow, sleet, rain, hail and a modicum of sun - a taste of all four seasons in a requisite 90-minute time scale.

One such display from the northeast elements on March 28, 1987 saw Tommy harness the weather to good effect. He picked up a loose ball on the touchline, sent over a speculative cross that was wind assisted and soared over the out stretched hands of Theo Snelders to give Saints the points.

Tommy's continual thirst for team colours of a black and white pattern were satisfied with that contentious move to Dunfermline.

Life with The Pars gave Tommy another visit to Hampden, the 1991 League Cup final seeing the trophy head back to Easter Road and not unfortunately to East End Park. Still, two cup final sorties for a provincial full-back are highly rated insertions in the Wilson memoirs.

Cartilage problems then reared their head before Tommy headed for Tynecastle, where he was earmarked by Joe Jordan as potential full-back cover.

Sitting on the bench is never going to assuage the aspirations of an ambitious player and Tommy was no different. He wanted first-team action and another Thomas - one Mr Burns - had no doubts, and took Wilson's talents to Rugby Park. His spell with Kilmarnock helped the Ayrshire club to win promotion to the Premier League in 92-93.

After the promotion party, a broken bone in his foot all but ended the Wilson playing career, and the curtain finally came down after a short spell with Dumbarton under Murdo McLeod.

While a continuing career in engineering was a possibility, the football bug had bitten deeply. Here was a player who had played at the top level, competed in Europe, enjoyed two national cup finals and gleaned considerable knowledge from his former bosses - Eddie Hunter, Rikki McFarlane, Alex Miller, Alex Smith, Tony Fitzpatrick, Jim Leishman, Iain Munro, Jocky Scott, Joe Jordan, Tommy Burns and Murdo McLeod - a Who's Who in the Scottish game.

And the expertise didn't go to waste. The SFA were expanding their development of the game in Glasgow and harnessed the Wilson know how to make the appointment of a Football Development Officer for Glasgow.

Tommy explained: "My remit is to set up participation centres for youngsters, to coach adults to work with young players, to set up indoors and outdoor playing arenas and to expand the concept of 7-a-side games".

Tommy's task is similar to the iceberg scenario - you only see one ninth of his work in open vision, but who would bet against more of his endeavours breaking the soccer surfaces in the future.

DAVID WINNIE

THE occasion was vintage surrealism. It was the end of season awards Dinner. The location was Reykjavik in Iceland. The local KR side had just won the national championship and David Winnie, in his first season with the club, had agreed to stay on to sample the celebratory menu on offer.

He revealed: "I was promised a good night. It was, but most of the proceedings were conducted in Icelandic. I hadn't a clue as to what was happening. Come the awards presentation, I heard my name mentioned and then bedlam seemed to break out. I'd just won their top award, the equivalent of Scotland's PFA award.

"Some very good players had won it in the past – players like Guni Torfason, well remembered at Love Street, Siggi Jonsen, who played for both Dundee United and Arsenal, and Eidur Godjohnsen at Chelsea. I was following in some pretty famous footsteps and to put it bluntly, I was more than chuffed."

That sense of self satisfaction was compounded by the fact that David was the first ever overseas player to win the Icelandic accolade.

There are, however, numerous other baubles on the Winnie mantelpiece. Pride of place is that winners medal from the Scottish Cup success in 1987, St Mirren narrowly edging out Dundee United at Hampden.

Equally, while not meriting access to the winners rostrum, David picked up runners-up gongs with Aberdeen in the 1992 Skol Cup final and the Premier League in that same season, with Rangers being the unconquered final hurdle.

Born in Bellshill with an early family homestead in Chapelhall, David made the transition to Renfrewshire, and Bridge of Weir in particular, as an eight-year-old. St Aelred's provided the base camp in his search for proficiency in the three "Rs", culminating in a clutch of Highers and a midfield role in the school side.

A tall lad in his teens, it was Jim Clunie's scouting team who spotted the latent potential with David happy to endorse an "S" Form for Saints.

The Winnie St Mirren debut is registered as being November 9, 1983, the 17-year-old – still wrestling with his academic studies – being pitched into a League Cup clash with Hearts at Tynecastle.

David recalled: "St Mirren had beaten Forfar Athletic in the third round and it was off to face the Jambos in the then sectionalised format in Edinburgh. My one abiding memory of the game was not the fact that we lost 3-1, but of being launched into orbit in a crunching tackle by the redoubtable Walter Kidd that scattered me on the red blaize trackside. It was pretty painful and a severe welcome to the big boys' game."

David went on to develop a taste for European competition, savouring the delights of Slavia Prague, Tromso and Mechelen with Saints.

Further Euro games came on board after David's transfer to Aberdeen – a move brokered by former Saints boss Alex Smith.

Winnie went on: "I spent over four years at Pittodrie with some great cup and league moments. However, one that wasn't so pleasing was a first round knockout in the 1991 UEFA Cup at the hands of BK 1903 Copenhagen. We took a lot of media stick at our inability to even score against the Danish side, but what was subsequently forgotten was the fact that BK were a good team. They went on to beat the mighty Bayern Munich in the next round."

Games against Valur and Torino were also inked into the Winnie scrapbook before he was sent south on loan to Middlesbrough. Life at Ayresome Park saw David sustain a severe injury, which jeopardised any firm transfer negotiations. A fee had been agreed with Boro but the injury sent David back up the A92 to the Granite City.

Thereafter, a succession of clubs found space on the Winnie CV. A season with Hearts, again reliving painful memories with that man Kidd, was followed by a spell at Dens Park, before Tony Fitzpatrick brought Winnie back to St Mirren Park.

David explained: "St Mirren had a very young team at the time and one of their failings was the inability to communicate. My remit was getting them to talk on the park. In effect, it wasn't David Winnie doing the talking, it was experience mouthing off."

That experience was taken to the wire as Saints just retained their 1997-98 First Division status courtesy of a wonder Hugh Murray goal against Stirling Albion at Forthbank Stadium.

After St Mirren, David was enticed to try his luck in Iceland with KR Reykjavik, the Icelandic scene being rich with former St Mirren associations. Former Love Street winger Alan Prentice played for Vikingur, while KR once had renowned Paisley icons in Torfason and Tottie Beck.

With the Icelandic season only lasting from May through to the end of October, David felt the need to augment his career with some playing activity during the northern hemisphere's winter months. That need was satisfied with an eight-month stint with the Canberra Cosmos in Australia, and a short term contract with Ayr United.

He said: "I was only filling in time at Ayr. KR wanted me back and in particular to play in the UEFA Cup, and I was always concerned I might pick up another debilitating injury."

That particular UEFA Cup tournament provided a high degree of embarrassment for David.

He explained: "KR were drawn to play Kilmarnock in the 1999 competition. We beat them 1-0 in Reykjavik but, for my sins, I was red carded in the first half in the return game at Rugby Park and it was only a Paul Wright goal in injury-time plus a David Bagan strike in extra-time that cost us the tie."

David left the Icelandic shores on amicable terms and was eventually approached to return by Peter Petersen to take on the role of assistant manager, later to assume the full managerial responsibility on Petersen's departure.

The previous KR success graph now tended to dip alarmingly and David's remit was to simply keep the team in the league. He managed it, but only just.

A return to Scotland saw him succeed Tom Carson as manager of Dumbarton and while the Sons started well, having won promotion to the Second Division in 2002, the quality of the playing staff wasn't strong enough for the job in hand.

David's Dumbarton departure was clouded in acrimony, which probably provided a determination to finish with football in all active spheres.

The undoubted Winnie energy content is now being channelled into attacking an Honours Degree in Law and Economics.

FRASER WISHART

ST MIRREN players over the years gifted with outstanding defensive traits have never been willing contributors to the shrinking violet club. Davie Lapsley regularly inflicted pain and torture on the match ball. Jimmy Drinkwater and Davie Lindsay generated fear amongst the opposition wingers.

Additionally, Kirk Broadfoot's physique of pure Drongan muscle was aptly constructed to suit the Latin motto of the former Kings of Scotland - Nemo Me Impune Lacessit - or in the Caledonian vernacular, Whae dare meddle wi' me!

Fraser Wishart was manufactured from a different mould. At 5'-8" and a mere 10 stones, Fraser's defensive expertise was fashioned on the exactitudes of speed and timing.

Born in Johnstone on March 1, 1965, the Wishart family home was once in Foxbar, before heading east to the Newlands area on the south side of Glasgow. That was the location of Hillpark Secondary School, Fraser's soccer skills being manufactured on Glasgow Council red ash pitches where one's knee caps tended to be well endowed with copious quantities of the red grit.

The school team assuaged the morning football thirst while the Eastercraigs club satisfied the afternoon need. Andy Millen was a playing colleague at the time and well remembers Wishart, not only at Eastercraigs but also on the senior stage.

Andy said: "Fraser was a player who showed enthusiasm and a desire for every club he played for. Anyone who played against him would be in no doubt he was a determined team player If you attract interest from Motherwell, St Mirren, Rangers and Hearts you have something positive in your football make-up."

Fraser developed an early appreciation of his future football career path in his teenage days.

He explained: "I played as a winger in my younger days when I was a bit quicker but my scoring record confirmed I had a better future as a wing back."

After trials with Clydebank and Hamilton, the teenager found favour with Pollok Juniors thanks to the neighbourly intervention of Dickie Brock,

303

who became the assistant manager at Newlandsfield Park.

Fraser's academic credentials saw him at university for a year before Bobby Watson signed him on a full-time contract for Motherwell.

The Wishart appearance stats at Fir Park were prodigious after his claret and amber debut against Hearts in September 1986. He only missed two games in his four-year spell, a testimony to his fitness and ability to escape injury.

However, later life at Fir Park was more sour than sweet.

Fraser recalled: "I left Motherwell under a slight cloud. Looking back, I think I handled it the wrong way. There was no malice involved. I had been tapped by Celtic. I think everybody in football knew, including the manager Tommy McLean, and of course I was denying it.

"I refused to accept Motherwell's re-signing offer. I didn't have an agent and received virtually no advice from anyone. I thought Celtic were going to sign me but it fell through as Chris Morris, who was supposed to be leaving, ultimately re-signed."

Motherwell's loss became St Mirren's gain as Tony Fitzpatrick, Fraser's school playground hero, signed him for Saints during the 1989 close season.

Despite over 50 appearances in black and white, things didn't quite work out for Fraser at Love Street.

He said: "I was so hyped up to do well with St Mirren. But in my second or third game, I played a simple one-two with Frank McGarvey and ruptured my thigh muscle. After missing only a couple of matches at Fir Park, I couldn't get a run of games going for St Mirren."

It was here that Fraser's travelogue in the Scottish soccer scene took over. A season with Falkirk preceded a handful of games with Rangers before he signed for Hearts. Then, with no recriminations, he signed for Alex McLeish at Motherwell.

Despite the full cycle, even then Fraser wasn't finished with his club collection. Four playing terms were spent with the slowly sinking Clydebank side, where he became the assistant manager to Ian McCall.

Wishart's final senior fling took place in Airdrieonian colours, Fraser playing in the Diamonds' trouble torn match with Ayr United at Somerset Park in the last match of the 2000-01 season.

Wishart's contacts in and around the Scottish leagues stood him in good stead in his role as assistant secretary to Tony Higgins in the Scottish Professional Footballers Association. So how did the entry to the trade union world materialise?

Fraser explained: "The background situation stems from the fact that my family were all staunch socialists. It all started when nobody would do the shop steward thing at Motherwell.

"I was only 19 at the time and basically it was all about collecting the union dues at £1 per week and taking the cash to Tony Higgins' office at Charing Cross.

"I joined the SPFA when I became a professional player in 1984. The job at the union was a part-time affair when I was playing. I would train for four mornings a week, which would give me a union working week of one day and four afternoons plus some occasional evening work."

Union activities for the Wishart attention are more profuse in the close season when clubs begin to off load unwanted players from their wage bills.

He went on: "Clubs in the past would release six and take on six. But in the strained climate of football finance, they now dispense with six and take on only two.

"Perhaps the biggest part of our job is fixing up redundant players with other clubs. We produce a definitive list of free transfers, provide a thumbnail career sketch of each player and send the database out to all clubs in the UK and to agents abroad.

"We don't receive any money for any of the transactions as we are not licensed agents. It's different in England as their PFA get 10 per cent of TV money that comes into the game. The system is much more advanced south of the border. If clubs here are in trouble they will phone the SPFA, yet we have little or no financial clout to help."

Wishart's heritable background ensures his family have remained as true but exiled Buddies.

He revealed: "I was at the 1987 Scottish Cup final supporting Saints at Hampden and the first result I always look for on a Saturday night is that of St Mirren."

Now there's devotion for you..

MARK YARDLEY

HE became a cult figure during his eight seasons in St Mirren colours. His 72-goal tally places him well up on the post-war scoring ladder and at the 2005 Premier Awards Dinner he was inducted to the Saints Hall of Fame. He is Mark Yardley.

A late starter on the senior circuit, Mark was 19 when he joined Livingston Juniors and spent five seasons with the West Lothian club, before some meteoric goal scoring activity saw Mark step up to the senior stage with Cowdenbeath.

His debut for the Central Park side bordered on Roy of the Rovers material.

Cowdenbeath are at home to Arbroath and Yardley nets four goals in a 6-2 drubbing of the Red Lichties.

A month later he bagged a hat-trick against Queen's at Hampden. Indeed, in his first seven games for the Blue Brazil, Mark amassed an impressive 11-goal return.

Here was a striker with an outstanding physique, displaying an emerging potential to the senior Scottish scene.

It was the English-based scouts who were soon scouring the travelogues for route one directions to Fife. Mark initially opted to go south for a trial with Rotherham, followed by an interest from Stockport County.

He recalled: "I felt I'd done really well in my week with Stockport, so much so that they invited me over to play in the Isle of Man pre-season tournament.

"Stockport boss Davie Jones, who later went on to manage Southampton and Wolves, wanted to sign me but only two firm bids of £25,000 were received by Cowdenbeath - one from Barnet plus one from St Mirren - and I was happy to choose Saints."

The St Mirren connection was conceivably fashioned outwith the playing arenas. Mark worked as an accountant with the Russell Athletic organisation - a company who handled substantial business with Gilmour Sports, the daily grind of St Mirren chairman Stewart Gilmour.

The weekly business chat Stewart and Mark enjoyed was such that Mr Gilmour was unaware he was addressing Yardley the footballer. The penny apparently dropped when there was no Mark on the other end of the line - because he was down on trial at Stockport.

Yardley's initial outing for St Mirren was neatly pigeon holed in the sensational tray.

Signed on the Friday, he was in the St Mirren line up the following day for a trip to Firhill to face the then nomadic Hamilton Accies. Mark was soon in action - within a couple of minutes to be precise.

He explained: "The first thing you want to do as a striker is get off the mark as quickly as possible. I'd made the step up from part-time football and didn't know much about my team-mates for that first game.

"Fortunately, I managed to get on the end of a cross from John Boyd to score and I reciprocated for him to get the second. Two goals up, but I've never forgiven Paul McIntyre for an illicit kick on a Hamilton lad. He was sent off, we were down to 11 men and just managed to hold out for a 2-2 draw. Cheerio to my debut win bonus."

As goals go in the Yardley scrapbook, that was highly rated, as was the first he netted in the 2000 title-clinching game against Raith Rovers. But the one strike firmly etched in the Yardley memory cells, and his last for St Mirren, saw off county rivals Morton at Cappielow in a first round League Cup clash at the start of the 2002-03 season.

He said: ""We were two down when Martin Cameron and Simon Lappin scored to get us back on level terms. I was fortunate to grab the winner after beating three men in a mazy dribble. The goal must have figured largely with the Morton fans as they gave me some reflective pelters when I played against them with Albion Rovers."

The Yardley penchant for profound articulation has seen him carry many a banner in various delicate negotiations.

He added: "I think I've always had the respect of the players and I'm more than happy and available to offer advice and maybe even counselling."

That charismatic approach combined with a gift of the gab has seen him on the box, guesting on Tam Cowan's irreverent show Offside. No doubt the Yardley verbosity, his scoring prowess and his stature triggered off the TV invitations.

It was that physical presence which, in time, contributed largely to bouts of annoyance and frustration.

During Mark's time at Love Street, the regular Monday morning step onto the scales revealed an avoirdupois reading of 13 stones, one pound, not a bad packaging content for a 6'-2" frame.

The 13-stone figure was regularly promulgated over the years in that austere publication The Scottish Football League Review. Much to Mark's concern, on his move to Albion Rovers, that same Review listed his weight as being 15st 7lb, to be followed in season 2004-05 with an OTT weight measurement of 16st 8lb.

He said of the stats: "Absolutely remarkable. I have to tell you that in all my time at Cliftonhill with Albion Rovers, I was never weighed once, so it follows that the listings in the Scottish Football League Review are a trifle fictitious."

That title-winning campaign in the millennium season looms large in Mark's more memorable moments. Not only did he top the First Division scoring charts with 19 goals, his striking ability also netting him the coveted accolade of First Division Player of the Year.

He recalled: "That season was a magical experience. Winning the championship at Love Street was a tremendous thrill. In fact, I'm under considerable pressure to take out a safety deposit box at the bank to keep my medal in - that's how much it means to me.

"Just to add to he sense of occasion, the video of that season is always being played on my parents' TV when we visit them."

Mark's registration with Rovers was retained with the Coatbridge club until the end of the 2004-05 season, thus preventing him from moving on. However, it's an almost cast iron certainty representatives from the Juniors would welcome further goal scoring exploits from the big man...

Now acting as the manager of the credit team on the retail side with The Royal Bank of Scotland in Edinburgh, Mark still manages a weekly five-a-side stint on Wednesday evenings.

But outwith his banking business, as well as playing and training, there is still adequate space in his leisure time diary to oversee the needs of his wife Paula, step sons Christopher and Andrew and young daughter Sophie.

JOHN YOUNG

"IF things in football go pear shaped, particularly when you sign a less than satisfactory player or have a bad game, simply just turn another page."

These are the philosophical effusions of John Young, whose soccer CV is well endowed with positive visions in both playing and managing.

The youngest of three, his first appearance on the Edinburgh skyline was in October 1951. Ten years later he was knocking the ball around for St Peter's Primary, his emerging skill as a potential striker then satisfying the Secondary needs of the St Anthony's School.

John's introduction to the senior scene was a simple case of being in the right spot at the right time.

He explained: "I saw myself as a late developer and was playing with the Albion Boys' Club. I played in a charity game in the Saughton enclosure in Edinburgh and in our team were Tommy Preston, Tommy Younger and Willie McFarlane, three Hibernian icons.

"Willie was the Easter Road manager at the time and as I managed to score a hat-trick, I was invited to play a trial for Hibs. That was against Hawick Royal Albert and again I managed to score three.

"I was a dashing centre-forward at the time and played in another trial up in Fife. I didn't play particularly well and on the way back the team bus broke down. That was when Willie McFarlane asked me to sign on as a full-time player with Hibees."

John only had a couple of seasons at Easter Road before McFarlane gave way to Dave Ewing, formerly of Manchester City. He in turn was replaced by the enigmatic Eddie Turnbull, he of the colourful phraseology.

Young joked: "Eddie knew a player when he saw one – he knew I wasn't a player and was sent packing!"

A period of soccer downtime saw John playing for Broxburn Juniors before an offer came in from Falkirk.

He recalled: "I played a trial on the Tuesday night for them against Hearts and was asked to return on the Thursday night to meet manager Willie Cunningham. He signed me in time to play on the Saturday for the first team. My striking partner in that game was the one and only Alex Ferguson."

Following the truism that nothing is forever in football, Cunningham was sacked and joined St Mirren, Ferguson was released and moved to Ayr United while John was given another free transfer.

A phone call from Love Street saw John embark on a more secure footing in his soccer career, with Cunningham appreciating that here was a player more gifted in the defensive arts than in bulging the opposition nets.

An eight-year association in St Mirren colours followed and John clocked up over 250 appearances over the period 1974-1982.

A League Cup sectional match against Stirling Albion at Love Street in August 1974 saw John make his St Mirren debut. Saints won 3-2 and the Buddies team selection that day read: Morrison, I. Reid, Beckett, Young, R. Reid, Johnston, McKean, Walker, Biggar, Borthwick and Lawrie.

John Young wore the No.4 shirt on that occasion and went on to wear shirt numbers 2, 3, 6, 8, 9 and 10, displaying a degree of versatility greatly appreciated by his managerial mentors in Messrs. Cunningham, Ferguson, Clunie and McFarlane.

The Young memory bank is well endowed with a host of outstanding St Mirren games. Being a member of the 1976-77 title-winning squad encompassed many memorable fixtures, particularly in the title-clinching game up at Dens Park, Saints winning 4-0.

John recalled: "I lived over in the east and travelled up to Dundee by car. The team arrived by bus and after the game they all went down to the Swallow Hotel for a substantial liquid celebration. But the beggars didn't tell me of their plans and left me to motor home on my own!"

John was also an integral cog in the 1977 Centenary celebratory match against Liverpool at Love Street.

He said: "Alex Ferguson told us it was only a friendly and not to get too involved, but the Liverpool lads soon got stuck in and it changed our approach to the game. It suited me as I was always a 'get stuck in' type of player.

"I've also fond memories of playing against Elsborg and St Etienne in the 1980 UEFA Cup. Playing against the likes of Michel Platini and Johnnie Rep was a master class in football education."

A remarkably fit man, John appeared in every Saints line up in his first two seasons. But a disastrous match against the Ayr United Reserve side at Somerset Park heralded a downturn in his career.

It was 3.20 pm on November 21, 1981 – John has the time and date heavily implanted in his memory cells – when he suffered a severe leg break.

He said: "I was 21 weeks in plaster, during which time the board decided to release me. Craig Brown, then the Clyde manager, had seen me play in a reserve game and offered St Mirren £5,000 for me. But it was Jimmy Bone who persuaded me to go to Hong Kong."

Life in the Orient was particularly attractive for John and his family but his registration with the Hong Kong club hit a snag. The league teams were only allowed seven European players. John was the seventh to arrive at the club. His documentation was also held up pending the arrival of an eighth Euro based player. The player was George Best. Enough said.

On his return to the UK, John had (whisper it) a short spell with Morton, followed by stints with Queen of the South and Brechin City.

John's time at Glebe Park was effective in sowing a seed leading to a rung on the management ladder, and his initial coaching apprenticeship was served at Arbroath under Bone.

Young explained: "When Jimmy moved to become Alex Smith's assistant at St Mirren, I took over and was there for five years as manager.

"One sure fire thing about managing in football is that one fine day you'll be presented with the dreaded P45. It happened to me at Arbroath and I was out of football work for about a month until John Ritchie asked me to join him back at Brechin City.

"I was eventually manager there for almost seven years. In truth, at one time I was the longest serving manager in Scotland. Working out of Glebe Park conditioned you to the highs and lows – you were well versed in both promotion and relegation dog fights."

John fully endorses the philosophy of those in charge of football clubs. He said: "Working Sunday to Friday, football management is a brilliant career, it's the Saturdays I hate most. They can seriously damage your football health!"

Spells at Dunfermline and again with Bone at Stenhousemuir followed before Ian Campbell, having guided the wee City team to the First Division in 2005, invited John back as his assistant at Glebe Park in January 2005.

With such an array of soccer experience in his CV, home stability has been the rock on which his career has been founded.

Married to Ann in June 1974, John was particularly concerned his honeymoon in Aviemore would clash with the World Cup Finals in Germany.

A television set would be required to monitor Scotland's fortunes. Whether TV or romance won the day is a secret Mr & Mrs Young didn't divulge – but clearly here was commitment on both sides.

Some with passports and short St Mirren stays

EVERYTHING with Brazilian connotations was exceedingly rosy. The Samba kings had just won the 1965 World Cup for the second successive occasion in beating Czechoslovakia 3-1 in Chile. All Brazilian players were, therefore, top dollar.

St Mirren manager Doug Millward apparently thought so – but was completely conned. He was persuaded to take on board **Fernando Azevedo** as a sure-fire Brazilian centre-forward against Morton on September 11, 1965.

The Cappielow club won 1-0 and Azevedo's contribution was considerably less than abysmal. The Brazilian never played for Saints again.

....

MANY will take the trek to the UK to learn and expand their grasp of the English language. Few will travel to Paisley to play football and enhance their language capabilities. **Victor Munoz** did.

Born in Zaragoza, the former captain of Spain, who earned 61 international caps, was on the books of the Italian club Sampdoria but was keen to play in Scotland and have the opportunity of improving his English speak.

Manager Tony Fitzpatrick was given the go ahead to sign the high-profile Spaniard and Victor – also a former captain of Barcelona – made his St Mirren debut against Celtic at Celtic Park on November 17, 1990. Regretfully, the Buddies lost 4-1.

Generally the confirmed midfield playmaker, wearing the No.5 shirt, Victor played 18 league games for St Mirren before leaving at the end of the 90-91 season with a handful of Caledonian memories and an improved English vocabulary.

Never one to contribute greatly to the "goals for" column, he did have one outstanding strike for St Mirren, firing in a blockbuster against

Stranraer in that 5-1 third round win in the 1991 Scottish Cup.

In his later days, Victor turned to management and successfully looked after the affairs of Villareal and Real Zaragoza.

……………………………..

A PLAYER with dual nationality, embracing both France and the Ivory Coast, **Moussa Dagnogo** started his playing career in Paris, before trying his luck across the English Channel with Bristol Rovers. A move north and a short stay with Aberdeen preceded manager Tom Hendrie giving him a short-term Saints contract at the back end of the 2000-01 season.

The potential augured well. A goal in an Under-21 match at Kilmarnock's Rugby Park was followed by a place on the bench for an SPL game with Dundee at Love Street.

The clock was running down. Only a few minutes to go. The score is tied at 1-1 and St Mirren are in desperate needs of points for SPL survival.

Moussa gets the nod from Hendrie, vacates his sedentary placement on the bench and proceeds to knock in the winner on his senior debut.

It was dream material but the dream only encompassed a total of four further league outings before the Paris-born frontman left Paisley.

……………………………..

PERHAPS not quite the full academic, **Kelechi Okorie** was an educated lad, having gained a qualification in finance in Huddersfield and had high hopes of a legal career in his post-playing days.

Born in Nigeria, Kelechi arrived in the UK in 1991. Football played second fiddle to his studies but a Norwegian friend had faith in his soccer ability and advised him to contact some Scottish clubs and St Mirren in particular with a view to playing on a regular basis.

A big lad with central defensive leanings, he did play a trial for Partick Thistle. But on his own admission, he didn't do himself justice, having not fully recovered from a bicycle accident when he wasn't wearing a crash helmet.

Manager Jimmy Bone was interested after some training pitch sorties and Kelechi made his St Mirren debut against Hamilton on December 3, 1994.

The match sponsors liked what they saw and nominated the Nigerian lad as their Man-of-the-Match. When the Stadium announcer intimated the accolade, Kelechi's felicitations went into over drive as he went on to shake as many congratulatory hands as possible – while the match was still going on!

Bone was incandescent. Saints were one down and play was almost suspended during the hand shaking party. The worthy Saints manager then ensured that never again would such an announcement be broadcast until the match had finished.

As for Kelechi, he made one more appearance before returning to serious study.

....

HE was elegant, athletic, a confirmed playmaker, a fans' favourite. He was **Tomas Stickroth.**

Born in Stuttgart on April 13, 1965, Tomas was a star player for Bayer Uerdingen in the German league.

Boss Tony Fitzpatrick was in need of some bolstering of his midfield and secured Tomas on the back of a reported fee of £400,000 – a record for St Mirren.

He came off the bench for his Saints debut against Rangers at Ibrox, the game ending in a scoreless draw.

Some 55 league matches were recorded in Tomas' favour, with only a couple of goals to his credit. The first came in a home match with Motherwell.

Some would say he flattered to deceive but for a continuing series of niggling injuries, Tomas would surely made a bigger impact during his three-season spell at St Mirren Park.

....

THE Finnish football season operates from May to October. Outwith these months, with the severe snow and frost conditions, the players either seek alternative sports or investigate short-term playing contracts in warmer climes.

Buddies manager Jimmy Bone opted to explore the latter Scandinavian soccer scene and his immediate need was for a quality defender.

Step forward **Janne Makela**. Born in Tampere and 24 years old during the 95-96 season, Janne started playing with his hometown team, Ilves Tampere, before moving on to MyPa and then to FinnPa. Both teams won promotion to Finland's Premier League in 1991.

A full-back with a serious track record, Janne had some formidable international appearance entries on his CV, boasting 11 Under-21 outings plus 18 full Finnish caps.

Much was expected of him when he faced Airdrie at Love Street in October 1995. Regretfully, a crunching Scottish tackle after only 30 minutes generated knee ligament damage and the Finnish lad left the pitch on a stretcher.

He went back to Finland for the requisite operation and recuperation. Janne played no further games for St Mirren but later returned to Scotland on trial with Hearts.

....

THE decibel ratings in the dressing room tend to be high when **Jose Quitongo** is in residence. The little man from Angola is a bundle of laughs, his effervescence clearly a calming influence on any pre-match tension.

Jose arrived in the UK in the mid 1990s and played one match for Darlington before joining Hamilton in November 1995.

That season Hamilton were relegated to the Second Division and St Mirren drew the Douglas Park side in the League Challenge Cup. Clearly Saints were clear favourites to win – but they didn't, thanks to two goals from the diminutive Jose.

A move to Hearts followed but he didn't last long at Tynecastle and went on to portray his skills in the soccer shop window at Morton. Saints played our Greenock rivals in a pre-season game, with the mercurial Jose again on the scoresheet.

Manager Tom Hendrie signed the little Angolan and Jose played almost 60 games for St Mirren over the 2000-02 period.

Perhaps a lasting memory of Jose occurred in a midweek cup tie against Ross County up at Dingwall. The match was tight and extra-time was on the horizon. Jose appeared agitated on the park and uttered a whisper to the referee before running off the pitch. A severe call of nature beckoned! When you've gotta go, you've gotta go!

There were frantic pleas from the St Mirren bench urging the Angola one to hurry up. He did and Saints went on to win.

It could only happen to Jose Quitongo, the confirmed mad hatter.

....

HE was only a toddler when he left Surinam, **Maikel Renfurm's** parents moving over to Holland. The rudiments of street football helped to develop his early skills in the Netherlands before joining Dynamo 67.

It was while at Dynamo 67, a youth club winning everything in sight, that the major clubs such as Feyenoord, Sparta Rotterdam and Den Haag began to take notice.

It was Sparta who won the race for Maikel's autograph. He was only 16 at the time. What wasn't so clever was to go on and spend 11 seasons with the Rotterdam club.

A move was required and Jimmy Calderwood, of Dunfermline and Aberdeen managerial fame, offered him a two-year contract at NEC Nijmegan.

From the flat lands of Holland, it was then over to the volcanic landscape of Iceland, where Maikel teamed up with former Saint David Winnie at KR Reykjavik.

Their combined contribution won the Icelandic league for KR and Winnie provided a glowing report of one readymade striker to Saints manager Tom Hendrie.

The articulate and likeable man from Surinam arrived to help save St Mirren from SPL relegation. Some 16 appearances were accorded to Maikel but as to a load of goals? Well, only one was recorded in the match with Dundee United on December 5, 2000.

100 Great Saints A–Z

Gerry Baker
Therolf Beck
Alex Beckett
Tom Black
Eddie Blyth
Jimmy Bone
Walter Borthwick
Tommy Bryceland
Gerry Burrell
Ian Cameron
Bobby Carroll
Steve Clarke
Jim Clunie
Denis Connachan
Tony Connell
Neil Cooper
Jack Copland
Alex Crowe
Willie Cunningham
Billy Davies
Jimmy Drinkwater
Tony Fitzpatrick
Bobby Flavell
Campbell Forsyth
Les Fridge
Mark Fulton
Willie Fulton
Tommy Gemmell
Archie Gemmill
Ricky Gillies
Peter Godfrey
Brian Hamilton
Ronnie Hamilton
Bobby Holmes

Derek Hyslop
Peter Kane
Donnie Kerrigan
Archie Knox
Paul Lambert
Davie Lapsley
Barry Lavety
Tommy Leishman
Alfie Lesz
Alex Linwood
Alan Logan
Frank McAvennie
John McCormack
Frank McDougall
Kenny McDowall
Donnie McDowell
Andy McFadden
Steven McGarry
Frank McGarvey
Kevin McGowne
Jack McGugan
Bobby McKean
Barry McLaughlin
Hugh McLaughlin
Ally McLeod
(of Scotland fame)
Ally McLeod
(of four goal fame)
Gordon McQueen
John McTurk
Norrie McWhirter
Brian Martin
Junior Mendes
Andy Millen
Alistair Miller

Arthur Milne
Campbell Money
Iain Munro
Cammy Murray
Hugh Murray
Jackie Neilson
Malcolm Newlands
Bobby Pinkerton
Gerry Queen
Bobby Reid
Willie Reid
Lex Richardson
Ian Riddell
Jim Rodger
Sam Smith
Dougie Somner
Gardner Speirs
Billy Stark
George Stewart
Willie Telfer
Billy Thomson
Jim Thorburn
Guni Torfason
Robert Torrance
Tommy Turner
David Walker
John Wilson
Tommy Wilson
David Winnie
Fraser Wishart
Mark Yardley
John Young
Some with passports
and short St Mirren
stays